Shakespeare and Son

Shakespeare and Son

A Journey in Writing and Grieving

Keverne Smith

 PRAEGER

AN IMPRINT OF ABC-CLIO, LLC
Santa Barbara, California • Denver, Colorado • Oxford, England

Library of Congress Cataloging-in-Publication Data

Smith, Keverne.
    Shakespeare and son : a journey in writing and grieving / Keverne Smith.
        p. cm.
    Includes bibliographical references and index.
    ISBN 978–0–313–39230–6 (hardcover : acid-free paper) — ISBN 978–0–313–39231–3 (ebook)
1. Shakespeare, William, 1564–1616—Knowledge—Psychology. 2. Shakespeare, William, 1564–1616—Family. 3. Grief in literature. 4. Loss (Psychology) in literature. 5. Dramatists, English—Early modern, 1500–1700—Family relationships. I. Title.
PR3065.S57   2011
822.3′3—dc22   2011010622

ISBN: 978–0–313–39230–6
EISBN: 978–0–313–39231–3

15 14 13 12 11   1 2 3 4 5

This book is also available on the World Wide Web as an eBook.
Visit www.abc-clio.com for details.

Praeger
An Imprint of ABC-CLIO, LLC

ABC-CLIO, LLC
130 Cremona Drive, P.O. Box 1911
Santa Barbara, California 93116-1911

This book is printed on acid-free paper ∞
Manufactured in the United States of America

Contents

Preface

So much has been written about William Shakespeare that it might seem there is nothing left to say, but the possible effects on his writing of the death of his only son, Hamnet, in 1596, while engaging many commentators, have rarely been explored in detail. And there's a good reason for this, as Richard Wheeler points out in one of the few attempts to do so: Shakespeare never refers to this death directly. I hope to show, however, that *cumulative evidence from repeated structural patterns* in works written over many years suggests that this most extraordinary writer was indeed an ordinary father when it came to bereavement—searching, not necessarily consciously, for ways to place his loss in perspective with his life. To retrace this path it is necessary to bring together areas of knowledge not normally connected: literary and historical studies on the one hand, and explorations of the experience of grief on the other. This unusual combination can illuminate many features of Shakespeare's writing after his young son's death. I hope this journey will be of interest to the general reader as well as to the academic, and have therefore tried to avoid technical language which might be opaque to such a reader whenever possible.

Counselors and therapists have shown that, when a new grief occurs in someone's life, earlier losses feed into it. In writing about the possible effects of Hamnet's death I am not suggesting that Shakespeare's works reveal that anguish alone; but I am arguing that there are moments when grief for Hamnet contributes to the emotional intensity of Shakespeare's writing, and that a recognition of these moments will deepen our understanding of the appeal of his wonderful plays, and perhaps may even help those who have found, as some of Shakespeare's protagonists find, that their grief isolates them from their fellow beings. This can be particularly true for men who, for a variety of historical, cultural and physical reasons, often find deep emotion difficult to deal with and so don't deal with it but try to push it aside.

Indeed, I think that, for Shakespeare, one of the many functions of writing after Hamnet dies is therapeutic. As practitioners of creative writing tell us, our lives are narratives in which we are the main character, and inventing fictions allows us to interact with that narrative and explore other possibilities. It might seem anachronistic to apply this idea to a writer who died in 1616; surely the concept that writing can be therapeutic is a modern one? But actually the earliest detailed account of drama—Aristotle's *Poetics*—suggests that tragedy arouses pity and fear in the audience in order to bring about a catharsis, a purifying purging, of the excess of these potentially overwhelming emotions. The way Aristotle refers to catharsis is revealing: elsewhere he goes into considerable detail about aspects of tragedy he discusses, but the comment about catharsis is almost a throwaway line, as if he is stating something so obvious that he need not elaborate further. Aristotle recognized that *one* of the purposes of theatrical performance was therapeutic, helping us to cope with the emotional rack which life stretches us upon. He implies, however, that it is primarily a conscious process, but the evidence suggests that often catharsis takes place at levels deeper than conscious thought. Certainly many recurring and developing patterns in Shakespeare's works seem to be present below the level of consciousness, and I have used the phrase "at some level" to indicate the impossibility of separating out the different layers involved in creative writing at a given moment. Moving through grief is a complex process which involves all levels of emotion and thought interacting, conscious and unconscious.

Most research in literary, historical and bereavement studies is similarly complex, requiring the interpretation and weighing up of evidence to reach a probable or possible, rather than a definitive, conclusion. For complete accuracy, almost every sentence I and anyone else writes about Shakespeare's works should include words like "probably," "perhaps," "the likelihood is," and so on; but I think such constant repetition would irritate, especially as this account is aimed at the interested general reader as well as the specialist, and I have therefore used such words and phrases sparingly. I hope, however, readers will take it for granted that this qualification applies throughout.

For about half of Shakespeare's plays there are at least two different texts from his period. The single play quarto editions usually seem to be based on draft or early versions of the play in question, whereas the texts in the huge *First Folio* collection of almost all his dramatic writings generally appear to incorporate later changes. Sometimes the different versions are revealing in relation to the presentation of grief. This is especially true in the cases of *Hamlet* and *King Lear*.

All quotations from Shakespeare are taken from Gwynne Blakemore Evans and John Tobin's excellent *The Riverside Shakespeare: The Complete Works*, second edition, abbreviated to *The Riverside Shakespeare*. Quotations from plays are followed by the act, scene, and line number in that edition; quotations from the *Sonnets* are followed by the sonnet number and line number. All other quotations are referenced briefly in the notes at the end of each chapter with full publication information of each source-text in the bibliography. These notes contain further details which could interrupt the flow of the main text, but which some readers may wish to follow up, in part or in whole. They are indicated by a small superscript number and can easily be ignored by those who only wish to read the main text.

Spellings have been modernized in texts from earlier centuries, except where there is a good reason to keep the original.

Acknowledgments

One of our culture's caricatures is the starlet who wins an Oscar and wishes to thank everyone, from her earliest teacher onward. But beneath the cliché is a truth. I have been fascinated by the topic of grief in Shakespeare since I was an undergraduate more years ago than I care to disclose, and many people have indirectly contributed to my project, even before I started to investigate the topic consciously almost a decade ago (as far as the demands of teaching—very enjoyable and rewarding—and ever increasing administrative duties—decidedly not—allowed). So in writing an acknowledgment list that is not as long as a chapter, I am aware that there is an injustice towards, for instance, the excellent English teacher I had from the age of 13 onward, Keith Stevens.

More recently, my wife Caroline, David Bevington, Silvia Holden, René Weis, Stanley Wells, and the late Stephen Wenman have very kindly read the whole of my draft manuscript at various stages in its development, and Sarah Brown, Valerie Wayne and Katrin Wilhelm have generously read sections. I have gained beyond measure from reflecting on their helpful comments and suggestions, although of course, I have not always agreed with them. It is a particular sadness that Stephen, who was an excellent mature student, has not been able to see how my final revision bears the imprint of his friendly honesty. Indeed, I have been overwhelmed by the generosity of colleagues in the international community of scholarship in responding to e-mails and other requests for information from someone, in most cases, they did not know. This is very encouraging in a world where communal values are increasingly under attack from purely competitive forces. At the appropriate moment in the notes I have recorded an individual's support. One e-mail that does not easily fit into the chapter notes I will mention here, representative of so many: I contacted Peter Donaldson, whom I did not know, at MIT, about the issue of which edition or online source to use for quotations from Shakespeare's plays; almost before I had time to draw breath I received a detailed, lucid discussion of the various possibilities that could not have been bettered. This has been my general experience, with hardly any exceptions. Similarly, this has been my experience with librarians, who have ordered items for me and replied to requests for information with exceptional speed and good will.

I have been very lucky too on the degree courses I've been involved in at the University Centre, College of West Anglia, King's Lynn, and Anglia Ruskin University, Cambridge, England, to have received early encouragement especially from Mary Joannou, and to have had departmental colleagues in English, History, Psychology, and Sociology who have formed a true community helping and supporting each other, despite the outrageous time pressures they have been subjected to by unnecessary bureaucracy. I am very grateful to Anglia Ruskin for awarding me two sabbaticals of one semester each and to the College for allowing me to take them. Without these, finishing my research and writing it up fully would not have been possible.

I am also very grateful to my editor, Dan Harmon, for seeing the potential in my project and with the help of Dharanivel Baskar for supporting me through all the technicalities involved in producing a typescript that could be translated into book form.

As with people, so with books: I could specify many more here, as my text and bibliography show; but below are the ones that have had most direct impact on my work. When I started to think seriously about this project in 2001, approaches to Shakespeare that had a psychodynamic and/or biographical element were, for the most part, unfashionable. This was understandable, given the looseness and generality of some of the worst of such readings; but I thought there was a place for a more disciplined and detailed application of such approaches in conjunction with a clear historical awareness. At just the right time in 2004, when I had my first chance to research the topic thoroughly, I came upon Richard Wheeler's wonderful paper, "Deaths in the Family: The Loss of a Son and the Rise of Shakespearean Comedy" and was encouraged to find someone who had an overview similar to mine, who had managed to combine these apparently disparate approaches, and who had noticed some pieces of evidence I had not. I read Stephen Greenblatt's *Will in the World: How Shakespeare Became Shakespeare* the following year and later saw his 2004 *New York Review of Books* article, "The Death of Hamnet and the Making of *Hamlet*." It was especially heartening to find someone linked to a critical approach which had been hostile to psychodynamic/biographical essays incorporating elements from such readings, albeit circumspectly and with sensible reservations. The gradual widening of perspective which the above works attest to is investigated in Takashi Kozuka and J. R. Mulryne's thought-provoking *Shakespeare, Marlowe, Jonson: New Directions in Biography*. Of the many Shakespeare biographies of recent years, the most helpful one for me has been René Weis' *Shakespeare Unbound* (U.S. title)/*Shakespeare Revealed* (British title). I particularly admire his ability to encourage the reader to reconsider matters taken for granted or ignored previously. When my final version was nearing completion I read Sean Benson's insightful *Shakespearean Resurrection: The Art of Almost Raising the Dead*, which helped me increase the precision of my text.

Finally, but definitely not least, I have been very lucky in having parents and a family who had faith in me and supported and encouraged me, and I dedicate this work to them. As I think we'll find when we look at Shakespeare's writing after the death of Hamnet, another unfashionable feature, faith, becomes an increasingly important element in his coming to terms with his grief.

Chronology

None of Shakespeare's plays can be dated exactly, but there is evidence to suggest which plays were written approximately when, based on:

1) allusions to individual plays by his contemporaries,
2) topical references within the plays, and
3) developing features of style as his career progresses, which computer analyses have confirmed.

1. Works written several years before Hamnet's death in August 1596: ***Henry the Sixth, Parts 1*** (Chapter 6) and ***3*** (Chapter 6).

2. Works probably started or completed close in time to Hamnet's death: ***King John*** (Chapter 4); ***Romeo and Juliet*** (Chapter 4); and ***Henry the Fourth***, especially ***Part 2*** (Chapter 6).

3. Works probably written after Hamnet's death but before *Hamlet*: ***The Merchant of Venice*** (Chapter 5); ***Much Ado About Nothing*** (Chapter 5); and ***As You Like It*** (Chapter 5).

4. Works written in the last years of Elizabeth the First's reign: ***Twelfth Night*** (Chapter 5); ***Hamlet*** (Chapter 7); and ***Troilus and Cressida*** (Chapter 8).

5. Works written or finalized in James the First's reign: ***Sonnets*** (Chapter 9); ***Measure for Measure*** (Chapter 10); ***King Lear*** (Chapter 10); ***Macbeth*** (Chapter 10); ***All's Well that Ends Well*** (Chapter 11); ***Pericles*** (Chapter 11); ***The Winter's Tale*** (Chapter 12); ***Cymbeline*** (Chapter 13); and ***The Tempest*** (Chapters 3, 14)

Thou Boy of Tears

Shakespeare's only son Hamnet died aged eleven in August 1596, cause unknown. How did Shakespeare react to this loss? Unlike his contemporary Ben Jonson, who composed moving elegies to two of his children, Shakespeare never wrote about it directly, despite the advice he puts in Prince Malcolm's mouth a decade later, "Give sorrow words. The grief that does not speak/Whispers the o'erfraught heart and bids it break" (*Macbeth*, Act 4, Scene 3, lines 209–10). Many critics have battled with, and been baffled by, this surprising absence of direct response, which might seem to confirm a current image, heightened by *Shakespeare in Love*, of a man who forgot about his family in Stratford while he lived, and had affairs, in London. I hope to show, however, that Shakespeare's reactions to the loss of his young boy are in his plays, but that they are buried like fossils and require an understanding of grief processes to unearth them.

Why buried? The answer lies in Shakespeare's period, in attitudes to maleness, and in Shakespeare himself. One of the targets of the Protestant reformers was the emotional demonstrations of grief that had evolved in the burial rituals of Medieval Catholicism. The reformers thought mourning should be moderate, rational, as befitted people believing in Christ's promise of resurrection. Many sermons and other documents from the sixteenth and seventeenth century teach what increasingly became the official line; for instance, John Chardon's sermon at the funeral of Sir Gawen Carew in 1584, argues that it is un-Christian to display excessive grief.[1] The implication, however, is that a substantial number of people found this difficult; if they were finding it easy, there would be no need to keep preaching about it. An anonymous letter published in 1630, *A Handkercher for Parents' Wet Eyes upon the Death of Children*, specifically addresses how a father should respond to the loss of a beloved son: "He is not clean gone, but only gone before. His mortality is ended, rather than his life. You have lost him for a time, God hath found him for ever." Further, "Rejoice and bless God, that you had such a son. Had him, did I say? You have him still. Not one child the fewer have you for his taking hence. . . . There [in heaven] you shall one day see him again face to face." "Lamenting and sorrowing" are not condemned to the mourning father in the letter; but they must be moderated.[2] Two of Shakespeare's characters express this same official view: one is Claudius, the murderer of Hamlet's father—a doubtful witness with his own agenda—but the other is the wise Lord Lafew, who states, "Moderate lamentation is the right of the dead," not "excessive grief" (*All's Well that Ends Well*, 1.1.55–6). Such sentiments were frequently stated in Tudor and Stuart England. (See Chapter 3 for a more detailed account of responses to bereavement in this period.)

Similarly, in Shakespeare's society, as in many others, it was thought "natural" for women rather than men to display grief in public. This idea was supported by contemporary medical knowledge, still derived primarily from the Ancient Greeks. Men were thought to be "naturally" hot-blooded; and this heat was supposed to burn away both moisture, such as tears, and the need to unpack the heart with words and lamentations. Hamlet famously berates himself for failing to meet this manly ideal. Women supposedly had cooler blood, and thus retained liquid. They were like sponges, so when bereavement squeezed them, they leaked both moisture, in the form of tears, and mournful words and cries, rather than burning these away as men were thought to do.[3] This theory put strong social pressure on men to repress, hide, and disguise grief in case they should be thought effeminate or lacking in self-control. What does and does not become a man is something that many of Shakespeare's protagonists ponder, often in relation to a sense of the social pressure to be manly—"manly" and "unmanly" occur 26 times in his works, illustrating this preoccupation. And although medical ideas nowadays are in many ways different, this pressure on men to be rock-like still persists in most societies, and hinders many men, as can be heard in these words of a father whose daughter had died. His friends and well-wishers' advice focused on ways in which he could support his wife through the loss, with no concern for his need to mourn. He exclaims:

> When is it my turn to cry? I'm not sure society or my upbringing will allow
> me a time to really cry, unafraid of the reaction and repercussion that might

follow. I must be strong, I must support my wife because I am a man.
I must be the cornerstone of our family because society says so, my family
says so and until I can reverse my learned nature, I say so.[4]

This father wants to cry and knows that he needs to cry, and this admission marks a beginning of his journey through loss; but external and, even more important, internalized social pressures prevent him, as they do many men, not from mourning, but from *mourning fully*, and encourage him, force him even, to repress some of his deepest feelings because of the need to be the strong male.

We might expect that with the advent of the "new man," this emphasis would be decreasing, but Niobe Way's 15-year research shows that it is still painfully strong. She has found that, in early adolescence, boys do share deep emotional experiences with friends, but in their later teens they shut down that side of themselves under pressure from the social ideology of the strong, independent, silent male. Several young men questioned showed an awareness that this shutting down of emotion would harm them, but felt they had no choice, if they weren't to appear "wussy."[5]

At first sight, then, there's nothing unusual in the fact that Shakespeare too habitually associates the most obvious sign of deep emotional disturbance—tears—with women and boys, rather than with adult men. For example, Aufidius calls Coriolanus "thou boy of tears!" when Coriolanus is moved by a plea from his mother (5.6.100). When King Lear cannot prevent himself from crying, he prays, "let not women's weapons, water-drops,/Stain my man's cheeks!" (2.4.277–8). When Mark Antony makes his and Cleopatra's troops weep after their defeat in battle, Enobarbus tells him, "Transform us not to women" (4.2.36). And so on.[6]

But what is unusual is a *change of emphasis* in Shakespeare's presentation of crying in the latter part of his career: references to tears in the plays from *Hamlet* onwards are predominantly negative and are strongly associated with boys and women, as in the examples above. In his earlier plays tears are indeed sometimes associated with weakness, but at other times they are presented as a healthy reaction, even from a grown man, to, for instance, the tragic horror of civil war. In *Henry the Sixth, Part 3*, a son who has unintentionally killed his father and a father who has unintentionally killed his son weep copiously, without any misgiving that this somehow makes them less like men. Crying is presented as the "natural" thing for these men to do, as if at this stage in his career Shakespeare can see the value of tears, even for a man, as an outlet for the extreme inner turmoil produced by grief. (This scene is discussed in detail in Chapter 6.)

Yet from *Hamlet* onwards two-thirds of Shakespeare's plays contain one or more references that show unease with the idea of a man crying. No such emphasis occurs in his most famous contemporary dramatists, Christopher Marlowe and Ben Jonson, even though they were subject to the same general social conditions. We've seen that Jonson had lost children, but also that he wrote directly about the experience, suggesting (as many other details confirm) a different temperament to Shakespeare's, and an ability to deal with issues more simply.

It is interesting to relate this preoccupation of Shakespeare's to research into grief; Tom Lundin found that there was "more evidence of persisting tearfulness and mourning among parents who had lost a child than among widows and widowers," and Geoffrey Gorer, that the loss of a child was "the most distressing and long-lasting of all griefs."[7] Catherine Sanders compared adults who had lost a child, adults who had lost a spouse, and adults who had lost a parent, and discovered those who had lost a child experienced a greater sense of despair, of anger, of loss of control, and of anxiety about death, as well as more physical symptoms of disturbance.[8] These findings probably do not surprise us because it seems common sense that the loss of a child, always an untimely death, is the hardest of all absences to accept. In themselves they prove nothing; but they offer the first clue towards the many connections between pronounced features of Shakespeare's later plays and research into the long-lasting effects of the loss of a child on many parents.

What, then, is the result of trying to do what many of Shakespeare's characters, and many men even nowadays, try to do—repress tears rather than express them, and the emotions associated with them? We cry because all human beings, men as well as women, need on occasion a channel for overwhelming emotion. But research such as William Schatz' confirms that men often cannot allow themselves this outlet: "The significant difference [between fathers and mothers] is that much of what goes on inside a man concerning the loss of a child *stays inside and only becomes apparent in some indirect way.*"[9] This aspect of male behavior needs to be seen in a wider perspective, however. It's sometimes erroneously concluded, from this lack of direct expression by fathers, that they feel the loss of a child much less than mothers do, and that because fathers usually spend less time with a child, they will miss that child less. Jean Scully started her counseling work with this presumption, and her surprise that it was not true comes across in this comment, "My work with grieving fathers spans more than 10 years, and during that time I have learnt from them. I have had to confront the prejudices I once held. Prejudices such as, 'men don't feel as much as women,' and 'fathers aren't as close to children as mothers.' "[10]

Jean Scully's experience suggests that many fathers do grieve as strongly as mothers but, as William Schatz indicates, cannot *complete* the process of mourning because they feel that they must hold in their emotions, that they must hide/disguise them. This can create a circular pattern because as counselors and therapists since Freud have emphasized, the most obvious effect of repressing grief is to make it even more inward and unshared, so repression leads to depression, melancholy, despair. Shakespeare of course produced the most famous of fictional melancholics in Hamlet, a character whose name is just one letter different from that of his dead son Hamnet, and I shall argue in Chapter 7 that repressed grief for Hamnet is a major element in that strangest of all Shakespeare's plays.

Notes

Full publication details of each source are in the bibliography.

1. Houlbrooke, *Death, Religion and the Family in England*, 1480–1750, p. 308.

2. Young, *Family Life in the Age of Shakespeare*, p. 225.

3. Insightful works about Renaissance medical theory include McLean, *The Renaissance Notion of Woman*, and Paster, Rowe and Floyd-Wilson, *Reading the Early Modern Passions*.

4. Quoted in Jacque Taylor, John DeFrain, and Linda Ernst, "Sudden Infant Death Syndrome," pp. 159–80, in Rando, *Parental Loss of a Child*. The quotation is on p. 172.

5. I am grateful to Niobe Way for sending me three draft chapters from *Deep Secrets: Boys' Friendships and the Crisis of Connection* before publication. Her work draws on interviews across cultural and class boundaries. Although there are obvious differences between the United States now and Shakespeare's England, there is also an underlying continuity in the linking of maleness with repression of tender emotion.

6. Further examples from *King Lear* are discussed in Chapter 10. Other instances of tears troubling men and being associated with women in the plays from *Hamlet* onwards include Claudius in *Hamlet*, 1.2.94, Hamlet himself, 3.4.127–30, and Laertes, 4.7.185–9; Sebastian in *Twelfth Night*, 2.1.40–2; Troilus in *Troilus and Cressida*, 1.1.9; Second Lord in *All's Well that Ends Well*, 4.3.107–8; Timon in *Timon of Athens*, 5.1.155–8 (a scene ascribed to Shakespeare rather than his possible collaborator, Thomas Middleton); Macbeth in *Macbeth* 1.7.72–4, and Macduff, 4.3.230–5; Coriolanus in *Coriolanus* 5.3.129–30; and Posthumus in *Cymbeline* 1.1.93–5.

7. Both quotations are from Parkes, *Bereavement*, pp. 121–22.

8. Sanders, "A comparison of Adult Bereavement in the Death of a Spouse, Child and Parent," p. 309.

9. Schatz, "Grief of Fathers," pp. 293–302, in Rando, *Parental Loss of a Child*. The quotation is from p.294. My italics.

10. Scully, "Men and Grieving," p. 97.

Conceal Me What I Am

But there are other factors that may have encouraged Shakespeare to hide, rather than express, his feelings about the death of his son. These factors predate the start of Shakespeare's career as an actor and playwright in the mid- to late 1580s, since from the first his plays are full of disguises, double, multiple, and ambiguous meanings, and intricate wordplay. In the early comedy, *The Two Gentlemen of Verona*, the heroine disguises herself as a page-boy to pursue her love. Behind this, amongst other things, is pragmatism: as women were played on Shakespeare's stage by older boys or young men, the disguise allows the actor a rest from the difficult task of attempting to portray a woman, and other playwrights use the same device.

As with images of men crying, however, it is a matter of degree. Throughout his career Shakespeare was attracted to wordplay and disguise more than his contemporaries. And it is not literal disguise that interests him most: symbolic disguise, pretending to be someone else, acting a role and *hiding your true feelings*, theater itself, fascinate him even more. "I am not what I am," says the blasphemous Iago, recalling God's self-revelation in the *Old Testament*, "I am that I am" (*Othello*, 1.1.65; *Exodus*, chapter 3, verse 14).[1]

Of course it's common in the drama of the period for a character to hide his or her feelings, but this is most usually a villainous or revengeful character like Iago; Shakespeare, however, is also strongly drawn to good characters who have to hide their feelings because they are too painful to be expressed *directly*. In *The Two Gentlemen of Verona* Julia, in her disguise as a page-boy, tells Silvia about her own sufferings as if they were someone else's. Silvia is drawn into the account, and asks how tall Julia was. The page-boy replies, "About my stature" (4.4.158). This makes us smile, as we know why the page-boy and Julia are the same height. But then the page-boy tells Silvia of a pageant in which he played a woman crying after she has been abandoned by her lover, and reports that Julia "moved there-withal,/Wept bitterly; and would I might be dead/If I in thought felt not her very sorrow" (4.4.170–2). Again, we know why the page-boy can report Julia's pain so feelingly; but rather than creating laughter, these lines plunge us into the depths of Julia's heartache. Indeed, the fact that she has to preserve her disguise and speak in character makes our sense of her sorrow even stronger; the only emotional outlet for her is to behave like a playwright and *invent a fiction that indirectly mirrors her own experience.*

A more famous example occurs about five years after Hamnet's death. Hamnet had a twin sister Judith (who survived into old age), and in *Twelfth Night,* Viola thinks her twin brother, Sebastian, is dead (as Judith's actually was). To survive in Illyria, Viola disguises herself as a young man, Cesario, and finds a place in Duke Orsino's court. She quickly falls for Orsino, but as Cesario has to hide this love, and also her mourning for her twin brother, a further burden Julia did not have. Yet the pain from these emotions is so strong that she cannot entirely conceal it and finds herself inventing a fictional sister and telling Orsino about her. But we know it is her own love she is talking about when she says, "My father had a daughter lov'd a man/As it might be perhaps, were I a woman,/I should your lordship" (2.4.107–9). The Duke is intrigued and asks for this lady's history.

> A blank, my lord; she never told her love,
> But let concealment like a worm i'th' bud
> Feed on her damask cheek; she pin'd in thought,
> And with a green and yellow melancholy
> She sate like Patience on a monument,
> Smiling at grief. Was this not love indeed? (2.4.110–15)

Orsino is moved by the story and asks whether the sister died. Viola/Cesario replies enigmatically, "I am all the daughters of my father's house,/And all the brothers too" (2.4.120–1). These last words are deeply moving, for they confirm the intensity of Viola's love for Orsino and her fear of taking that unspoken love to the grave; but they also confirm her isolation, for the use of "brothers" where we would expect "sons" recalls the (apparent) loss of Sebastian as well. Typically, for Shakespeare in his comedies, however, he does not dwell on this moment of deep emotion; the next lines forward the plot.

Viola and Julia are engaging in what nowadays might be called narrative therapy—they are making a fictional story of their own agony, pretending it is someone else's, as a means of survival, a means of *expressing but also of distancing themselves from their pain*. We'll see there is evidence that Shakespeare does the same thing with his own grief for Hamnet, and that when we really understand these moments they are even more heartbreaking than the one here when Viola briefly remembers her utter solitariness in life, and dissembles so she can endure the moment and carry on living. Yet more isolated is Hamlet, who upbraids himself for falling short of proper manliness, and who has "that within which passeth show," a disguised/hidden identity that cannot be expressed to others, even to Horatio; even, fully, to himself (1.2.85—the *Folio* wording).

The word "hide" and its cognates (excluding hide in the sense of animal hides) occurs more than 200 times in Shakespeare's works and "disguise" and its cognates occurs more than 60 times. It might be thought that the latter would only be found in a few works, but actually "disguise" and its compounds occur across 27 plays and one poem, or over two-thirds of his output. It's no surprise to find that the great poet of metamorphosis, of transformation of identity—Ovid—is the classical writer whose influence is most pronounced in Shakespeare's works, from the early *The Two Gentlemen of Verona*, where the word "metamorphis'd" occurs in the first scene (l.66), to the last scene of his final sole-authored play, *The Tempest*, where Prospero's climactic speech celebrating and renouncing magic is based on Medea's invocation to supernatural forces on behalf of Jason's dying father. In 1598 Francis Meres connected the authors in print, writing that Ovid's soul resided in Shakespeare.

Why might Shakespeare have been so strongly drawn to people who have to transform and hide their feelings behind a role, and whose words have hidden meanings? Clearly there can be no certainty, but there are possibilities worth exploring. When Shakespeare was young, his father John was one of the most important and wealthy citizens in Stratford, rising to the role of alderman and then bailiff, or chief administrative officer. But in 1576–1577, when William is 12–13, a very sensitive time for many children, and perhaps especially those who know they are their father's heir, things begin to go wrong. John stops attending council meetings, probably to avoid creditors, and starts to mortgage property, including some of the land inherited by his wife Mary.

David Thomas has traced the evidence in the public records. These show that the authorities took an interest in John as early as 1570, when he was twice accused of breaking the usury laws by charging interest at 20 and 25 percent, so it seems that well before his fall he was already sailing close to the wind. In 1575 John was twice accused of illegal wool-trading, the first time being fined 40 shillings—more than £400 in modern money, and very definitely a firm warning; the second case was inconclusive. In 1578 he changed from creditor to debtor, borrowing £40 (about £8000 in modern money) from Edmund Lambert on the security of a Wilmcote property inherited from his wife's family; he did not pay the debt when it fell due in 1580, and ended up in a legal dispute with Edmund's son, which was still going in 1597. In the mid 1570s he abandoned his application for something necessary to confirm his status as a gentleman—a family coat of arms. In the early 1590s he was listed among those not attending compulsory communion because of fear of creditors.[2]

Many men in such a situation would try to disguise what was happening from their children, but inevitably time reveals what the debtor has tried to conceal. Whatever the exact details, Shakespeare experienced a home moving from optimism and comedy to (hidden) tragedy, and this is likely to have been a cause of grief. Although death is the most obvious cause of mourning, any disturbing loss, such as a humiliating fall in community status and financial security, can cause someone to hide their pain in public and to internalize grief. Shakespeare could reasonably have expected to go to university—he was clearly clever enough—but his father's financial difficulties may have added this to the losses he had to endure. His first biographer, Nicholas Rowe, states that financial circumstances led to Shakespeare being withdrawn from school because his assistance was required at home. While Rowe's source and its reliability is not known, it does fit the later evidence given above. (Even had John's financial situation improved, Shakespeare's marriage at 18 in 1582 finally scuppered any chance of attending university because Oxford and Cambridge would only allow bachelors to become bachelors of arts). Further, Shakespeare may have seen other families suffering financially because there was an economic recession in Stratford and the surrounding countryside in the last quarter of the sixteenth century. Certainly the sense of the loss of the Garden of Eden, of Paradise, recurs in Shakespeare's works, and this may well be one of the experiences that contributed to this preoccupation.

So one cause of his interest in hidden emotion and meaning might be his father's declining status and financial difficulties. Family disgrace can be unbearable to children today, but in Shakespeare's more communal society it was an even greater source of public shame and humiliation. When Shakespeare became successful, he acquired the coat of arms and rank of gentleman his father had wished for, bought the second biggest house in Stratford, and started to acquire land and property, which in practice replaced that lost by his father; this suggests a strong desire to re-establish his own, and his family's, honor and social position. His plays, too, are riddled with men concerned, often obsessed, with questions of honor and status; honor and its cognates occur nearly 1000 times in his works.

A further need both for concealment of his earlier life and for establishing his status as a gentleman may have arisen when he arrived in London in the mid-to-late 1580s. By the early 1590s he had had some success, since at least one of the university-educated playwrights, Robert Greene, looked down on this man from rural Warwickshire as an "upstart crow" and social climber.[3] Indeed, some of Shakespeare's own *Sonnets* show embarrassment at the fact that he was an actor in, as well as a writer of, plays, an activity Greene viewed with contempt, comparing actors to puppets; for instance, "Alas, 'tis true, I have gone here and there,/And made myself a motley to the view" (Sonnet 110:1–2). Shakespeare might also have wished to conceal the exact circumstances of his marriage to Anne Hathaway, since he was one of only three Stratford men between 1570 and 1630 known to have been married before the age of 20—the average for sixteenth century men was 27/28—and the only one of the three known to have been marrying a woman already pregnant. There was much for a man eager to improve his status to wish to conceal.[4]

Interestingly, Shakespeare is not the only giant of literature concerned with hidden meanings and emotions, and questions of status, whose father fell from grace: Charles Dickens, Henrik Ibsen, and James Joyce all had fathers who descended into financial difficulties, leading to a loss of social position for their families, and all three share Shakespeare's preoccupation with hidden and disguised truth. Of course, problems with money and loss of status were, and are, common occurrences, and most who experience them do not become great writers. I think, however, it is more than coincidental that, of those who gained high status by writing, several had this same motivating experience in childhood or early youth.

A more contentious possibility concerns religion. In 1757 a Spiritual Last Will and Testament was found in the roof of John's house on

Henley Street. The original has unfortunately disappeared, and the Testament is only known through a copy, so it could be a forgery; but its language has been shown to come from Shakespeare's period rather than the period in which it was discovered, which argues that at least some authentic document is behind it. The language is also Catholic rather than Protestant, being based on the last testament of Charles Borromeo, one of the founders of the Counter-Reformation. Against this apparent indication of Catholic faith, in the years when he was in power, John did not openly oppose the Reformation and its iconoclasm; but to acknowledge yourself a Catholic in Elizabeth the First's England was to court fines and persecution, so it is no surprise that such a faith might be hidden in a roof. Perhaps John did what many people do under an oppressive regime: conform outwardly, but not (completely) inwardly. As Stephen Greenblatt suggests, Shakespeare "might have sensed that his father was playing a part, without ever knowing securely where the boundary lay between fiction and reality."[5] In other words, he might have learned to be wary about exposing his inner self to the public gaze.

Further, Shakespeare's elder daughter Susanna was charged for not taking the compulsory Easter communion in 1606, a few months after the Gunpowder Plot. Her marriage to the staunchly Protestant John Hall in 1607 could in part have been a way of answering this social unorthodoxy. And Shakespeare's mother came from Catholic stock. Thus there is at least circumstantial evidence of Catholic sympathies within Shakespeare's wider family. In addition, his close friends, Hamnet and Judith Sadler, after whom his twins Hamnet and Judith were named, and who probably acted as godparents, were among the others charged with Susanna in Easter 1606; and Hamnet petitioned that they needed time to clear their consciences, which suggests they had difficulty accommodating themselves to the more belligerent religious orthodoxy that followed the arrest of Guy Fawkes and his fellow conspirators the previous November. Stratford, on the surface, became increasingly Protestant after 1584, when Richard Barton became vicar at Holy Trinity, to be followed by a succession of vicars, such as John Bramhall and Richard Bifield, with puritanical leanings. Ann Hughes notes that in 1602 the puritan bailiff, Daniel Baker "imposed on any member of the Corporation who allowed any plays or interludes to be performed on corporation property" a 10 shillings fine, more than 100 pounds nowadays.[6] We can imagine how uneasy a playwright and, possibly, his father would have felt with this latter development in their native town.

Moreover, recent research has shown that the area around Stratford, particularly to the north and west, was one of the strongholds of Catholicism in the second half of the sixteenth century; and many of Shakespeare's Stratford neighbors, such as the Reynolds and the Badgers, were overtly or covertly Catholic. René Weis gives a useful summary of the evidence of Catholic sympathies in Stratford, which reinforces Stephen Greenblatt's suggestion that one of the things Shakespeare learned as a child was the wisdom of keeping your views, whatever they were, to yourself in a society in which both a Catholic and a Protestant queen might inflict unimaginable suffering on your body for believing what was out-of-fashion.[7] The great modern poet Seamus Heaney, who grew up in a Catholic family in Northern Ireland in the 1940s and 1950s, learned the same attitude, as he records in his poem "Whatever You Say, Say Nothing."

So there is circumstantial evidence about Catholic sympathies among Shakespeare's family and neighbors and in his locality, but is there evidence of his own religious sympathies from his plays? Whole books have been dedicated to investigating this matter, since famously, notoriously even, you can find things for and against almost any belief, including religious belief, in Shakespeare—further evidence to support the conclusion that Shakespeare learned to keep his personal emotions locked within. But while it is not surprising to hear anti-Catholic sentiments from a writer in an officially Protestant England, it *is* surprising to find as many sympathetic references to the old religious beliefs and practices as we do. In *Hamlet*, for instance, the Ghost has come from Purgatory, which did not exist, according to Article 22 of the Church of England's 39 Articles of Faith. Interestingly, though, Shakespeare does not announce that Purgatory is the Ghost's abode; rather the Ghost says that by day "the foul crimes" of the Ghost's "days of nature/Are burnt and *purged* away," (1.5.12–3; my italics). Of course, the reference does not prove that Shakespeare believed in Purgatory, but it certainly suggests familiarity with the basic doctrine; interestingly, however, the reference is in disguise and might be heard differently by people with different beliefs, or might be lost altogether in the excitement of the plot. As David Bevington points out, there are also two direct references to Purgatory, in *Othello* and *Romeo and Juliet*; but again, these do not draw attention to themselves in theological terms.[8]

One of the most striking suggestions of Catholic sympathies is in Shakespeare's last sole-authored play, *The Tempest*, which ends with an epilogue that is much more serious in tone than the ones in earlier plays such as *A Midsummer Night's Dream, Henry the Fifth,* and *As You Like It*.[9] The actor playing Prospero reveals, "And my ending is despair,/Unless I be reliev'd by prayer," and his final words are, "As you from crimes would pardon'd be,/Let your indulgence set me free" (*The Tempest*, Epilogue, 15–6; 19–20). The last line, of course, is an invitation to the audience to show its appreciation and may also be a request for James the First to indulge him by releasing him from the obligation to be the playwright for the King's Men, as David Beauregard notes.[10] But as he also comments, "indulgence" may have other connotations as well, particularly in the context of the need to be pardoned from the crimes, or sins, we have committed. Indulgences lay at the heart of the split between Catholics and Protestants in the Reformation. In Catholic teaching there was a Treasury of Grace (or Merit) built up primarily by the sacrifice of Jesus on the cross, but also added to by the sacrifices of the saints; and this abundant goodness could be set in the scales against the crimes of ordinary sinners. The beneficiaries could be people who had died and were being purged in Purgatory, as well as those still living. Prayers of intercession from believers could aid the purification of sinners in Purgatory and on earth, and these prayers could help to obtain for sinners an indulgence (a full or partial remission of the punishment due for sinful behavior). In other words, another person's fervent prayer might win an indulgence that could help to "set free" a penitent person despairing because of his awareness of his own "crimes" or sins. The epilogue seems to hint at something very close to traditional Catholic doctrine; but again it does so indirectly, so that a Protestant could understand it in a more general sense.

Further, as historians such as David Cressy and Ralph Houlbrooke have pointed out, one of the additional effects of the Reformation was to shorten funeral services and to make them more impersonal. Stephen Greenblatt has noted that Shakespeare's strangest play, *Hamlet*, is preoccupied with the inadequacy of the established burial services, Ophelia and Laertes (as well as Hamlet) complaining about their brevity, in both cases on behalf of their father and, in Laertes' case, when Ophelia too has died.[11] Unsurprisingly, no record survives of the burial service used for Hamnet in 1596, but almost certainly it followed the shorter and more impersonal Anglican text, even if Shakespeare and/or some members of his family preferred the longer, traditional ceremony. (As we'll see in Chapter 3, it is possible that Shakespeare was not even present—what effect might that have had on a grieving father in later years?).

There is indeed evidence from the next decade to suggest that the nature of the burial service was important to Shakespeare. His youngest brother, Edmund, was just three years older than Shakespeare's elder daughter Susanna and four and three-quarter-years older than Hamnet and Judith. Edmund, Susanna, Hamnet, and Judith grew up in the same house and almost certainly played together as children of similar ages. When Hamnet died in 1596 Shakespeare might have seen Edmund as the nearest thing to a son remaining to him, and it is interesting that Edmund was the only brother to follow Shakespeare into the London theater. When we look at Shakespeare's will in the next chapter, we'll find that he went to elaborate lengths to try and ensure that his property passed eventually to a male, rather than a female, descendant; and substitute sons become crucial figures in Shakespeare's later plays (see Chapter 10 onward).

Edmund died at the young age of 27, in late December 1607, and a partial record of his funeral has survived. It was expensive, costing 20 shillings, a substantial amount in Shakespeare's day, and included a knell rung before noon on the great bell of St. Mary Overy, in Southwark, and burial in the church, not the churchyard, a great honor for a mere player. To put the expense in perspective, tolling of the lesser bell cost, at the most, one shilling; and a common burial such a player might usually receive, cost 2d., one-one hundred and twentieth the cost of this one![12] Someone clearly wanted Edmund to have an elaborate send-off into the next world, involving some elements of ritual associated more with the traditional Catholic faith than with the more austere Protestant approach. Further, the ringing of the funeral bell before noon was unusual; it normally took place in the afternoon. But if Shakespeare were involved in preparations for a performance in the afternoon or evening, the morning would be the only time he could attend. The most likely provider of this costly funeral is Edmund's prosperous eldest brother William, and it is possible that one reason for it was that Edmund's death recalled Hamnet's in Shakespeare's imagination. We will find that in several plays written after Edmund's death, Shakespeare seems especially concerned with fathers trying to come to terms with the apparent, and in one case actual, death of a child.

So we have circumstantial evidence that Shakespeare had more sympathy with the traditional, more elaborate ceremonies and beliefs of the Catholic Church than he could openly acknowledge, and this may be a further reason for his fascination with hidden and disguised emotion.

Another factor that probably increased Shakespeare's focus on double and hidden meanings was his fathering of twins. As they were of different sexes, they were not of course identical, unlike the fictional Viola and Sebastian. Nevertheless, there are always similarities between twins, especially as babies, when Shakespeare probably saw his most, before his departure for London. In one of his early works, *The Comedy of Errors*, he takes a play by the Roman dramatist Plautus, which has one set of twins, and doubles this to two. There's an obvious advantage from a theatrical viewpoint in doubling the opportunities for farcical confusion, and it is the farce of the situation that Shakespeare highlights. But there may have been a psychological attraction as well; if he were already missing his young twins, he could at least have them doubled in his imagination, in rehearsal, and in performance. Indeed, the end of the play reunites a family separated for more than 20 years. Shakespeare had split apart his own family by going to London in the mid- to late 1580s and may have found some comfort in the idea that a family long separated could eventually be reunited, because he must have realized it would be many years before Stratford became his main domicile again, and may have already felt some guilt about the separation. All four twins in *The Comedy of Errors* are male; but as noted above, about five years after Hamnet's death in *Twelfth Night*, he creates his most memorable twins who are of different sexes. In Shakespeare's theater a boy or young man playing a young woman already introduced a twinlike image in which both sexes were present in the *same figure*; disguising the young woman as a young man, as Viola was disguised in *Twelfth Night*, was a kind of double twinning, which may have had considerable psychological appeal.

It's also worth noting, as Katherine Duncan-Jones and Germaine Greer point out, that before birth, twins are in one sense rivals for the nutrients from their mother's body, and that it is common for birth to be premature and for one twin to be healthier than the other.[13] Judith lived to be 77, nearly 25 years more than the average span of her Stratford contemporaries; so if either twin were born weaker, it is likely to have been Hamnet. David Bevington notes that several deaths of sons, most famously those of the young princes in the Tower in *Richard the Third*, occur in plays definitely written before Hamnet's death.[14] Such scenes are of course very effective theatrically, but it could be that they are also colored by personal experience of a weak male child. Certainly across Shakespeare's career there are many vulnerable young boys who do not make it to manhood, while young baby girls under threat, like Perdita in *The Winter's Tale* and Miranda in *The Tempest* survive, as his two daughters did.

Interestingly, "twin" and its cognates occur 15 times in Shakespeare's dialogue, only four times as a literal reference. Of the other 11, eight are linked with negative ideas of division, burden, or loss, all but one of these in works completed after Hamnet's death. "Twain," meaning two, often in terms of two people or beings forcibly separated, occurs 45 times; and it is likely that someone as alert to puns as Shakespeare would have linked the words at some level, especially after his twins were twain.

The aforementioned seem to me the most likely contributory factors to Shakespeare's fascination with concealed emotion and double/hidden meanings; but the really important matter for this exploration of grief is the *fascination itself*, whatever its cause.

Notes

Full publication details of every source are in the bibliography.

The biographical information in this and subsequent chapters comes from Chambers, *William Shakespeare: A Study of Facts and Problems* and Schoenbaum, *Shakespeare: A Documentary Life* and *William Shakespeare: A Compact Documentary Life,* except where otherwise stated. The interpretations are my own.

1. Both the *Bishop's Bible* and the *Geneva Bible* have the same translation.

2. Thomas, *Shakespeare in the Public Records*, pp. 2–5. As Nicholas Knight points out in *Autobiography in Shakespeare's Plays: Lands so by His Father Lost*, Edmund Lambert's attempt to gain property which, in the Shakespeare's eyes, was not legitimately his, might be an influence on the choice of the name Edmund for the villainous usurper in *King Lear* (p. 13).

3. The "upstart crow" reference occurs in *Greene's Groatsworth of Wit* (although, since it was published posthumously, it is possible that part or all of the text is by someone pretending to be Robert Greene). Shakespeare is not named, but that he is intended is shown by the fact that this "upstart crow" thinks he is the only "Shake-scene in a country," and by the parody of a line from *Henry the Sixth, Part 3*. For a fuller discussion of Shakespeare's response to Greene after Greene's death, see Chapter 12.

4. Jones, *Family Life in Shakespeare's England*, p. 10, and Young, *Family Life in the Age of Shakespeare*, p. 41.

5. Greenblatt, *Will in the World*, p. 102.

6. Ann Hughes, "Building a Godly Town: Religious and Cultural Divisions in Stratford-upon-Avon," in Bearman, *The History of an English Borough*, pp.97–109. The quotation is from p.103.

7. Weis, chapter 3, both editions, and also *Shakespeare Unbound* pp. 331, 336 and 416–7, and *Shakespeare Revealed*, pp. 293, 298, and 370–1.

8. Bevington, *Shakespeare's Ideas*, pp. 112–3.

9. In Beauregard, "New Light on Shakespeare's Catholicism: Prospero's Epilogue in *The Tempest.*"

10. Beauregard, *Catholic Theology in Shakespeare's Plays*, p. 156.

11. Greenblatt, *Hamlet in Purgatory* (throughout) and *Will in the World*, especially pp. 312–3. Matthew Greenfield has also written an illuminating account of the way the Reformation changed burial services, "The Cultural Functions of Renaissance Elegy."

12. I am grateful to Julian Litten, author of *The English Way of Death*, for an e-mail containing this information about funeral costs.

13. Duncan-Jones, *Ungentle Shakespeare*, pp. 90–1, and Greer, *Shakespeare's Wife*, pp. 195–7. In giving an account of a shipwreck in *The Comedy of Errors*, Egeon states that his wife was "more careful for the latter-born" of her twins (1.1.78). This of course is most likely to be just a detail to forward the plot, but it might also be based on a (not necessarily accurate) memory of maternal partiality.

14. Bevington, *Shakespeare and Biography*, pp. 102–3.

I'll Seek Him Deeper Than E'er
Plummet Sounded

Shakespeare and his contemporaries knew by experience how precarious human life was. Robert Burton writes that, after the loss of friends and family members, "brave discreet men otherwise oftentimes forget themselves, and weep like children many months together . . . and will not be comforted."[1] Especially fragile were young lives. The figures of childhood mortality from Shakespeare's England make grim reading: a third of children failed to reach the age of 10 (including Shakespeare's two elder sisters, Joan and Margaret, and his younger sister, Anne). Indeed, 40 years ago it was thought by some historians, for instance, Lawrence Stone, that the frequency of infant and child death meant that a parent would not have felt much sorrow, but more recent research has recognized this view as naïve. Particularly relevant is Michael MacDonald's investigation of the records of Richard Napier, a clergyman who acted as a combination of astrologer, doctor, and counselor for more than 30 years, starting in 1597. MacDonald tabulated Napier's case histories, and these show that bereavement was equal second as a cause of distress and anxiety for Napier's patients. 134 out of the 717 (mainly ordinary) people who came to Napier, felt inwardly disturbed by grief they could not control or resolve. MacDonald comments that in this period "bereavement was a common explanation for madness and despair."[2] In 85 percent of instances this uncontainable grief was for a close family member. Out of these cases, just under 50 percent were for a child, more than for either a spouse or a parent. As we might expect, the mother was the more frequently affected parent; but fathers too are amongst those needing to consult Napier because they could not come to terms with the pain and disturbance they were suffering.

Clearly, the loss of a child in these cases was far from easy to deal with. In *Birth, Marriage and Death* David Cressy summarizes the change of perspective in relation to Tudor and Stuart England brought about by primary source research like MacDonald's: "Historians once advanced the notion that people in the past did not love each other and were coldly unemotional in the face of a death in their family. But the bulk of the evidence indicates that love, pain, and grief were deeply and widely experienced."[3] There is some indication that the frequency of stillbirths and deaths shortly after birth meant that these were less disturbing for most parents than they are nowadays; for instance, "We both found the sorrow for the loss of this child, on whom we had bestowed such care and affection, and whose delicate favor and bright grey eyes was so deeply imprinted on our hearts, far to surpass our grief for the decease of his three elder brothers, whose dying almost as soon as they were born, were not so endeared to us as this was."[4] (But even in a case like this we need to remember that most responses we have from this period come from fathers rather than mothers, and that at least some mothers may have felt much deeper pain for miscarriages and stillborn babies than has survived in the historical record).

Surveying the remaining evidence, Ralph Houlbrooke concludes that, in sixteenth and seventeenth century England, "After babies had survived a few days their deaths certainly caused sadness."[5] Indeed, Shakespeare probably felt relief when Hamnet completed his first decade and seemed to be heading for manhood: between the ages of 10 and 14 deaths were less frequent than for any other age group. It would have been a mortifying blow when the boy died the following year. Houlbrooke refers to the experience of Jeremy Taylor, a seventeenth century divine, that parents who could endure the loss of an infant, were often unable to cope with the loss of an older child, and summarizes, "Deaths in later childhood were far less frequent than in infancy and early childhood, and often harder to bear."[6] (Interestingly, in 1986 the clinical psychologist Therese Rando reported that the intensity of a mother's grief for a dead child does not seem to vary according to the child's age, but that a father's often does: the older the child, the more difficult the grief for many fathers).[7] Linda Pollock quotes an example from a sixteenth century shopkeeper called Wallington, whose four-year-old daughter died. This instance is especially interesting because inevitably fewer records remain for people of his social rank: "The grief for this child was so great that I forgot myself so much that I did offend God in it, for I broke all my purposes, promises and convenants with my God, for I was much distracted in my mind, and could not be comforted, although my friends spoke so comfortably to me."[8]

And Hamnet was not just any child for Shakespeare: he was his only son, his heir. This was a period when a male child was valued more highly than a female one by most fathers, and when the absence of a son meant a loss of social prestige: a daughter, when she married, gave up the family name and became a part of her husband's family. There is clear evidence that Shakespeare wanted a male heir. In his will he made a determined effort to ensure that his property passed eventually to a male, even though, or perhaps because, he had no son to leave it to. His property was to go to his elder daughter, Susanna, but on her death it was to pass

> to the first son of her body lawfully issuing & to the heirs Males of the body of the said first son lawfully issuing & for default of such issue to the second son of her body lawfully issuing & to the heirs Males of the body of the said second son lawfully issuing & for default of such heirs to the third son of the body of the said Susanna lawfully issuing. . . .[9]

And so on, to the seventh son, all for the hope of a male grandson to inherit! This will was made in 1616, when Susanna was 32, had been married for more than eight years, and had only had one child, a daughter. But Shakespeare still had a desperate fantasy of a clutch of grandsons: clearly a granddaughter was not enough. It seems probable that he would have agreed with Polixenes in *The Winter's Tale* that, for a father, his "joy is nothing else/But fair posterity" (4.4.408–9).

This is evidence of one way in which the loss of Hamnet must have pierced Shakespeare to the quick. What might have comforted him? Colin Murray Parkes notes that, for all "social animals," not just human beings, "the principal behavior pattern evoked by loss is searching."[10] This process of searching, physically and/or mentally, for the absent one is often helped by remaining in the vicinity of the bereavement. In the terrible Aberfan disaster in Wales in 1966, 116 children were buried when a tip of coal waste collapsed onto their village. Afterward, each bereaved family was offered the chance to move elsewhere, but most did not take this, giving as the main reason "the wish to stay close to the dead children."[11] Many counselors and therapists link this searching behavior with the comfort received by mourners from regular journeys to the loved one's grave. Evelyn Gillis, for instance, records her own need to keep returning to her daughter's grave: "Sometimes I sat by her grave for five to six hours. Although I knew I should leave . . . I could not find the strength to go . . . Nor did I want to."[12] Dennis Klass notes how a self-help group for bereaved parents developed various rituals to help participants with their grief, one of which was a Saturday cemetery visit to the graves of each other's children. When the idea was first introduced at a meeting "it turned out that many of the members had been doing it informally for many years."[13] Shakespeare also seems to have understood the comfort a churchyard could give: in Act 5 of *Hamlet* the Prince, when musing in the graveyard with Horatio, is calmer than we have seen him before in the face of the facts of physical decay.

Shakespeare, however, did not have this form of comfort available after Hamnet died in 1596, because his life had become London-based; (Shakespeare did not watch his children grow as most of his neighbors did their children). It is not known how often he returned home. In the seventeenth century John Aubrey, whose reliability is open to question, records him as going home only once a year, without saying for how long. The distance from London to Stratford is more than 90 miles, and it has been estimated that the shortest route and most hurried journey to Stratford, and back again to London, would have usually taken three or four days in the Elizabethan period, so it is improbable that Shakespeare undertook the journey frequently, especially after he became an estab-lished and busy man of the London theater. What is likely is that he was already experiencing some feelings of guilt over his absence from his wife and children, and that these would be increased by his son's death. And even if he were at home for the funeral, when he rejoined his fellow actors, he would have been coping with his grief with no family member, favorite playplace of his son's, or burial place, to support him. This need for com-fort is not just a modern phenomenon; Ralph Houlbrooke records several instances from the sixteenth and seventeenth centuries in which "The sharing of grief with a spouse equally affected by bereavement was a mit-igating factor for parents who suffered the loss of children."[14] If there was such comfort for Shakespeare, it would have been of short duration. Similarly, there was little possibility of a further child to take Hamnet's place within the family: William and Anne had had no children for 11 years, and Anne was now 40.

Perhaps initially Shakespeare felt he could cope best with Hamnet's death not by being in places associated with his son, but by moving away from them. In the year after Hamnet's death, he took his family to a new and bigger house, New Place. Of course, there were many reasons for the change, not least, as we have seen, the desire to restore the family status lost by his father and to show the townsfolk of Stratford that the young man who set off for London having achieved little had made it and could now afford to buy its second biggest residence. But the (mistaken) belief that he could erase the pain of bereavement by a change of location might also have contributed. Certainly, in practical terms, the *effect* of the move would have been to erode another set of physical and emotional connections with the boy.

Indeed, it may be that if Hamnet's death were sudden, Shakespeare was not at home when it occurred, and he may not have even have reached Stratford in time for the burial, on Wednesday, 11 August. The company Shakespeare belonged to, the (Lord) Chamberlain's Men, was in a difficult situation. Its patron, Lord Hunsdon, who had supported the theater against the attacks from the puritanical aldermen and preachers of London, died on 23 July. The players must have been apprehensive about their future, especially when the following month, William Cobham, Lord Brooke, was appointed Lord Chamberlain; he was not the supporter of players that his predecessor had been. Thomas Nashe wrote to William Cotton in September, "now the players, as if they writ another *Christ's Tears*, are piteously persecuted by the Lord Mayor and aldermen, and however in the old Lord's time they thought their state settled, it is now so uncertain they cannot build upon it."[15] Because we know that the theaters did survive and playwrights such as Shakespeare and Jonson (the latter unperformed at this date) went on to write some of the greatest works of world drama, it is easy to forget how precarious the survival of a theatrical company was in a world where puritanical ideas were growing ever stronger, and how anxious its members, especially those who had invested money as Shakespeare had, must have felt at such times.

A second blow had occurred the day before Lord Hunsdon's death. After a meeting of the Privy Council on 22 July, letters were sent to the JPs of Middlesex and Surrey to prohibit theatrical performances for fear of the plague.[16] (It turned out not to be a major outbreak in London, but that is with the benefit of hindsight; there were also strong outbreaks in Reading, Salisbury, and Exeter). In the previous two plague-free summers the diary of impresario Philip Henslowe records payments for plays for his company, The Admiral's Men, through August and into September, so it must have been a bitter blow to Shakespeare's company as well to have its income cut off at a stroke.[17] The usual reaction to such a closure was to go on tour, and the likelihood is that Shakespeare's company left London either before (if they saw it coming) or soon after the closure, with the further incentive of getting away from the plague; (if the former, they may not have learnt of their patron's death till they were on the road). By early August, at least some of the company were performing at Faversham, in Kent.[18] Was Shakespeare with his fellow actors?

We cannot know for sure, but the likely answer is yes. Shakespeare was not only a founder member, actor, and playwright of the Chamberlain's Men, but also an investor, or sharer, roughly equivalent to a modern shareholder, helping to meet the expenses and sharing in any profits. The company was only two years old, and was in the business of establishing itself against Henslowe's rival, and previously preeminent troupe, The Admiral's Men. Shakespeare's own financial future was bound up with the success of the company in London and adjacent counties, so at this stage in his career it was in his interest to travel with them, especially given the precariousness of income and patronage in London. And if he were on tour, it would have taken a day, and more probably two days, for a message from Stratford to reach London, and who knows how long for a messenger, a stranger, to locate a traveling company somewhere in Kent. Then Shakespeare would have had to return to Stratford, probably via London. All told, it could well have taken at least a week for Shakespeare to reach Stratford. Robert Bearman writes that from "the evidence we have in other cases, a delay of even three days was unusual" before burial, to prevent the spread of disease and the sight of bodily decay, a risk which was highest in summer.[19] And if Shakespeare had stayed in London rather than traveled with his fellow players to Kent, it would still have taken at the very least three to four days for a message to reach London and for Shakespeare to travel home (assuming he could leave at once).

All in all, then, there is a strong chance that Shakespeare was not present when his son died and a possibility that he was not even at the funeral. He was unusual for his time in having three children by the time he was 21, and no (known) children thereafter. Because of the threat of infant and child mortality, large families were common: his friends the Sadlers had 14 children, and his leading actor Richard Burbage, eight; but for Shakespeare all his hopes for a male heir rested in Hamnet. Why did the Shakespeares have no more children? The traditional suspicion has been that Shakespeare and Anne grew apart after he went to London, perhaps before then, and the absence of any warm words about his wife in his will, in contrast to many other wills of the period, seems to support this. But giving birth was very hazardous in the late sixteenth century, and the birth of twins even more so. It may be that Anne suffered an injury that prevented her from bearing further children. Whatever the reason, the outcome is clear.

What other effects might Shakespeare's general absence from Stratford have had on his inner emotions? Roberta Woodgate found that parents with fewer good memories of "normal child-parent activities or interactions" found coming to terms with a child's death "more of a struggle." She also discovered that physical contact plays an important part in accepting such a loss, quoting one father as saying, "I regret not holding him. That is one of my big regrets."[20] Joan Arnold and Penelope Buschman Gemma confirm that "Respondents who had not been able to see or touch their child expressed deep remorse."[21] Shakespeare may have been in this position. He certainly shows an awareness of the importance of seeing and touching a child in *King Lear*, combining the two absences in one line, when the blinded and guilt-ridden Earl of Gloucester addresses the absent son he will never see again: "Might I but live to see thee in my touch/I'ld say I had eyes again" (4.1.23–4).

Whether a parent has mainly positive memories or not, much research confirms what common sense would suggest: that guilt is prominent among the emotions experienced when a child dies. Parents inevitably ask themselves, what could I have done to prevent this happening, even when the answer is nothing. Therese Rando's work with bereaved parents led her to conclude that guilt "appears to be the single most pervasive parental response to the death of a child."[22] Bob Wright quotes a bereaved parent as saying, "I must have done something really wicked to deserve this."[23] How much more guilt might parents have felt in Shakespeare's day, when the idea that God punished people directly for their sins was more common than nowadays? And how much more guilt might a father have felt if he was not even there, or was only there at the end, and had spent most of his child's 11 years of growth away from him in London?

There was another reason why Shakespeare might have felt guilty about his absence. From 1592 to 1596 had been an especially difficult period for most of the inhabitants of Stratford, with burials outnumbering baptisms in all but one year. 1594 began a series of cold, wet summers, with poor harvests and scarcity, culminating the year after Hamnet's death with 161 more burials than baptisms, the highest deficit in Stratford since the plague year of Shakespeare's birth. Because food is readily available to many of us nowadays, we can fail to realize how dependent an area like Stratford and its surrounding countryside was on the harvest and its effect on the staff of life, bread. As well as this dearth, Shakespeare's neighbors and friends had had to grapple with the further hardship and damage caused by extensive fires in 1594 and 1595.[24]

We'll find that guilt becomes a stronger and stronger element in Shakespeare's plays as his career progresses, and that the apparent or actual death of a child, and the need to ask for a child's forgiveness, are common features in Shakespeare's final plays. But I wish to argue more widely that the plays from the late 1590s onwards reveal the journey of a man who, like most bereaved parents, struggled to make sense of his devastating loss, and who provided himself with fictional resurrections of seemingly dead children as a way of introducing other possibilities into his life story, and of enduring his grief.

In other words, among many other things, he engaged in a kind of narrative therapy, though *not necessarily at a conscious level*. Although he revised at least some of his plays, Shakespeare generally seems to have written fluently and quickly, in contrast to Ben Jonson, who tells us he was criticized for writing slowly and carefully; indeed Jonson complains about Shakespeare's facility, indicating that he wrote *too* quickly and casually. In *A Midsummer Night's Dream* Theseus imagines the poet's eye "in a fine frenzy rolling," and this summarizes the effect that reading or listening to Shakespeare's plays creates (5.1.12). Afterward, reading through, or in rehearsal, their creator *may* have become conscious of patterns generated in the flood of composition that had personal, as well as theatrical, resonance; or he may not. Certainly, counselors and researchers such as Martin Payne, Cheryl White, and David Denborough confirm that it helps many people struggling with a desolating experience to create a transformed narrative of events from their life. In Jens Brockmeier and Rom Harre's words, such transformations "open us up to the hypothetical . . . taking into account many potential viewpoints."[25]

The evidence for an element of narrative therapy is strongest in Shakespeare's final plays, such as *The Tempest*, written 14 to 15 years after Hamnet's death. Here, Shakespeare, unusually, invents his own plot; and one of the characters he chooses to create is Alonso, alone in his grief for his apparently drowned son Ferdinand. He seeks his son everywhere, in line with the process noted by Parkes, and feels terrible guilt that his son has drowned because of his own "trespass," a word reminding us of the plea for forgiveness in the Our Father, or Lord's Prayer, (3.3.99).[26] When he cannot find his son, Alonso wishes for the only father and son reunion he believes is possible, that brought about by suicide. He thinks that because of his sins, "my son i'th' ooze is bedded; and/I'll seek him deeper than e'er plummet sounded/And with him there lie mudded" (3.3.100–2). What a moving and tender image—his son lying in bed—is set against the powerful horror of drowning in the oozy mud, and the yearning to be with his son again, (the falling cadence of the last line reinforcing the emotional impact). We are not told Ferdinand's age, but he is certainly old enough to marry Miranda, so at least a few years older than Hamnet was when he died. But the image suggests Shakespeare is picturing a young boy sleeping in bed rather than an adolescent. (See Chapter 14 for a more detailed discussion of *The Tempest*).

Even at the end of his career, then, there is evidence that a transformed Hamnet is still a ghostly presence in Shakespeare's plays. This corresponds with the findings of many counselors and researchers that the loss of a child leads to most parents, in the title of Roberta Woodgate's article, "Living in a World without Closure," and further, not wanting closure, if that is taken to mean forgetting their child, but rather wanting to move to a new relationship with the one they have lost, and often finding this extremely difficult to reach. Dennis Klass, Phyllis Silverman, and Steven Nickman present the same desire for continuity in *Continuing Bonds*, and Paul Rosenblatt finds that for "almost every" bereaved parent, "the child continued to be a presence" in his or her life.[27] The extent of this presence is highlighted by Jean Simons, when she notes that, after the free-phone Child Death Helpline went nationwide in England in 1995, many parents contacted it not just to talk about recent losses but about long-dead children, sometimes from as much as 50 years before, and that many were ashamed that they still felt grief.[28] This shows the other side of a continuing presence of a dead child in a parent's life: a positive experience can help the parent towards a new relationship with the lost one; but one that focuses on loss rather than a new relationship can hinder the parent from moving on in his or her journey. These troubled parents are the descendants of those who went to Richard Napier between 1597 and 1634 with disturbances of feeling that, in some cases, took them to the edge of what we normally label sanity.

Before we start to explore in detail individual works that suggest a continuing bond between Shakespeare and his dead child, it is important to emphasize that the evidence is *cumulative*: no single play reveals it in its entirety. Rather, the moments and patterns discussed are like jigsaw pieces that reveal a coherent picture only when all are in place. It is that jigsaw the following chapters will start to put together.

Notes

Full publication details of every source are in the bibliography.

1. Burton, *Anatomy of Melancholy*, Partition 1, p. 359.
2. MacDonald, *Mystical Bedlam*, p. 17. The statistics are from pp.77-8. I'm grateful to Stephen Greenblatt for telling me about the book in response to an e-mail.
3. Cressy, *Birth, Marriage and Death*, p. 393.
4. Simonds D'Ewes, quoted in Stone, *The Family, Sex and Marriage in England, 1500–1800*, p.106.
5. Houlbrooke, *Death, Religion and the Family*, p. 234.
6. Houlbrooke, pp. 8, 234.
7. Rando, *Parental Loss of a Child*, p. 223.
8. Pollock, *Forgotten Children*, p. 135.
9. Thomas, *Shakespeare in the Public Records*, p. 32.
10. Parkes, *Bereavement*, p. 59.
11. Parkes, p. 55.
12. Gillis, "A Single Parent Confronting the Loss of an Only Child," pp. 315–20, in Rando, *Parental Loss of a Child*. The quotation is from p. 319.
13. Klass, "The Deceased Child in the Psychic and Social Worlds of Bereaved Parents during the Resolution of Grief," p. 158.
14. Houlbrooke, *Death, Religion and the Family*, p. 237.
15. Nashe, *The Works of Thomas Nashe*, Volume 5, p. 194.
16. I am grateful to Sean Cunningham at the National Archives for the details here. The manuscript reference is PC 2/22, p. 317.
17. Foakes, *Henslowe's Diary*, pp. 23–4, 30–1.
18. Gibson, *Records of Early English Drama: Kent, Diocese of Canterbury*, p. 562. It's likely that the company played in other towns as well, but that records have not survived: Faversham was part of an established Kentish circuit which included up to ten other towns, such as Canterbury, Rye, and Dover.
19. Bearman, *Shakespeare in the Stratford Records*, p. 7.
20. Both quotations are from Woodgate, "Living in a World without Closure," p. 78.
21. Arnold and Gemma, "The Continuing Process of Parental Grief," p. 669.
22. Rando, *Parental Loss of a Child*, pp. 15–16.
23. Wright, *Sudden Death*, p. 53.
24. Alan Dyer, "Crisis and Resolution: Government and Society in Stratford, 1540–1640," in Bearman, *The History of an English Borough*, pp. 80-96, especially 90–2.
25. White and Denborough, *Introducing Narrative Therapy* and Payne, *Narrative Therapy*, are examples of recent texts focusing on the way narrative can help us come to terms with difficult experiences, especially loss.

Quoted in Bosticco and Thompson, "Narratives and Story Telling in Coping with Grief and Bereavement," p. 5, Brockmeier and Harre's words are from "Narrative: Problems and Promises of an Alternative Paradigm," *Research on Language and Social Interaction,* 30(4), 263-83, 1987.

26. There were many different translations of the Our Father, or Lord's Prayer, much to the consternation of Henry the Eighth; but the Edwardian Prayer Books established "trespass" as the standard English translation.

27. Rosenblatt, *Parent Grief,* p. 123.

28. Simons, "The Child Death Helpline," in Hockey et al, *Grief, Mourning and Death Ritual,* pp. 158-73. The information is on pp.161–2.

Possible Traces of Grief; I Would That I Were Low Laid in My Grave

What was the first play Shakespeare wrote after Hamnet's death in August 1596? It would be wonderful if we could date Shakespeare's plays so precisely, but we cannot. Further, we do not know whether Hamnet died suddenly, or whether he had been ill for some time; if the latter were the case, plays written before his death might contain anticipatory grief and be relevant to an exploration of Shakespeare's response to this loss. Interestingly, Catherine Sanders found that whether the death of a child was caused by a severe illness of some duration, allowing the parent to prepare for the probable outcome, or whether it resulted from a sudden illness or accident, made "little difference" to the intensity of a bereaved parent's experience.[1]

At first sight, however, there may seem to be nothing to explore because none of the plays written around the time of Hamnet's death concentrate on grief, and this might be taken as evidence that Shakespeare was not much affected by this loss. But a few years later comes *Hamlet*, full of death and unresolved mourning from top to toe, suggesting a welling-up of emotions associated with grief from deep within. And when we look closely at the plays probably written near the time of this death, we find that grief, especially grief for a lost child, features in several of them but that it does so in the background, as if it is being held back, until in *Hamlet* this is no longer possible.

In this chapter we will explore two plays, which may contain the first traces of Shakespeare's grief—*King John* and *Romeo and Juliet*. Because we cannot be sure whether they were completed before or after Hamnet died, some readers may wish to move straight to the next chapter. These two plays are not essential to my argument, which is based on works definitely finished after Hamnet's death. But even if one or both plays were completed before August 1596, I think they would still be relevant because they may contain anticipatory mourning—it is indeed the main expression of grief in both plays (although in *Romeo and Juliet* Juliet's parents do not know that she is not dead). Further, even if Hamnet was as healthy as could be when these plays were finished, and his father had no fears for his son beyond those felt by almost every parent, some of the lines we will examine would surely come back to haunt such an alert reader of double meanings as Shakespeare was, and may have influenced some of his later characterizations.

King John was definitely performed before September 1598, when it is mentioned in Francis Meres' list of Shakespeare's plays. How much earlier it was completed is uncertain. Most commentators, including John Tobin, editor of the forthcoming Arden edition, place it no earlier than 1596 on grounds of style and topical allusions.[2] It is unique among Shakespeare's early history plays because the others, covering the reigns of Richard the Second, Henry the Fourth, Fifth, and Sixth, and Richard the Third, form two linked sequences; but *King John* is a one-off rewriting of an earlier anonymous play, *The Troublesome Reign of King John*.[3] One clear reason for the interest in John's reign was that it raised issues of political legitimacy and succession that concerned contemporaries, as a childless monarch in her early sixties drew ever closer to death without naming a successor; but a part of its attraction for Shakespeare might also have been that one of its minor plotstrands deals with a young boy's tragic death.

King John has seized the throne on the death of Richard the First, although the young Prince Arthur has as good a claim as he does. Emotions associated with grief are presented through this young, doomed Prince, and through the reaction of his mother to her separation from him, as she rightly thinks, forever. Her predominant response is probably the predominant one for most parents at first: an overwhelming sense of loss.

Shakespeare makes intriguing changes to his source material. The historic Prince Arthur was 16 when he died, and he speaks like a macho 16-year-old in the source play, *The Troublesome Reign of King John*. But Shakespeare makes his Arthur much younger and gentler, a boy rather than a young man. Of course, there is a dramatic advantage in increasing an audience's sympathy by making the victim a child; but there are many young male victims in Shakespeare, culminating in the detailed and affectionate picture of Prince Mamillius in *The Winter's Tale*, and this recurrence suggests there may be more to it than simple theatrical considerations.

When the Earl of Pembroke believes Prince Arthur has been murdered on the orders of King John, he vows to "find th'inheritance of this poor child,/His little kingdom of a forced grave," and he imagines the coffin held in "*three foot*" of earth (4.2.97-100; my italics). A grave of three foot would, even in Shakespeare's time, suggest a boy rather than an adolescent, and Pembroke's use of "child" and "little" reinforces this sense. That this is not a slip of Shakespeare's pen is shown throughout. For instance, when King John takes Arthur prisoner, the Jailor calls the Prince "boy" frequently, and speaks of his "innocent prate," or chatter, not a term easy to use for the macho Prince in *The Troublesome Reign* (4.1.25).

Even more striking than Arthur's apparent age is his awareness of, even acceptance of, death; and it is possible that Shakespeare is, at some level, seeking comfort in the thought that his young son will accept, or has already accepted, his fate. In the early part of the play, when the Prince's mother is arguing with his grandmother about his claim to the throne, he says that he is not worth the commotion made on his behalf and wishes they would stop. And then he uses a very surprising image to try and stop their argument: "I would that I were low laid in my grave" (2.1.164). How strange that a young claimant to the throne should be thinking of his own burial. Then he weeps, not something a potential king should do, and something which we saw in Chapter 1 disturbs many Shakespearean adults. The unusual phrase "low laid" occurs only once elsewhere in Shakespeare, and there it is also in relation to a son (apparently) about to die, as we will see in Chapter 13; "laid low" also occurs only once, when Juliet is "laid low in her kindred's vault" (5.1.20). Further, this Arthur is self-effacing rather than assertive, making no strong claim to the crown, unlike his prototype in *The Troublesome Reign*. In this he anticipates Prince Hamlet, who is similarly uninterested in his Uncle Claudius' theft of the throne for the first four acts of that play. In both cases the expected behavior of a young prince is not what interests Shakespeare; indeed, he seems to be using prince in another sense—a prince of the ordinary rather than of the royal and political world.

This picture is developed in the horrifying scene when King John's henchmen are preparing to bind Arthur, so they can blind him. He promises to "sit as quiet as a lamb," reinforcing the picture of an idealized young, gentle boy who, like the Lamb of God, accepts his fate with resignation, something Hamlet also does eventually (4.1.79). Idealization of this sort is one of the commonest parental responses to the death of a child, and is an especially prevalent feature in Shakespeare's final plays, as we will see from Chapter 11 onward.

Certainly Arthur does not last much longer, dying as he thinks of escape. This is a moment crying out for heroic assertion—the boy standing on a high wall preparing to jump to possible freedom—yet what we hear is an acknowledgment of fear, a plea to the ground to take pity on him and not hurt him and, just before he leaps to his death, "As good to die and go, as die and stay" (4.3.8). No heroics here. This Arthur is a delicate and melancholy young boy, looking to the earth as to a mother who gently catches her falling child. He seems weary of life's struggle and pain, and in the last line appears to see death as unavoidable, almost to *desire* it; whether he tries to escape or stays in prison, death will come soon. There is a clear contrast with the Arthur of *The Troublesome Reign* here. He has the same fear, but his final lines before he jumps are very different: "And if I fall, no question death is next:/Better desist, and live in prison still./ Prison said I? nay, rather death than so:/Comfort and courage come again to me./I'll venture sure: 'tis but a leap for life."[4] Here is the heroic conquering of fear so absent in Shakespeare's lad. After fatally injuring himself *The Troublesome Reign's* Arthur has a final speech, like an aria before the hero dies in opera; by contrast Shakespeare's Prince, fittingly, speaks no more. His ending is of a piece with his beginning—"I would that I were low laid in my grave"—where he seems to anticipate and accept this conclusion. In his study of Shakespeare's presentation of children, Morriss Henry Partee finds that, "Unique among Shakespeare's child characters, Arthur demonstrates a consistent sweetness and gentleness."[5] Perhaps as well as receiving comfort at some level from this image of acquiescence, Shakespeare is also unconsciously exploring whether this might become his own reaction to the losses of life as well.

Shakespeare is obviously fascinated by anticipatory grief in *King John*. In an earlier scene Arthur's mother, Lady Constance, is sure that she will never see her son again, even though he is not yet dead. It is interesting that, for what may be his first dramatic response to Hamnet's anticipated or actual death, Shakespeare is using a plot that allows him to show a mother's rather than a father's grief and anticipatory rather than actual grief, although there were plots with bereaved fathers that he and his company could have chosen. But for many people, displacing painful emotion onto another, rather than dealing with it directly, is the easier option. The following lines may draw on Shakespeare's wife Ann's expressions of anticipated or actual grief. Certainly the anguish of Arthur's mother for her absent boy is presented in detail. In her agony she pleads for "amiable, lovely Death" to come to her, or for the relief of going mad (3.4.25):

> I am not mad, I would to heaven I were!
> For then 'tis like I should forget myself.
> O, if I could, what grief should I forget! . . .
> For, being not mad, but sensible of grief,
> My reasonable part produces reason
> How I may be deliver'd of these woes,
> And teaches me to kill or hang myself.
> If I were mad, I should forget my son,
> Or madly think a babe of clouts were he.
> I am not mad; too well, too well I feel
> The different plague of each calamity (3.4.48–50; 53–60).

In some of his later plays Shakespeare does present fathers who have lost sons, and Constance's words anticipate similar ones from the Earl of Gloucester in *King Lear* and Alonso in *The Tempest* (although interestingly both fathers have their sons restored to them). But for now it is a mother, and a mother who will not have her son restored. She continues the process of idealization we have already seen: "such a gracious creature" as her Arthur has never existed (3.4.81).

She is too sensitive, however, to be able to escape her *imagination* of his sufferings in the next life; and here again Shakespeare, as imaginative a writer as has ever lived, may well be exploring his own fears, fears that resurface in Hamlet's "To be, or not to be" soliloquy and in Claudio's anguished plea to his sister to commit mortal sin to save his life in Act 3, Scene 1 of *Measure for Measure*. Constance pictures her boy in the afterlife eaten away by sorrow, so that, even when they meet again, she will be deprived of the joy of recognizing him, "And he will look as hollow as a ghost,/As dim and meagre as an ague's fit,/ . . . never, never/Must I behold my pretty Arthur more" (3.4.84–85; 88-89). This reflects the terrifying fear that even the next world will not return the boy who has been lost, a fear many bereaved parents endure. But another fear might be present too: that the boy will not recognize, will be indifferent to, or will even reject the grieving parent, possibly an enactment of a sense of guilt for not protecting him better—a father frequently away from home might well feel that at some level. In the repetition of "never" there is an anticipation of the anguish of a later parent, King Lear, over the dead Cordelia, as we will see in Chapter 10. The image of "pretty" Arthur again suggests that Shakespeare is thinking of a young boy, not an adolescent.

When the Pope's legate behaves as a man is expected to behave and rebukes Constance for pouring out her grief, she replies, "He talks to me that never had a son," one of the many lines which, if written before Hamnet's death, must have come back to haunt Shakespeare if anyone tried to comfort him (3.4.91). Then come her most frequently quoted lines:

> Grief fills the room up of my absent child,
> Lies in his bed, walks up and down with me,
> Puts on his pretty looks, repeats his words,
> Remembers me of all his gracious parts,
> Stuffs out his vacant garments with his form . . .
> O Lord, my boy, my Arthur, my fair son!
> My life, my joy, my food, my all the world!
> My widow-comfort, and my sorrows' cure! (3.4.93–97; 103–105).

(The last line is literally true, as Lady Constance is a widow; but so in a way was Anne Shakespeare, for much of each year). Arthur's absence is a physical presence for his mother, everyday details continually reminding her that he is not there, and it may be that Shakespeare is drawing on his own and Anne's actual or anticipated suffering as he writes this. The speech begins with a vivid personification of grief, and Caroline Spurgeon notes that there are more personifications in *King John* and in *Romeo and Juliet* than in any other plays.[6] In personification abstract ideas like grief, or inanimate objects like a besieged city, are presented as if human and alive, and it may be that the imagination of a father who fears losing, or has lost, a child would find comfort in animating inanimate ideas and objects.

After the scene Arthur's mother is not seen again, and we learn later that she has died "in a frenzy," a fit of mad, uncontrollable passion, unable to cope with the absence of her beloved child, a fate only narrowly avoided by the apparently bereaved Alonso 15 or so years later (4.2.122). We may recall, too, that in *A Midsummer Night's Dream* Theseus thought the poet's eye rolled in a "fine frenzy," and that he linked the poet, the lover, and the lunatic as "of imagination all compact." Perhaps the borderline between a fine frenzy and true madness seemed to Shakespeare a relative rather than an absolute one (5.1.12, 8).

The accuracy of this picture of a parent's grief is confirmed by the therapist Murray Cox. A friend of his had just died:

> I called upon his mother ... who had scarcely heard the name of Shakespere [*sic*], much less read any of his plays ... among other things

I told her, in the anguish of her sorrow, that she seemed to be as fond of grief as she had been of her son. What was her reply? Almost a prose parody on the very language of Shakespeare—the same thoughts in nearly the same words.[7]

Romeo and Juliet may also reflect actual or anticipated grief for Hamnet. It was definitely finished before 27 March 1597, by which time the opening of the play had been discovered set in type during a raid on a printing press belonging to John Danter. How much earlier was it produced?

Stylistic analyses of changing features of Shakespeare's style indicate that it was written close in time to *King John*. The editorial consensus, based on a variety of factors, has been to place *Romeo and Juliet* prior to August 1596, but René Weis, who has prepared the new Arden edition, has drawn attention to evidence that suggests that it may not have been *completed* until after the boy had died.[8] The first, probably pirated, quarto of 1597 states that the play has been performed by the "Lord of Hunsdon his Servants." We would expect the more prestigious title of the Lord Chamberlain's Men because this is how the company was known from its inception in 1594, until the death of Lord Hunsdon in July two years later, and again after Hunsdon's son became Lord Chamberlain and patron of Shakespeare's company in March 1597. In between these dates the company was known as Hunsdon's Men, and this quarto reference suggests that the play may have been first performed after the death of the elder Hunsdon on 23 July 1596, later than previously thought.

Weis also highlights other intriguing features, such as the changes that Shakespeare makes to his main source material—Arthur Brooke's poem *The Tragical History of Romeus and Juliet*—which carry further implications for dating. One is that, despite the fact Shakespeare seems to have written the play quickly, using parts of the poem almost line by line, he is unusually specific about the time of year when he sets the action— mid July—and this leads on to references to Lammas-tide and Lammas Eve by the Nurse. In Brooke's poem, by contrast, the feast at the Capulet house for which Lady Capulet and the Nurse are preparing takes place at Christmas. Lammas was literally a harvest festival at the beginning of August, but the term referred more generally to the time of year (as Easter does nowadays). It is during the latter part of Lammas 1596 that Hamnet dies, probably no earlier than 8 August, given the fact that he was buried on the eleventh; if Shakespeare is writing shortly after this death, he may have deliberately altered the season to fit the event. The Nurse first asks Lady Capulet how long it is to Lammas-tide, and Lady

Capulet replies, "A fortnight and odd days" (1.3.17). This is an unnecessary exchange in terms of plot, but certainly fixes the time of year. Then the Nurse tells us that Juliet will be 14 on Lammas Eve, that is July 31; so although Juliet is a July baby, as befits her name, she is born in the very last hours of July, almost into August, as if Shakespeare is focusing on the coming month. In fact, the Nurse tells us about Juliet's birth on Lammas Eve twice. True, she is a repetitive character; but what she is repetitive about is up to Shakespeare, and the effect is to make this date and time of year stick in the mind, perhaps deliberately.

We saw in Chapter 3 that at least some of Shakespeare's company were performing in Kent during Lammas, 1596, and that Shakespeare may well have been with them. In the same speech the Nurse tells us that it is 11 years "since the earthquake" (1.3.23). There were several quakes and ground movements in England in the sixteenth century, and in one of them a field had collapsed into the earth at Mottingham in Kent. What might have caused the event to lodge in Shakespeare's mind is that it happened on 4 August 1585, that is, during Lammas, and it may have been mentioned to his company as it toured in Kent on the eleventh anniversary of the event: the main sixteenth century route from London to Faversham passes within three miles of Mottingham. Further, the collapse happened in the year of Hamnet and Judith's birth, and when Hamnet died may have become linked with that loss at some level. If this is so, it again suggests the play was not finished until after Hamnet's death.[9]

In Act 4 Juliet, wishing to avoid a forced marriage to Count Paris, receives a potion from the Friar to make her appear dead. Again, Shakespeare is unusually and unnecessarily precise about the day on which this event takes place. When the plan is devised by the Friar, the wedding is going to be on a Thursday, and she is to take the potion on the Wednesday evening. But in the following scene Capulet hastens the wedding to Wednesday, so Juliet takes the potion on Tuesday night and is placed in the family vault on a Wednesday. Hamnet was buried on *Wednesday*, 11 August, according to the Julian calendar in use in England till the eighteenth century, so again the day may not be accidental. Weis argues persuasively that Juliet's anticipation of the horrors of waking up in the vault—"To whose foul mouth no healthsome air breathes in," where "bloody Tybalt, yet but green in earth,/ Lies fest'ring in his shroud," amidst the "loathsome smells"—may reflect apprehensions Shakespeare anticipated or experienced about Hamnet's burial, and about the likelihood that his precious bones would be, at a later date, dug up and dumped in the Stratford charnel house (4.3.34; 42–43; 45). Further, Juliet has previously exclaimed that, rather than marry Paris,

> hide me nightly in a charnel-house,
> O'ercovered quite with dead men's rattling bones,
> With reeky shanks and yellow chapless skulls;
> Or bid me go into a new-made grave,
> And hide me with a dead man in his shroud—
> Things that, to hear them told, have made me tremble (4.1.81–86).

The child born on the cusp of Lammas is made to feel the physical horrors of the world after death, and this perhaps complements Constance's fear in *King John* of her son not being recognizable by, and not recognizing, his mother in the afterlife. Juliet would be played of course by a young male, and this would add further horror for the author as he wrote if he anticipated Hamnet experiencing this or, worse, knew that he already was. (For a more detailed discussion of burial practices, see Chapter 7).

Even secondary characters seem instinctively to think in images of death. The Chorus at the start of the second act, talking of Romeo's change of affection from Rosaline to Juliet, begins, "Now old desire doth in his death-bed lie." And the first time we see Friar Lawrence he evokes the paradox, "The earth that's nature's mother is her tomb;/What is her burying grave, that is her womb" (2.3.9–10). Romeo takes up the negative part of the Friar's image when he enters the Capulet burial chamber, thinking Juliet already dead: "Thou detestable maw [stomach], thou womb of death,/Gorg'd with the dearest morsel of the earth" (5.3.45–46). Indeed, if we take the three words "death, die, dies," they occur more times than in any other plays except *Richard the Third* and *Henry the Sixth, Part 2*. That the words should occur so frequently in two history plays dealing with civil war, death, and butchery is no surprise; but it is a surprise that occurrences in *Romeo and Juliet* should exceed those in other history plays dealing with similar events, such as the other two parts of *Henry the Sixth*, *Richard the Second*, and the two parts of *Henry the Fourth*, suggesting actual and anticipated death is much on Shakespeare's mind as he writes. *King John* does not have as many direct references, but it too contains images recalling the maw, or stomach, of death and the charnel-house: when wishing she were dead, Constance talks of the "odoriferous stench" of death, which is a "carrion monster" (3.4.26; 33); and Philip refers to "the rotten carcass of old Death" (2.1.456).

Another significant change in *Romeo and Juliet* is the age of the heroine—nearly 16 in Brooke's poem, 13 in Shakespeare. As we saw with Prince Arthur in *King John*, there's an obvious dramatic reason for making Juliet an even more vulnerable child, but again that may not be the only factor at work. Weis notes that Shakespeare's elder daughter Susanna was 13 in the year of Hamnet's death and argues that in some ways her sense of loss might be reflected in the play, as Judith's might be in Viola's grief for her twin in *Twelfth Night*. Juliet's age is mentioned by both her parents and by her Nurse, and again such an emphasis is unusual in Shakespeare, most of whose characters are of indeterminate age; it seems important to Shakespeare that Juliet is 13, that we are approaching Lammas, and that Juliet is placed in the vault on a Wednesday. Weis further notes that in *King John* we are given a picture of "maids of thirteen" talking familiarly "of puppy-dogs", a domestic detail that again might be based on the Shakespeare household and Susanna (2.1.460). As we have seen, Juliet's birthday is Lammas Eve; and in a way Susanna was born again at the age of 13 during Lammas 1596, for she now became her father's heir.[10]

Most families shorten names, and Susanna might well have been Susan in the family. Weis reminds us that the only two Susans in Shakespeare are in this play. Neither Susan appears onstage, so they are absent and present simultaneously, as Susanna is now absent and present in the life of a father based mainly in London. One is Susan Grindstone, who is mentioned by one of the Capulets' servingmen, but not seen. The other is the Nurse's baby, who was born in the same year as Juliet, but who died as a baby—another image of young death. The Nurse suckled both babies, suggesting a mother suckling twins; and one "twin" lived, and one died, as happened to the Shakespeares, too. This is not Shakespeare's only image of near-twins, in which one is dead and the other alive: in *The Winter's Tale* Mamillius dies in Act 3, while Florizel, born within a month of him, lives to become Leontes' substitute son (see Chapter 12).

In contrast to *King John*, *Romeo and Juliet* allows Shakespeare the chance to present both parents' grief. When Juliet appears to be dead in Act 4, Lady Capulet cries, "my child, my only life!/Revive, look up, or I will die with thee!" and when Capulet appears all his wife can do at first is repeat "she's dead!" After the initial shock, her words become more tender: "But one, poor one, one poor and loving child,/But one thing to rejoice and solace in,/And cruel Death hath catch'd it from my sight!" (4.5.19–20, 24, 52–54). Capulet too finds the death "Ties up my tongue, and will not let me speak," but is eventually able to give voice to his anguish, "O child, O child! my soul, and not my child!/Dead art thou! Alack, my child is dead,/And with my child my joys are buried;" buried may have a literal, as well as its obvious symbolic, meaning here (4.5.32, 62–64). Of course, Juliet is not dead at this point, as Arthur is not dead when mourned by his mother, so again, there may be an anticipation of, rather than actual, mourning. Previously, the Friar has described the effects of the drug given to Juliet to simulate death, providing another anticipation of its effects: "The roses in thy lips and cheeks shall fade/To wanny ashes, thy eyes' windows fall,/Like death when he shuts up the day of life" (4.1.99–101). And a third parent—Montague—brings the experience even closer to Shakespeare's own situation in the final scene when, in his anguish at seeing Romeo's dead body, he berates his son for pressing "before thy father to a grave" (5.3.215). Hamnet had done, or would do, just that.

This cumulative circumstantial evidence, then, supports Weis' argument that the mourning of Juliet's parents when she appears to be dead may draw on recent, raw family experience of anticipated or actual death. When Capulet thinks Juliet is dead, he says, "Death is my heir" (4.5.38). Interestingly, in a line only in the *Second Quarto*, which seems to present an earlier draft of the play than the *Folio* version, Capulet is a bereaved father who speaks to Count Paris in mournful tones before Juliet has even met Romeo—"Earth hath swallowed all my hopes but she" (1.2.14). It is as if Shakespeare is already thinking ahead to the fact that the father will be left heirless when Juliet does die in the final scene, and perhaps the image of earth swallowing all hopes links back to the swallowing of the field at Mottingham as well as to the more obvious image of a burial.

Typically for Shakespeare, however, a counter movement is also present, one we will find of developing importance in his comedies and romances—the hope of revival, of resurrection. As Sean Benson points out, Romeo "dreamt my lady came and found me dead—/Strange dream, that gives a dead man leave to think!—/And breath'd such life with kisses in my lips/That I reviv'd and was an emperor" (5.1.6-9). However, as Benson also indicates, the failed resurrection of the play is more accurately predicted in Juliet's horrified premonition, as Romeo prepares to descend from her balcony, "Methinks I see thee now, thou art so low,/As one dead in the bottom of a tomb" (3.5.55–56).[11]

We can say, then, that there is an accumulation of evidence that suggests these two plays either anticipate, or draw near to, Shakespeare's own experience, while maintaining a distance from it, as we saw Julia (in *The Two Gentlemen of Verona*) and Viola (in *Twelfth Night*) drawing near to their own pain, but distancing themselves from it by giving it a different "local habitation and a name" (*A Midsummer Night's Dream*, 5.1.17). In *King John* we saw a mother's anticipatory grief for a young son; in *Romeo and*

Juliet both parents' grief for the apparent death of a young daughter. But in neither, a father's for a young son. Further, as several feminist critics have noted, there is a move away from father-son to father-daughter relationships in the second half of Shakespeare's career, a development that reflects in part his own changed family situation. It is in Shakespeare's comedies that young women start to take on more prominence as characters, as the next chapter investigates. But the young women in the comedies after Hamnet's death are frequently transformed to young men, and adopt fictional young men's names—Balthasar, Ganymede, and Cesario. These nonexistent young men are present and absent simultaneously, as the dead Hamnet is now both absent and present in Shakespeare's life and imagination. In these comedies writing, whether consciously or unconsciously, begins to provide a means of taking some tentative steps in what will become a long day's journey through grief and mourning.

Notes

Full publication details of every source are in the bibliography.

I am grateful to Eugene Giddens for a helpful e-mail about *King John*.

1. Sanders, "A Comparison of Adult Bereavement in the Death of a Spouse, Child and Parent," p. 317.

2. I am grateful to John Tobin for an e-mail on this subject. Readers unfamiliar with, but interested in, the detail of stylistic analysis will find a helpful starting-point in Wells and Taylor's *William Shakespeare: A Textual Companion*, pp. 98–107, followed by discussion of individual plays. Examples of stylistic devices analyzed are Eliot Slater's examination of the distribution of rare words in the plays, John Fitch's work on the occurrence of mid-line pauses, Wells and Taylor's revised version of Karl Wentersdorf's metrical index. In recent years further excellent work has been done, especially by MacDonald Jackson.

3. Ernest Honigmann has won minority support for his view that *King John* precedes *The Troublesome Reign*, so was written before 1591 when *The Troublesome Reign* was published; but I agree with the majority of editors that the topical allusions, stylistic features, and the evidence that *King John* revises and tightens the earlier, more sprawling play, argue against this.

4. Bullough, *Narrative and Dramatic Sources of Shakespeare*, Volume 4, p. 120.

5. Partee, *Childhood in Shakespeare's Plays*, p. 69.

6. Spurgeon, *Shakespeare's Imagery and What It Tells Us*, p. 246.

7. Cox, *Structuring the Therapeutic Process*, p. 219. I am grateful to Robert Brown for lending me this book.

8. Weis, *Shakespeare Unbound* (U.S. title), pp.224–30, *Shakespeare Revealed* (UK title), pp. 200–5. He has kindly exchanged some further ideas with me by e-mail. See note 2 above re stylistic analysis.

9. I am grateful to Simone Harris at the Local Studies Library, Bromley, for the information about the landslip at Mottingham, Kent, and to Tony Burgess, an expert on old maps of Kent, for the information about the proximity of Mottingham to the main route from London to Faversham in Shakespeare's period. The Nurse's reference to 11 years "since the earthquake" has intrigued many critics by its strange specificity, suggesting a reference that some in an audience, or his fellow players, or Shakespeare himself, would recognize. If Shakespeare is writing in 1596, the earthquake might simply be the birth of twins in 1585, especially if Anne did not know she was carrying twins till they were born.

In *As You Like It*, while talking casually about the hours of the day, Jaques says, "And after one hour more 'twill be eleven,/And so from hour to hour, we ripe and ripe,/And then from hour to hour, we rot and rot" (2.7.25-7). Such a melancholy reflection is in character for Jaques; but it might also suggest a connection at some level in Shakespeare's mind of the number eleven and the idea of ripening then rotting, dying.

10. Weis, *Shakespeare Unbound*, p. 204, *Shakespeare Revealed*, p. 182.

11. Benson, *Shakespearean Resurrection*, pp. 43, 80, and 83.

The Partial Release of Comedy; Almost the Copy of My Child That's Dead

But even if *King John* and *Romeo and Juliet* bear traces of anticipated or actual grief connected with the loss of Hamnet, what has puzzled many critics is that the next few years are dominated by comedy: *The Merchant of Venice, The Merry Wives of Windsor, Much Ado About Nothing, As You Like It, Twelfth Night*. Even in the genre of history play, we have the antics of Falstaff, and although Shakespeare may have started *Henry the Fourth, Part 1* before Hamnet's death, almost certainly *Part 2* is written after it. Surely this shows that Shakespeare came to terms with this loss quickly and was relatively unaffected by it?

But I agree with Richard Wheeler that this increase in comic writing is not as strange as it might at first seem.[1] As Jeffrey Kauffman indicates, an early response to the pain of a traumatic death is often not denial, in the straightforward sense of that word, but dissociation, an unconscious need to escape from the trauma into a more pleasant imaginary world.[2] Indeed, he concludes that such protective dissociation is part of the normal course of mourning, although it can obviously last longer than is helpful and turn into repression of grief. Dissociation can also be linked to the desire to keep busy as a way of warding off unpleasant thoughts and memories. Shakespeare's workload seems heavy in the three years following

August 1596: two plays a year, perhaps three in some years, as well as acting, being a sharer and an organizer within the company.

Further, I would agree with Wheeler that the loss of Hamnet is actually present in these comedies, although again in disguise. In Shakespeare's first five comedies, written before Hamnet's death, only one—*The Two Gentlemen of Verona*—has a young woman disguised as a young man, and then only in the last two acts; but in the next five comedies finished after Hamnet's death, three use disguise to create a young man who does not exist, a fourth has a heroine with a sexually ambiguous name, leaving only one—*The Merry Wives of Windsor*—without any such feature. There is an oral tradition that this was written at the request of the Queen, who wanted to see Falstaff in love, rather than of Shakespeare's own volition. In the later two indeed—*As You Like It* and *Twelfth Night*—the disguise lasts for almost the whole play.

The first of the group is probably *The Merchant of Venice*. It was completed before July 1598, when it is entered in the Stationers' Register. Evidence points to it being written after Hamnet's death: for instance, the mention of the loss of the "wealthy Andrew" in the first scene seems to refer to the capture of a Spanish ship, the St. Andrew, during Drake's daring raid on the Spanish fleet in Cadiz in 1596 (1.1.27). News of the capture appears to have reached England at the end of July 1596, and the victory remained a matter of national celebration for the next year.[3] *As You Like It* is not mentioned in Meres' list of Shakespeare's plays published in September 1598, but it is entered in the Stationers' Register for 4 August 1600, so was written between those dates. Wheeler notes that both of these plays show that when the heroine is disguised as a young man she gains power. In the former, Portia becomes the young doctor of law, Balthasar, who outwits the unscrupulous Shylock in court; and in the latter Rosalind becomes Ganymede, with "a swashing and a martial outside," who brings separated people together at the play's end (1.3.120). These are actions they *could not have performed as young women*, a reminder to us and to Shakespeare as he wrote, that in his society a son can achieve much more than a daughter, and that the absence of a son is a social as well as a personal loss. Indeed, Shakespeare may not have differentiated between social and personal loss in the way we do nowadays.

Of course, on Shakespeare's stage the visual effect would have strengthened this sexual ambiguity, for it would have been a young male that Shakespeare and his audiences saw in the part of Portia or Rosalind and then in the disguise of Balthasar or Ganymede. Wheeler makes the perceptive suggestion that this sexual ambiguity might have enacted an even deeper satisfaction for Shakespeare, representing "more poignantly and disturbingly, a father's fantasy of transforming the surviving daughter [Judith] into the son."[4] He further points out that near the end of *As You Like It*, when Rosalind is still disguised as Ganymede, her father thinks he sees "Some lively touches" of his daughter's features in the boy, and Orlando replies that the first time he saw Ganymede he thought "he was a *brother* to your daughter" (5.4.27, 29; my italics). Hamnet is dead, but at some level Shakespeare is finding that he can alleviate his grief by conjuring up nonexistent young men onstage.

The beginning of *The Merchant of Venice* may also be relevant. Antonio tells Salerio and Solanio, "I know not why I am so sad;/It wearies me, you say it wearies you" (1.1.1–2). Salerio offers the rational explanation that Antonio is concerned about the risk of his ships sinking, and when Antonio rejects that explanation, Solanio says he must be in love; that explanation is also rejected. Many bereaved parents report sudden and apparently inexplicable feelings of gloom, so it may be that this strange mood reflects something Shakespeare was aware of in himself.

We can date *Much Ado about Nothing* more precisely than most of Shakespeare's plays. It is not in Meres' September 1598 playlist.[5] The first published *Quarto* version of 1600 seems to be based on a draft version of the play, since some of the speech prefixes refer to the comedian Will Kemp[e], rather than to the part he will be playing, Dogberry. Kemp[e] left the Lord Chamberlain's Men early in 1599, so almost certainly (most of) the play was written in late 1598 or early 1599. In it two further motifs that might be linked with Hamnet's death are present, albeit in a minor way: a father oscillating between love for and rage against a daughter, as if a daughter is not enough, and the resurrection of an apparently dead child or sibling. The second in particular will become a central feature in some of Shakespeare's later plays.

In *Romeo and Juliet* Capulet raged against Juliet when she refused to marry Count Paris, and it is possible that there is some personal feeling from a father who, in Wheeler's argument, might have preferred to lose a daughter rather than his only son; but the wrath there was already present in Shakespeare source poem, *The Tragical History of Romeus and Juliet*. In *Much Ado about Nothing*, however, Leonato's explosion of anger against his daughter Hero is not in Shakespeare's main source, *Timbreo and Fenicia*, in which Lionato does not believe the accusations against his daughter Fenicia; but Shakespeare's Leonato does believe them and becomes so angry and so violent that he almost kills Hero, who collapses, seemingly dead.[6] Her father's rage does not abate at this apparent death, however. Quite the reverse—he shouts at her that it would be better if she never rises, "Do not live, Hero, do not ope thine eyes;/For did I think thou wouldst not quickly die,/Thought I thy spirits were stronger than thy shames,/Myself would, on the rearward of reproaches,/Strike at thy life" (4.1.123–7).

Of course, when Leonato realizes his daughter is innocent, his anger turns back to love, a pattern that recurs with King Lear and Cordelia, perhaps reflecting Shakespeare's own ambivalence toward daughters he loved but who were not his son. Indeed, the vehemence here, going so far as to wish his daughter dead, is striking. Possibly it was like a further reliving of Hamnet's death for Shakespeare to be physically reminded, every time he returned to Stratford and saw Judith in particular, of the twin he would never see again, except in his imagination. This might add to any feelings of guilt he was experiencing because rationally he would know that Judith had no choice in her living and Hamnet dying. In *King Lear* deep guilt for the anger he displayed against his good daughter is the strongest feeling Lear experiences when he and Cordelia are reunited, and this may also draw, to an extent, on earlier negative feelings.

Support for this interpretation comes from the fact that Leonato, Capulet, and Lear are not the only fathers to disown a daughter or wish her dead. In *The Merchant of Venice* Shylock wishes Jessica dead when he thinks she has betrayed him, and in *Othello* a daughter's behavior actually causes her father's death. Desdemona marries Othello without her father's consent—Shakespeare's daughters were of marriageable age when he wrote this play—and he dies of grief. Again this is Shakespeare's addition to his source story, in which Desdemona's equivalent has no father. Certainly in several plays in the middle of his career the relationship between father and daughter is fraught and deadly. And even as late as *The Tempest* Prospero is strangely aggressive towards the gentle Miranda when telling her his history. It is as if, for Shakespeare's fathers, and for Shakespeare himself if we remember his will, a daughter is insufficient.

But the second, more positive motif in *Much Ado* that might reflect the loss of Hamnet is apparent resurrection. After Claudio and Don Pedro falsely accuse Hero of infidelity, she collapses, and appears to be dead when they sweep out of the marriage ceremony. When Hero revives, the Friar, recognizing her innocence, suggests they pretend that she is indeed dead to encourage the men to repent and to wish they could make amends. "Come, lady, die to live," he says, in a paradox that becomes increasingly important to Shakespeare in his final plays (4.1.253). Leonato continues the pretence that his daughter is dead, ostensibly to test whether their penitence is really heartfelt:

> I cannot bid you bid my daughter live—
> That were impossible . . .
>   My brother hath a daughter,
> *Almost the copy of my child that's dead,*
> And she alone is heir to both of us.
> Give her the right you should have giv'n her cousin,
> And so dies my revenge (5.1.279–80; 288–92; my italics).

Of course this "copy" of Hero does not exist, but what bittersweet emotions a hearing or rereading of this speech must have evoked in a writer as alert to double meanings as Shakespeare was, for he too has a daughter who is almost the copy of his child that's dead. Further, Shakespeare has had to alter his original intention in order to create Leonato's brother Antonio's imaginary daughter as their only heir: earlier Antonio had a son who was to provide music for the masked ball, but who is now conveniently forgotten (1.2.1–2).

The men do repent (although insufficiently for many modern readers and playgoers) and perform a night vigil at the family monument. As Sean Benson points out, one of the lines in the vigil, "Graves, yawn and yield your dead," is a premonition of the apparent resurrection which will follow the next day, when Claudio does what he should have done earlier—accepts the bride that is offered to him (5.3.19).[7] But she is wearing a mask, so he cannot know he is marrying Hero until after he has made his commitment. And when she removes her mask, he sees "the copy of my child that's dead," *in other words, an identical twin to Hero, an imaginative recreation of one seemingly lost for ever, but now raised from the dead onstage.* Seeing this, Don Pedro is as amazed as Claudio: "The former Hero, *Hero that is dead!*"—the continuous present tense reinforcing the sense of a miraculous occurrence (5.4.65; my italics). Shakespeare is feeling his way towards a pattern developed in later plays like *The Winter's Tale*: Claudio and Don Pedro have to *acknowledge their guilt, repent, and give themselves up, at least momentarily, to magic and faith* before the miracle of apparent resurrection can take place. They have to believe. Among other things, I would argue, they are in part Shakespeare's representatives onstage: what would he and other bereaved parents not give to stand or kneel where they are standing or kneeling, and to see what they are seeing?

So in a way Hamnet does still live—in his father's imagination. In creating this moment near the end of *Much Ado* Shakespeare is moving onward in his journey through mourning. Dennis Klass' work with bereaved parents led him to believe, "The end of grief is not severing the bond with a dead child, but integrating the child into the parent's life in a different way than when the child was alive."[8] Gail Ashton reports many parents who have had the same experience; for instance, "He continues on, the love . . . And I have this freedom to know that he lived, to know that he died, and to know that he is still part of our family." One comment is especially relevant: "My life is far richer; more fulfilled, I believe it has given me a level of understanding and a level of sensitivity that I didn't have prior."[9] From the first Shakespeare was a writer sensitive to his characters' painful inner experiences; but I would agree with Park Honan that the loss of Hamnet was a major reason why this sensitivity increased in his subsequent plays.[10]

Typically for Shakespeare, however, this "resurrection" is presented in disguise, in a metamorphosis—Claudio and Don Pedro witness a young woman, not a young man, apparently returning from the dead. Or they do in a modern production, but of course on Shakespeare's stage they would have seen a young *male*. And every new performance would have brought for its author a further catharsis as this figure, both male and female, unmasked himself/herself, and was alive once more.[11]

But the "resurrection" of Hero is very tentative in comparison to what we will find in some later dramas. It's as if Shakespeare has stumbled upon it here, rather than consciously chosen it or realized its power, and has to kill off Antonio's son to make the "resurrection" work. Further, the moment is soon left behind to concentrate on the more engaging Beatrice and Benedick. In *Twelfth Night*, however, such a moment is developed more fully, and this time the rebirth involves *twin* equivalents to Hamnet and Judith.

Twelfth Night is not mentioned in Meres' 1598 list of plays. There is a recorded performance at the Middle Temple on 2 February 1602, but whether this was a first night is unknown. As René Weis reminds us, Shakespeare's twins had been baptized on 2 February 1585.[12] The identical date is no doubt a coincidence, but it is hard to believe that Shakespeare's thoughts would not have returned to Judith celebrating her seventeenth birthday in Stratford, while he (presumably) was in London, and to Hamnet unable to celebrate his, and only alive and reunited with his twin by the magic of theater.

The name of Duke Orsino probably comes from Queen Elizabeth's guest of honor, Duke Orsini of Bracciano, at a performance of an unknown play on twelfth night, 1601. The Duke was also a Count, and similarly Orsino is referred to as a Duke and a Count on several occasions in *Twelfth Night*. The play may have been written shortly before the visit or in the following year. It is one of Shakespeare's funniest comedies, but is also marked by a melancholy that reaches its strongest expression in *Hamlet* (see Chapter 7). Melancholy was fashionable at the turn of the seventeenth century, and Shakespeare mocks it through the portrait of Jaques in *As You Like It*, though typically for Shakespeare there is not merely mockery in, for instance, one of his most famous speeches, "All the world's a stage." In *Twelfth Night* and *Hamlet* the pervasiveness and seriousness with which it is presented suggests that melancholy is not just something that Shakespeare is mocking or affecting in his writing. *Twelfth Night* is indeed the last of his plays which can easily be called a comedy. A variety of influences seem to have fed into this, including changes in audience taste and increasing social and political uncertainties; but the evidence from 1601 to the end of Shakespeare's career suggests as well that he is finding it more and more difficult to write comedy as his audience liked it.

Shakespeare is indeed drawn toward images of death and grief: two unrelated sisters, Olivia (in black) and Viola, grieve for "a brother's dead love" (1.1.30). The usual word order would be "a dead brother's love," but Shakespeare's change emphasizes that it is the love that is "dead, " which the mourner is missing. Olivia wishes to keep her grief "fresh/And lasting in her sad remembrance," and interestingly, this grief is for a father as well as for a brother (1.1.30–1).[13] We will meet a more prominent dead father in the next chapter, in *Hamlet*. Further, Viola's father died when she was 13, Juliet's age, and Susanna's age when Hamnet died (5.1.245). This emphasis on male death and resulting grief marks a significant change to Shakespeare's main source, "Of Apolonius and Silla," in which Olivia's equivalent Julina is a widow who has moved beyond mourning and might now be called feisty, and this suggests that male mortality is much in Shakespeare's mind as he writes this play.[14] When Viola hears of Olivia's grief, it reminds her of her own and draws her towards Olivia: "O that I served that lady" (1.2.41). As Sean Benson notes, Viola, in the disguise of Cesario, talks of the "deadly life" that strong passion for another human draws us into (1.5.265).[15] On the surface Viola/Cesario is referring to Orsino's unrequited love for Olivia, but it is reasonable to suggest that Viola's (and Shakespeare's?) deeper feelings after losing a brother (or son?) might be coloring her choice of words here.

Indeed, the main grief presented is Viola's for her twin brother. Perhaps at some level, and at this time in Shakespeare's journey, a sister's imaginatively experienced grief is more bearable to contemplate than a father's actual grief because it allows Shakespeare in part to deflect his own grief onto Judith's equivalent, again combining involvement and distance. The grief is intense: after she is shipwrecked, Viola's first fear is that her brother is drowned, and only then does she decide to disguise herself. In "Of Apolonius and Silla" Silla [Viola] has to disguise herself because Apolonius [Orsino] knows her already and will recognize her; but Viola does not have that or any other clear motivation, although by implication she may feel safer disguised as a man. Her first plan is to dress herself as a eunuch, and that this is not just a slip of the pen is shown by the fact that the Captain confirms the idea (1.2.52, 58). But when we see her disguised as Cesario, it is clear that Shakespeare has changed his mind and decided to disguise her as *her apparently dead brother*. As she says, "I my brother know/Yet *living in my glass*; even such and so/In favor was my brother, and he went/Still in this fashion, color, ornament,/*For him I imitate* (3.4.379–83; my italics).

So Viola is coping with her grief in part by deliberately recreating her brother's appearance. She is the copy of her brother that's dead, no almost about it, because in the feigning of the play the twins are identical, despite their different sexes. For most of *Twelfth Night* the disguised Viola represents both herself and Sebastian, two people in one body. When we finally see the two of them together, Orsino cannot believe it, exclaiming, "One face, one voice, one habit, and two persons" (5.1.216). This supports Wheeler's suggestion that one of the reasons Shakespeare was drawn toward young male actors playing women, then disguising themselves as men, was that it created an androgynous figure in which both a male and female child could be present and that the death of Hamnet made this kind of synthesis more important to him. It is as if the twins are as near "An apple, cleft in two" as possible, and this fits with the name Shakespeare chooses for Viola in disguise, Cesario, associated with caesus, from caedere, to cut (5.1.223). Interesting, too, is the fact that Cesario does not leave the stage in the final act and reappear as Viola, in contrast with Ganymede, who returns as Rosalind to speak the Epilogue at the end of the earlier *As You Like It*. Indeed, Orsino's last words address Cesario, not Viola, and draw attention to the male attire, as if this male image is the one Shakespeare wishes to leave in the mind of the audience, *and himself*. In terms of dress two Sebastians face us because in Shakespeare's period the distinction between male and female clothing would normally have been immediately apparent in a way that is not always true of modern productions, in which unisex attire can be chosen. Many counselors and researchers, such as Therese

Rando, report that a significant number of bereaved parents experience "some type of visual or auditory hallucination of the child," or feel "an intuitive, overwhelming sense of his presence," and we'll find that the evidence supporting this idea is even stronger in Shakespeare's final plays.[16] Dreams of lost loved ones are not new, but are also recorded in the sixteenth and seventeenth centuries; and most of the dreams Ralph Houlbrooke encountered in his research "seem to have been serene and comforting," rather than disturbing.[17]

Of course, we know as early as Act 2 that Sebastian has survived the shipwreck and may have been confident of this almost as soon as we met Viola, when the Captain reassured her that he had seen Sebastian riding the waves (1.2.10–15). And the play's two titles announce themselves as comic (although twelfth night also suggests the mixed mood of the play because it is the *last* day of celebration before we go back into the everyday world that the final song gives us). But Judith's equivalent is made to experience the full force of the possibility that Sebastian has died, while simultaneously having to hold in her feelings of love for Orsino and having to present herself as a man. This situation allows its author the therapeutic experience of living through Viola's anguish when she remembers her dead brother while simultaneously enjoying the reassuring fantasy that the brother will eventually be restored. Sometimes well-meaning, earnest people say we should always be truthful, but as Ibsen shows in *The Wild Duck*, this can have catastrophic effects in the wrong circumstances: everyone needs hope, and in the throes of a devastating experience a false hope may sometimes be better than none at all—it may help to keep the mourner going. Certainly, this image of an earthly restoration of the lost one seems to be battling with a melancholy, which we will find in *Hamlet*, is almost overwhelming. Indeed, one reason *Twelfth Night* moves audiences so strongly is that, in the course of a lifetime, virtually all of us find ourselves in situations in which we are desperate to believe that our lost ones are not really lost and that some time in the future we shall meet them again.

The other main plot in the play, the duping of the hypocritical pretend-puritan Malvolio, produces some of the funniest scenes in Shakespeare, such as the one in which Sir Toby's and Sir Andrew's nighttime revelry is interrupted by Malvolio, dressed in his nightshirt. But even in this scene, a mood of sadness and loss is also present: "Youth's a stuff will not endure" is the last line of Feste's song. This can be taken as a hint to Sir Toby that he should propose to Maria while there is still time, but it also represents a melancholy truth we all discover in our own lives (2.3.52). This tone is echoed at many moments, for instance, in the muted end to the scene of midnight revelry, when the foolish Sir Andrew states, "I was adored once, too," as if he realizes deep down that this is unlikely to happen again and that his attempts to woo Countess Olivia are futile, even though he is going to proceed with them (2.3.181). Another instance is when Olivia talks to Cesario of his "wit and youth" coming to "harvest," and then tells him, "There lies your way, due west;" the literal meaning is that she is dismissing him in the direction of the setting sun, but at a deep level we find Shakespeare associating the harvest of wit and youth with the west, the direction of the setting sun, the direction of death (3.1.132–4). As many critics have noted, at the heart of the witty, rumbustious, and farcical comedy there is a sense of time moving inexorably on toward the moment when we will be laid in the ground in the equivalent of "sad cypress" (2.4.52). And it colors the play's ending, which is unlike anything in Shakespeare's source materials.

On the surface this is an unmitigated triumph, especially the reunion of the twins. Many theatergoers would agree with Wheeler that this is the play's climax, rather than the marriages at the end: "I find the reunion of sister and brother in this play to be the most deeply moving moment in any Shakespearean comedy."[18] "Moment" may seem an odd choice for something that takes a few minutes to perform, but Wheeler is justified because time seems suspended as Viola/Cesario and Sebastian gradually allow themselves to believe that their twin is alive. The movement outside normal time can give in performance a sense of ritual, and we have seen in Chapter 2 how the erosion of traditional rituals of mourning brought about by the Reformation may have been of considerable concern to Shakespeare, encouraging him to create his own theatrical ceremonies.

Some general comments by Darian Leader are very helpful in understanding one of the many levels involved for Shakespeare in this "moment" of reunion:

> Very often you see moments in the mourning process where the person isn't just invaded by thoughts or images of the lost loved one, but is telling someone else about that person—*maybe on a stage* or in some kind of deliberately stylized context. This indicates that one may be turning a loss into a symbolized event . . . You could say it's exactly that presence of artificiality that will allow us to engage with our own grief, that to really engage with the one we have lost we have to be able to make a limit between the world of the living and world of the dead.[19]

As Leader implies, the theater with its disguises, is the perfect local habitation for such emotional exploration. Or, as a bereaved parent put it, "The loved one you lost is still living with you, inside."[20] Shakespeare is moving forward in his searching, his journey, although not necessarily consciously.

Hero's return to life in *Much Ado* was a muted experience; here, Shakespeare, at some level, lets himself go in presenting the full wonder of this "resurrection" that can never be experienced in our earthly life away from the magic of art. Indeed, it is significant that Shakespeare's final protagonist Prospero is a magician, who can open graves and *raise the dead*, much like a playwright (see Chapter 14). The final moments of Sebastian's and Viola's mutual recognition are rapturous:

> *Sebastian.* I had a sister,
> Whom the blind waves and surges have devour'd.
> Of charity, what kin are you to me? . . .
> *Viola/Cesario.* Such a Sebastian was my brother too;
> So went he suited to his watery tomb.
> If spirits can assume both form and suit,
> You come to fright us.
> *Sebastian.* A spirit I am indeed,
> But am in that dimension grossly clad
> Which from the womb I did participate.
> Were you a woman, as the rest goes even,
> I should my tears let fall upon your cheek,
> And say, "Thrice welcome, drowned Viola" (5.1.228–30; 233–41).

Benson quotes David Scott Kastan's perceptive comment, "Twins separated for only three months would hardly need to test their identities in order to re-establish their relationship."[21] The magic of the moment goes beyond the facts of the situation and suggests that a much longer and more complete separation is in Shakespeare's mind. The full impact of the last line above can easily be lost in reading or in performance if you already know the names of the characters; although we have heard Viola called Cesario many times, this is the first time the name Viola has been spoken, as if it is *only when her twin brother is restored to her that she regains her full identity.* Her name is repeated two lines later, which highlights this further, and Sebastian starts to believe. But Viola cannot yet allow herself to believe— understandably, since desolation would follow if it proved to be untrue— and attempts to keep control of the situation by referring to herself in the third person (as she had done when inventing her fictional sister). Continuing in the role of Cesario, she says that her father died "that day when Viola from her birth/Had numb'red thirteen years" (5.1.244–5). Concise explanation could sort this out—"Sebastian, I was saved by our ship's captain," "Viola, I was rescued by Antonio,"—but this is eschewed in favor of a sense of incredulous wonder, akin to a religious experience. Shakespeare's contemporaries knew their Bible much better than we do, so when Viola/Cesario says to Sebastian, "Do not embrace me," some may have been reminded of Jesus' words to Mary Magdalene, "Touch me not," after *the* resurrection (5.1.251).[22] The tenderness of the scene, and the transformation of devouring waves to tears of happiness, make this especially moving. From a Christian perspective, it could be seen as an image of the next life; but it is presented to us (and longed for?) as if it could happen in this one.

After this the proposed marriages can seem an anticlimax, a convenient way of closing the play, like the fortuitous appearance of Fortinbras and his army at the end of *Hamlet*. True, Viola's deep grief has been counterbalanced by deep love for Orsino; but where are the signs that he loves her deeply or indeed is capable of love at all? Olivia's grief for her father and brother has given way to love for Viola/Cesario; how convenient that this love is purely external and so can be transferred easily to Viola's identical twin brother. How convenient too that Sebastian is perfectly happy with Olivia and remains unaware of how much he is loved by another character in this apparently light-hearted play who is caught up in the "deadly life" of passion—Antonio, who risks imprisonment and death because "I do adore thee so" (2.1.47). Antonio is left alone at the end of the play while the others are celebrating, and he might in part represent Shakespeare's own longing for *his* Sebastian, his adorable boy, to be restored to him. Interestingly, Shakespeare does allow Sebastian to reciprocate Antonio's passion for a moment when they meet again in Act 5: "Antonio, O my dear Antonio!/How have the hours rack'd and tortur'd me,/Since I have *lost* thee" (5.1.218–20; my italics). But the plot requires Sebastian to accept the aristocratic and beautiful Olivia, so this striking image of the torture of separation, unmatched by any expression of love towards Olivia, is left hanging in the air. Antonio is Shakespeare's own creation, rather than coming from his source stories, and echoes the Antonio in *The Merchant of Venice* who is also passionately fond of a young man but left alone at the end. (For further discussion of this idea, see Chapter 9).

Other features of the ending undercut the festivity too. Malvolio stalks out, saying, "I'll be reveng'd on the whole pack of you," reminding Shakespeare's audience that the puritanical forces Malvolio has aligned himself with are growing in strength as Elizabeth's reign and power ebb away (5.1.378). It is indeed the *end* of festivities, in various different ways, which *Twelfth Night* is presenting. And it closes with a further song from the ambiguously-named Feste, a name that is close to festive but even closer to fester, representing the mixture of celebration and mortality in this bittersweet play. His melancholy mood throughout is in part Shakespeare's response to a new, more thoughtful comedian joining the company—Robert Armin—and it is possible that Armin had a hand in, or even wrote, some or all of the songs. Nevertheless, Feste's mood fits many other features of the play, is not only present when he is present, and will become increasingly prominent in Shakespeare's next plays, and not just in roles probably written for Armin. Feste's last song, like the graveyard scene near the end of *Hamlet*, takes us through the whole of a man's life. Of course, it is normally performed comically, but if we look at the words, a dispiriting journey it is from the foolishness of boyhood to the shut gates, fear of thieves, swaggering, and hangovers, which seem to constitute the whole of manhood, accompanied continually by "the wind and the rain . . . /For the rain it raineth every day" (5.1.390, 392 and following stanzas).

It's a measure of how wonderfully enjoyable much of *Twelfth Night* is that playgoers sometimes do not register the negativity of these words; the reunion of the twins has been so heartfelt that for some it banishes this distasteful picture of the fears and inadequacies of much adult male experience. Taking both elements together, however, *Twelfth Night* suggests an author struggling to come to terms with the losses of life which have culminated in death in the family, and realizing at some level that the theater is the only place now where he can see a representation of his boy moving and breathing. Indeed, one of the appeals of fiction for audiences *and authors* is that in it events can be shaped and directed as they cannot in real life; what the author wills can actually take place.

And here, it is worth considering an interesting feature of some character names noted by many critics: Malvolio, Viola, and Olivia—all names of Shakespeare's invention rather than from his source material—are close to anagrams. The root is clearest in Malvolio, a man of ill volition, ill-will toward others (as Benvolio in *Romeo and Juliet* bears good will). The names show an interest in volition, in willing things to happen, which these three characters try to do, and remind us that the play's other title, and possibly its first one, is *What You Will*. The playwright and lover of puns is Will Shakespeare, and I think this word play may illustrate Shakespeare's awareness of our, and his, attempts to will things to be true that may not be.

But the reunion here, miraculous as it is, is not enough to close Shakespeare's need to present grief for a lost child and, consciously or not, he returns to magical "resurrections" of apparently lost siblings and children later, especially in his final plays, where fathers will be involved as well as sisters, suggesting that the expression of pain through the proxy of a sister/daughter provided an inadequate catharsis. The repeated enactment of what is at heart the same event conforms to patterns noted by counselors. David Malan writes of the stage in the normal grief process "in which the grief begins to come to the surface and needs to be expressed over and over, until every aspect of the loss has finally been worked through."[23]

But for Shakespeare, as for many others, it has to be worked through in disguise. And this takes us back to *As You Like It*, and the jester and would-be pastoral poet with a very interesting name—Touchstone— who is Shakespeare's own invention, rather than a product of his main source, Thomas Lodge's *Rosalynde*. The clown does indeed seem to act as a touchstone to the worth or otherwise of several characters. And he is one of the few speakers in Shakespeare's plays to comment on the nature of poetry.

The word "poetry" occurs in only five other plays, in which the references are either pejorative, as in the macho Hotspur's "mincing poetry" (*Henry the Fourth, Part 1*, 3.1.132) or link poetry with a young woman, such as Bianca (*The Taming of the Shrew*, 1.1.93). These other references also occur in plays which predate *As You Like It*. Touchstone's comment is altogether more intriguing. In Act 3, Scene 3 he is wooing the country lass Audrey and says he is there as "the most capricious poet honest Ovid was amongst the Goths" (3.3.7–8). Certainly, the transformations and complexities in the comedies we have been exploring are worthy of Shakespeare's favorite classical poet. The major playwright during Shakespeare's early years in London, Christopher Marlowe, was also bewitched by Ovid and had translated his erotic *Amores*, and written what is probably the best known poem in the pastoral tradition, 'The Passionate Shepherd to His Love." Although Marlowe had been dead for six years, Shakespeare is clearly meditating on him and later makes Phoebe quote from his *Hero and Leander*: "Dead shepherd, now I find thy saw of might:/'Who ever lov'd that lov'd not at first sight?' " (3.5.82–83).

Marlowe had been murdered in a private room in a tavern in 1593, apparently in an argument over the bill, or reckoning, but Charles Nicholl demonstrated that he had been involved in spying for the government and was more likely assassinated. Touchstone tells Audrey, "When a man's verses cannot be understood, nor a man's good wit seconded with the forward child, understanding, it strikes a man more dead than a great reckoning in a little room. Truly, I would the gods had made thee poetical" (3.3.12–16). This seems to be a reference to Marlowe's murder and also to Barabas' image in his first speech in *The Jew of Malta*, "Infinite riches in a little room," but what the references imply is problematic (1.1.37). Audrey is as baffled as an audience is likely to be, and asks whether poetical is "honest in deed and word? Is it a true thing?" "No, truly," Touchstone replies, "for the truest poetry is the most feigning, and lovers are given to poetry" (3.3.18–20). The surface meaning becomes clearer as the scene develops. Touchstone hopes Audrey will not be honest in the sense of defending her honor, will agree to couple with him, preferably in marriage. But if that is not possible in time, coupling "in bawdry" will do, for, as Touchstone says, "man hath his desires" (3.3.97; 80–1). It is also possible, however, that, in thinking of these two great predecessors, Marlowe and Ovid, Shakespeare has said indirectly something about his own poetry—that it is at its truest when apparently it is most feigning, most fictional, most in disguise.

Notes

Full publication details of every source are in the bibliography.

1. Wheeler, "Deaths in the Family: The Loss of a Son and the Rise of Shakespearean Comedy," is particularly stimulating on the move towards comedy in Shakespeare's output, and its relation to Hamnet's death.

2. Kauffman, "Dissociative functions in the normal mourning process," pp. 31–2.

3. I am grateful to the Arden editor of *The Merchant of Venice*, John Drakakis, for an e-mail sent while preparing his new edition stating that all the evidence he had discovered supported late 1596 or 1597 as the date of composition.

4. Wheeler, "Deaths in the Family," p. 146.

5. Meres' list includes *Love's Labours Won*, which is usually thought to be a play now lost. It is possible, though unlikely, that it is another title for *Much Ado About Nothing* or even *As You Like It*; but stylistic analysis confirms that both these plays are post 1596, and so written after Hamnet's death.

6. "Timbreo and Fenicia," Bullough, *Narrative and Dramatic Sources of Shakespeare*, Volume 2, pp. 112–34.

7. Benson, *Shakespearean Resurrection*, p. 44.

8. Klass, "The deceased child in the psychic and social worlds of bereaved parents during the resolution of grief," p. 170.

9. Both quotations from Ashton, "Pebble on my Wing," p. 10.

10. Honan, *Shakespeare*, p. 236.

11. It is also interesting to consider the choice of the ambiguous name Hero for Leonato's daughter. A hero is normally male. Shakespeare could have stayed with Fenicia, Hero's equivalent in his main source story, as he did with Juliet

and with Rosalind in other plays. True, Hero is a female name in the Greek myth of Hero and Leander, and Shakespeare certainly knew the story, and knew Christopher Marlowe's unfinished poem on the subject, published with a completion by George Chapman in 1598. Hero in this story is the epitome of faithfulness in love—very appropriate to Shakespeare's Hero—so there might seem no more to be said. But there were 1,001 faithful heroines whose names Shakespeare could have chosen—indeed, faithfulness was one of the patterns of behavior which (male) authors tried to instill in women—so why choose Hero rather than any of the others? And when we look carefully the story of Hero and Leander, in which Hero commits suicide after her faithful lover Leander drowns, is not really close to the story of the immature, jealous Claudio and his false accusations against Hero. But given that Hero was played by a young male, a sexually ambiguous name might have satisfied Shakespeare's inner needs for a resurrection at some level. It is worth noting too that Ophelia and Hermione were also male as well as female names (see Chapters 7 and 12).

12. Weis, *Shakespeare Unbound*, p. 300 and *Shakespeare Revealed*, p. 267.

13. In wanting to grieve for a long period Olivia is not following the Protestant reformers' requirement for moderate grief. As Suzanne Penuel points out, Olivia secludes herself "like a cloistress," which recalls the world of the nunnery some reformers wished to abolish, and she "water[s]" her chamber with "eye-offending brine," suggesting her tears are like sprinkled holy water (1.1.27–9; Penuel, "Missing fathers: *Twelfth Night* and the Reformation of Mourning," pp. 87, 91). Feste conducts a mock-religious catechizing of Olivia which presents the reformers' logic. "Good Madonna, why mourn'st thou?" She replies, for her brother's death. Feste then mischievously says, his soul is in hell, and Olivia responds, she knows it is in heaven. "The more fool, Madonna, to mourn for your brother's soul, being in heaven" (1.5.66–71). This is witty and entertaining stuff, but the rigorous catechism lays bare the emotional poverty of an approach to mourning based purely on reason. "Madonna" is of course the Italian for "my lady," but in this mock-religious context evokes *the* Madonna, her profound grief for her dead son, and her role as intercessor on behalf of those in Purgatory, rendered obsolete by the reformers' abolition of Purgatory.

14. "Of Apolonius and Silla," Bullough, *Narrative and Dramatic Sources of Shakespeare*, Volume 2, pp. 345-63.

15. Benson, *Shakespearean Resurrection*, p. 50.

16. Rando, *Parental Loss of a Child*, p. 17.

17. Houlbrooke, *Death, Religion and the Family in England, 1480-1750*, pp. 231-2.

18. Wheeler, "Deaths in the Family," p. 147.

19. Leader's words are from his interview with Pointon, p. 19. My italics.

20. Quoted in Schwab, "Paternal and Maternal Coping with the Death of a Child," p. 414.

21. Benson, *Shakespearean Resurrection,* quotes Kastan's comment on p. 56. It is from p. 577 of Kastan's paper, *"All's Well That Ends Well* and the Limits of Comedy," Journal of English Literary History, volume 52, 572–89.

22. *The Gospel of John*, chapter 20, verse 17, in both the *Bishop's Bible* and the *Geneva Bible.*

23. Malan, *Individual Psychotherapy and the Science of Psychodynamics*, p. 139.

6

Grief, Anger, and the Difficulty of Mourning; Then Get Thee Gone and Dig My Grave Thyself

So far in Shakespeare's plays we have found two unsurprising main reactions to the death of his son: a deep sense of loss and a developing interest in moments of (apparent) resurrection. But grief often brings with it other, more disconcerting emotions—anger and a sense of abandonment, even betrayal, are commonly reported. This can take the obvious form of rage against God and the universe for allowing the death to happen, but it can also appear in the subtler form of anger against the dead person for dying, for abandoning the mourner to carry on alone. It may at first seem impossible that a parent could feel angry toward a dead child, but many counselors and therapists report that the pain caused by the loss of a child can produce rage, even though the child has clearly not chosen to die. For example, Hazel Danbury records a case where a mourning parent's "overwhelming grief carried with it rage and also a sense of outrage that the child could do this," that is, could be so hurtful as to die.[1] Bob Wright records a mother addressing her dead child, "Why have you left me and hurt me in this way?"[2] William Worden gives the example of the words of a father whose son died suddenly at the age of two months: " 'I let him into my life for two months and he left me.' At first he felt guilty about these feelings."[3] These examples confirm the depth of the hurt when the love the parent has offered seems to have proved insufficient to keep the child alive. Worden's continuation may surprise some readers: "At first he felt guilty about these feelings, but through counseling, he was helped to understand that they were normal." Normal is the key word here. It is normal to feel anger as well as more tender emotions when deprived of something we love; loss is experienced as loss, *regardless of its cause*.

As Worden notes, parents overcome with rage are likely to experience guilt, and there is evidence that Shakespeare too struggled to come to terms with similar emotions. His most intense play, *King Lear*, starts from the wrath of two fathers against their favorite children. The children have not literally died, but in both cases their fathers feel abandoned and betrayed by them, and in Gloucester's case, he fears that his son wishes to kill him. In Chapter 10 I will argue that this situation allows Shakespeare, among many other things in this very complex play, to explore at some level the anger, and the resulting sense of guilt when the anger proved to be unjustified, which followed Hamnet's death, and to act out, via intermediaries, these disturbing emotions. It isn't just children who explore challenging experiences through play; adults do this too.

King Lear was not written until nine or so years after Hamnet's death, but we have an anticipation of that explosion of anger in the *Henry the Fourth* plays. *Henry the Fourth* is mentioned in Meres' list of 1598, but he does not indicate whether there were yet two Henry plays in existence. *Part 1* was entered in the Stationers' Register for 25 February 1598, and is generally thought to date from one or two years before. Nothing in the entry, however, nor on the title page of the *Quarto* text published in the same year, suggests there is a completed second play from which it needs to be distinguished. *Part 2* is entered in the Register on 23 August 1600. This cumulative evidence is usually taken to mean that *Part 2* was not finished until after 25 February 1598.

In both parts the relationship between King Henry and his son, Prince Harry, allows Shakespeare, as a son and a father himself, to explore the psychological complexities involved in father-son relationships. As we saw in Chapter 2, Shakespeare's youth had not followed a socially-acceptable model: he had made an older woman pregnant and had had to marry her at 18, had had three children by 21, an age when most respectable young men in Stratford were still unmarried, let alone fathers, and soon afterwards had set off for London, leaving Anne and her children at home. But by early 1596 he was the most successful and prosperous playwright in London, and could afford to acquire the coat of arms his father had aspired to. It would have been easy for Shakespeare to identify with Prince Harry, for he too had been an apparent wastrel, staying away from court and mixing with rogues; and he too had proved himself a worthy son by the end of *Part 1*, as Shakespeare had proved himself. But Shakespeare had also felt the pain of a son's absence, at first self-inflicted when he went to live in London, and then in a much deeper way when that absence became permanent. We know that Shakespeare was not the main actor in his company and, from *The Scourge of Folly* by John Davies, that he sometimes played the role of king. Henry the Fourth is not the main character in the plays that bear his name; there would be an added poignancy if, as he wrote, Shakespeare knew he would personate this world-weary father onstage.

Henry already yearned for his absent son in *Part 1*, but *Part 2* is much more somber and heavy in mood, presenting a father who is literally dying under the cares of fatherhood and kingship. Now his son-and-heir has returned to his old ways and absconded from court, and Henry's grief is intensified by his despair that even his approaching death is not enough to bring his son to see him: his son is as good as dead to him. The father imagines the pain of this absence continuing into the afterlife, as Prince Arthur's mother had done, "therefore my grief/Stretches itself beyond the hour of death./The blood weeps from my heart" (4.4.56–8). Several fathers in Shakespeare's later plays are similarly near to death, and I would argue that one reason why Shakespeare is drawn so frequently to such moments is that he senses, as René Weis suggests, that now his son has died, a part of himself has also died, and a purpose in life is much less clear to him.[4]

And worse is to come for the exhausted King. When Prince Harry finally appears and is supposed to be watching over his father's disturbed sleep, he takes the crown away to another room. Henry is horrified when he wakes:

> This part of his conjoins with my disease,
> *And helps to end me.* See, sons, what things you are! . . .
> For this the *foolish over-careful fathers*
> Have broke their sleep with thoughts, their brains with care,
> Their bones with industry;
> For this they have engrossed and piled up
> The cank'red heaps of strange-achieved gold; . . .
> When, like the bee, tolling from every flower
> The virtuous sweets,
> Our thighs pack'd with wax, our mouths with honey,
> We bring it to the hive, and, like the bees,
> Are *murd'red* for our pains (4.5.63–4; 67–71; 74–8; my italics).

It is difficult to believe that the father's hurt, anger, and frustration that all his diligent, painful work on his son's behalf has come to nothing does not draw on feelings deep inside Shakespeare: by hard work he had raised himself from a provincial nobody to a successful man in the country's capital who was beginning to accumulate a respectable inheritance, including property and a coat of arms, for his son to enjoy; but now there was no son to enjoy it: "Are murd'red for our pains," may not be an exaggeration of Shakespeare's unconscious feelings.

When Prince Harry returns and tries to explain his behavior—"I never thought to hear you speak again"—Father cuts him short: "Thy wish was father, Harry, to that thought:/I stay too long by thee, I weary thee . . . / Then get thee gone, and dig my grave thyself" (4.5.92–3; 110). The metaphor of murder is taken even further. The son's behavior is the equivalent of digging the father's grave; and for Shakespeare as a father himself this could have two, probably unconscious, associations—the father feeling he will die of grief and the father feeling his family line and name is at an end because he now has only daughters, and they will change their name when they marry.

Indeed, the image of a son killing a father is not confined to this play. Shortly after it comes *Julius Caesar*, in which Julius is assassinated by a group of senators led by Brutus, whom in many ways he regards as his protégé, and who, in ancient gossip, was Julius' illegitimate son: the rumor that "Brutus' bastard hand/Stabb'd Julius Caesar" is referred to in the earlier *Henry the Sixth, Part 2*, so Shakespeare certainly knew it (4.1.136–7). And when Ulysses is predicting the horrors that can arise from social disorder, one of them is, "And the rude son should strike his father dead" (*Troilus and Cressida*, 1.3.115). In *King Lear* Gloucester mistakenly believes that this is what Edgar wants to do to him, and soon. Fatherhood is presented in many of Shakespeare's plays as a lacerating experience.

The main plot of civil unrest in *Henry the Fourth, Part 2* introduces other aspects of a bereaved father's emotions, and a situation is presented that is about to become unusual in Shakespeare's plays—a father mourning the actual (rather than the apparent) death of a son. This paternal grief, however, is expressed more briefly than the maternal grief in *King John*, is for a grown man not a child, and is soon contained and directed in a typical male manner. The elderly Earl of Northumberland has been awaiting news of the rebellion against the King led by his son, Harry Hotspur. When he knows for certain that his son is dead, he rages not as King Henry has against his son, blaming him; instead he rages against the universe, wanting all human life obliterated. "Let heaven kiss earth! now let not nature's hand/Keep the wild flood confin'd! let order die! . . . / And darkness be the burier of the dead!" (1.1.153–4; 160). His first response is to want to annihilate the world, for what is the point of living without his child? We'll find Lear and Macbeth wanting a similar destruction, in Lear's case because he feels abandoned by his children, in Macbeth's because he has no son to inherit the crown he has risked his immortal soul to grasp. This double recurrence of Northumberland's emotions suggests that Shakespeare is drawing on something deep within, and in all three cases it is linked with a sense of paternal powerlessness. A similar reaction is reported by counselors and therapists dealing with bereaved parents, especially fathers; for instance, "I wanted to destroy the world that had hurt me in this way: my mind kept filling with images of myself tearing at walls, at buildings, at people, destroying, hurting, killing even."[5] It is revealing too, as Richard Wheeler notes, that Northumberland's agony is increased by the fact that he was not with his son when he died, as Shakespeare may not have been with his.[6] But the release of feelings here is not developed much further; Northumberland reverts to one of the traditional male responses to loss— to displace emotion by violent activity—and is soon bent on revenge.

This brief scene of a father mourning for his son is near the midpoint of Shakespeare's theatrical career, and it is helpful to put it in context with what is to come and what has preceded it. It will be eight or so years before Shakespeare can face again a father mourning a child who is actually dead, and then, in *King Lear*, it is a *daughter*, not a son, who has died. After a further four to five years, in *The Winter's Tale*, Prince Mamillius dies, but very surprisingly Leontes does not (appear to) mourn for him, but only for his wife Hermione. In fact, it is not until 13 to 14 years after *Henry the Fourth, Part 2* that Shakespeare, in his final sole-authored play, *The Tempest*, can bear to present directly and at some length a father mourning an only son, and even then we know before we experience Alonso's grief that his son is really alive.

So in no play after *Henry the Fourth, Part 2* do we see a father mourning an only son who is actually dead; it seems to become too painful an experience to contemplate directly, without the benefit of disguise. Yet in the plays before Hamnet's death, there is no such avoidance. In *Henry the Sixth, Part 3*, when Shakespeare wants to encapsulate the horror of the divisions created by civil war, he presents a son who has unwittingly killed his father and a father who has unwittingly killed his son. The son appears first, carrying his dead father, and the climax is reached when the father enters, carrying a corpse, and then recognizes his victim: "Ah, no, no, no, it is mine only son!" (2.5.83). Then he weeps, without feeling the unease that many of Shakespeare's later males feel. "Mine only son" has religious associations with Abraham's potential sacrifice of Isaac and with God the Father's sacrifice of His only son; the allusion emphasizes the enormity of the deed, as if every son is as important and special to his father as Isaac was to Abraham and Jesus was to God. The onstage picture of a father carrying his dead son recalls the most famous of such parental images: the Virgin Mary holding the body of the dead Jesus after his crucifixion, again underlining the horror of the situation, but also suggesting that the father here is feeling as intensely as a mother would. We will see Shakespeare return to this pietà image even more movingly in *King Lear* and in *Cymbeline* (Chapters 10 and 13).

The father is then given a long valedictory speech. Even this early in his career Shakespeare can intuit the despair of a father who feels responsible for his son's death, and perhaps he is already feeling at some level guilt for leaving his son and the rest of his family in Stratford. The father mourns, "These arms of mine shall be thy winding-sheet;/My heart, sweet boy, shall be thy sepulchre,/For from my heart thine image ne'er shall go" (2.5.114–6).

A second early play reaches a climax in a father's mourning for a dead son. *Henry the Sixth, Part 1* may be what we now call a prequel, written after what we know as *Parts 2 and 3*, because of the earlier plays' popularity. In it we see an ideal of absolute loyalty between father and son. The father, Lord Talbot, who died in the middle of the fifteenth century, is not a well-known figure to us; but for Elizabethans he was as famous as Nelson is now and was known as the scourge of the French. When the English are outnumbered by the French near Bordeaux, both Father and his son John are willing to sacrifice themselves so the other can escape. Each rescues the other from certain death at different points; and it seems both might survive against the odds, until a youthful rush of adrenalin sends John back into the battle, where he perishes in a "sea of blood" (4.7.14). So Father has the unendurable experience of outliving his son, if only for a few moments. Talbot asks for his son's body to be placed in his arms—another pietà image: "Soldiers, adieu! I have what I would have,/Now my old arms are young John Talbot's grave" (4.7.31–2). Then he too dies, of weariness and grief.[7]

So stage fathers mourning dead sons disappear after *Henry the Fourth, Part 2*; but not stage fathers disturbed in other ways, and in the next chapter we'll meet one of the most fascinating of them all.

Notes

Full publication details of every source are in the bibliography.

1. Danbury, "Narcissism and Bereavement," in Cooper and Maxwell, *Narcissistic Wounds*, pp. 101–14. The quotation is from p. 110.

2. Wright, *Sudden Death*, p. 54

3. Worden, *Grief Counseling and Grief Therapy*, p. 102.

4. Weis, *Shakespeare Unbound*, p. 300 and *Shakespeare Revealed*, p. 266.

5. Staudacher, *Men and Grief*, p. 31.

6. Wheeler, "Deaths in the Family," pp. 142–3.

7. It is possible that there are other moments in tragic and historical plays in the years immediately following Hamnet's death, which in part are influenced by the boy's loss. For instance, in Act 4, Scene 2 of *Julius Caesar* Brutus knows of his wife's death, then seems not to know, and needs to be told again. It is sometimes thought that this reflects rewriting on Shakespeare's part, and that he only intended one of the two moments to be included, but both were printed inadvertently; but as Sarah Brown suggested to me, the apparent inconsistency might be deliberate, to show how difficult it is to take in the fact that a loved one has died.

Grief on Grief; That Within
Which Passeth Show

What's in a Name?

In previous chapters we have seen features and patterns in Shakespeare's writing that could be linked in part to the loss of Hamnet; but these have not dominated the plays discussed. There's been a sense of partial rather than full engagement with the pain of mourning, a sense of repression, and this can often lead to a time when grief pours out as from a breached dam. I would argue that, for Shakespeare, this process is shown in *Hamlet*. There is an intensity of grief hinted at before, but never pervasive as it is here, where the universe is nightblack as the hero's mourning cloak. Even before the Ghost of Hamlet's father appears commanding his son to avenge his murder, Francisco, on sentry duty, is not just frozen by the bitter night but is also, inexplicably, "sick at heart," preparing us for the large number of images of inner unease and sickness that Caroline Spurgeon was the first to try and quantify in this strange, strange play (1.1.9). As Jeffrey Kauffman notes, one aspect of repressed grief can be to "engender in another person what is in oneself denied," whether it be engendered in a real person or in a fictional character.[1] Therese Rando's research into the differences between mothers' and fathers' reactions to the loss of a child revealed that, for fathers, the main distinguishing responses are "a great sense of isolation and desolation, accompanied by feelings of loss of control and a considerable fear of death," all features strongly present in this play and in many of those to come.[2]

Many commentators would agree with T.S. Eliot's famous comment that *Hamlet* "is full of some stuff that the writer could not drag to light, contemplate or manipulate into art . . . Hamlet (the man) is dominated by an emotion which is inexpressible because it is in excess of the facts as they appear." At the heartsick heart of the play is something "which passeth show" or utterance, no matter how many words Shakespeare uses.[3]

And he does use many words. A draft version of *Hamlet*, which forms the basis of the *Second Quarto* text, takes about four-and-a-half hours to perform, two hours longer than the average play of the period. As a playwright of 10 or more years' experience, Shakespeare must have realized that he was writing *much, much more than his company was likely to perform*. In other words, although he was writing one of his most theatrically and verbally inventive plays, he was not writing *merely* with performance in mind. Indeed, a shorter, revised version that seems to have been prepared for performance survives in the *Folio* text, though even this is much longer than the average playtext of the period and, as well as omissions, contains some additions not in the *Second Quarto* text. A third version survives in the *First Quarto*. It is a garbled, probably pirated, text, perhaps intended for a traveling troupe like the one that comes to Elsinore. A little over half the length of the *Second Quarto*, it shows amongst other things how much of the play can be omitted without losing the basic plot. In the *Second Quarto* indeed Shakespeare was letting himself go, letting himself improvise freely on a plot that, as usual, he had borrowed, knowing that perhaps as much as a quarter of his draft would not reach the stage. Something buried needed to emerge into the air.

The survival of three texts adds to the difficulty of dating *Hamlet*. It is not mentioned in Meres' 1598 list, and is entered in the *Stationers' Register* on 26 July 1602, so these are the time limits. The revised *Folio* version has a topical reference to the "war" that broke out between rival theater companies in 1601; this is not present in the draft *Second Quarto* text, so the latter may predate this "war" and be from 1599 or 1600. As the play has been revised at least once, however, it seems best to regard it not as the work of a single occasion or even year, but as a text that emerged from draft to *Folio* version in the period from three to five years after Hamnet's death.

As always with Shakespeare, a range of influences seem to have fed into the play. A number of social factors almost certainly contributed to its mood of paralysis, including the fact that the childless Queen Elizabeth was losing ground and had refused to name a successor, and the fact that Shakespeare's former patron, the Earl of Southampton, had aligned himself with the Earl of Essex, who had fallen out with Elizabeth and her ministers (and, after Essex's failed coup of February 1601, ended up in the Tower of London). But I do not think external factors alone account for the way in which *Hamlet* is, overall, so radically different from any of Shakespeare's previous plays. Personal experiences enter into it too.

In 1600 Shakespeare's father, John, was about 70, and had lived 20 years longer than his average Stratford neighbor—a modern equivalent might be 90. Even if John was in good health for his age, it is probable that Shakespeare, like most children, imagined his father's coming death and the effect it might have on him. John died in September 1601, and the weight of evidence suggests that *Hamlet* existed in at least one text by that date, so I think we are dealing, as perhaps in *King John*, with anticipated rather than actual death, and an awareness on Shakespeare's part of his powerlessness to prevent it. I agree with the theory first sketched by Georg Brandes that this further woe took him back to earlier losses in his life, especially the devastation of losing a son—indeed, increased his sense of isolation, for when his father died, the male generation either side of his own would be gone.[4]

This sense of isolation in grief is vividly conveyed when we first see Hamlet, who is in black while everyone else is in bright colors, celebrating the marriage of his mother and his uncle. Once again Shakespeare is presenting what many mourners experience. In *The Bereaved Parent* Harriet Sarnoff Schiff quotes the blunt comment, "Grief can't be shared. Everyone carries it alone, his own burden, his own way," and she agrees that this was her experience also when she lost a child.[5] I think it was Shakespeare's too, and that it is no coincidence that he invents a protagonist who cannot articulate his deepest feelings to anyone, even, fully, to himself. Shakespeare is doing what we saw Viola do in Chapter 2: inventing a fictional character to represent emotions that cannot be expressed directly because they are too painful. Indeed, one of the ways in which this play marks a decisive change in Shakespeare's writing is that after it, as Park Honan and others have noted, he becomes increasingly concerned with characters whose pain separates them from their fellow creatures, like Othello, Lear, and Macbeth. As we saw in Chapter 2, Stephen Greenblatt has explored the possibility that this sense of isolation was exacerbated for Shakespeare and some members of his family by the brevity and impersonality introduced into the process of mourning (especially the rituals associated with preparation for death, burial, and post-burial) by the Protestant reformers. The Ghost, Hamlet, and Laertes complain about abbreviated burial ceremonies, the Ghost is afraid that he will be forgotten after his death, and his son berates himself for his impotence in enacting the Ghost's wishes. Further, the mad Ophelia starts singing a traditional ballad, but it soon becomes a simple sung dirge for her dead father. "He is dead and gone, lady,/He is dead and gone,/At his head a grass-green turf,/At his heels a stone" (4.5.29–32). The singing of dirges was another matter disapproved of by reformers because it went beyond the ideal of moderate grief. Greenblatt argues further that Shakespeare gradually came to realize at some level that theater could explore some of the emotional space left empty by the abandonment of traditional religious ritual.[6] This corresponds to what we saw at the end of *Twelfth Night*, where Shakespeare begins to invent his own ritual moments linked with death and (apparent) rebirth. The strongest examples of this process occur in *The Winter's Tale* and *Cymbeline* (see Chapters 12 and 13).

Observations from many counselors and therapists support the idea that a later (actual or anticipated) death can isolate a mourner further, and take him or her back to unresolved issues from an earlier loss. For instance, Christopher Clulow and Janet Mattinson state: "There is much clinical evidence to show that when a major loss is not properly mourned at the time, a subsequent loss rebounds on the first, and then a double grief breaks through the defensive barriers. Double grief can be quite overwhelming, out of proportion to the later loss and unduly persistent."[7] In other words, "in excess of the facts," as T. S. Eliot put it. When a further loss occurs, even an expected one, it can lead to trauma. David Malan writes, "traumatic events often owe their damaging effects to the fact that they are a repetition of something similar that has happened in the past. . . . One of the important roots of depression is concerned with feelings of loss and *particularly with grief that has in some way miscarried and has never been worked through*."[8] Sidney Zisook and Richard DeVaul similarly found that unresolved grief tends to take on a life of its own. In cases where grief was worked through, "grief-related feelings and behaviors peaked in intensity between the first and second years, and gradually diminished thereafter. Unresolved grief, on the other hand, did not significantly change over time. Once present, it tended to remain."[9]

Therese Rando confirms Zisook and De Vaul's conclusion with specific reference to bereaved parents: "In the third year of bereavement there may be an intensification of the grief experience, suggesting that bereavement may actually worsen with time."[10] We should not take this as a scientific measure, which does not vary from one parent to another. It means that at a time when we might expect a bereaved parent to have started to come to terms with the devastation of loss and be moving onward in his or her process of mourning, the grief sometimes increases, and I think this is one of the many things happening in *Hamlet*, probably begun three to four years after Hamnet's death. For most of the play we are presented with a man who cannot progress in his emotional life, who seems stuck in a moment of trauma while the world around him moves on, indifferent to his inner pain.

Several features of the play support this idea of grief for Hamnet resurfacing. Firstly, many critics have commented on the protagonist's name, Hamlet. It is important to note that this comes from a lost play and is not Shakespeare's invention, but as Stephen Greenblatt argues, I think the very act of writing the name so frequently would have affected him deeply.[11] Shakespeare's twins were named after Shakespeare's Stratford neighbors Hamnet and Judith Sadler. Spelling of names was much less fixed in Shakespeare's period, and in several contemporary documents Hamnet and Hamlet are *interchangeable*. For instance, in Shakespeare's own will, he leaves a bequest to Hamlett Sadler to buy a ring, yet the will is witnessed by Hamnet Sadler. Presumably "Hamlett" is the name Shakespeare dictated to his lawyer, Francis Collins; perhaps even near to death the name Hamnet was too painful to pronounce (as Mamillius' name is for King Leontes 16 years after the boy's death in *The Winter's Tale*).[12]

What can we deduce from this? That when Shakespeare was writing Ham*l*et, it would have been the same as writing Ham*n*et, especially for a man obsessed with puns, similar sounds and double meanings. Further, Shakespeare's earlier draft version preserved in the *Second Quarto* has "Ham" as the usual speech prefix when Hamlet speaks. Many people's first names get changed into nicknames by family and acquaintances— Shakespeare is Will in some contemporary documents and in punning references to himself in the *Sonnets*—so it is likely that Hamnet was not always referred to so formally by the family. Perhaps he was Ham, in which case there would not even be the one letter difference that there is between Ham*l*et and Ham*n*et whenever Shakespeare was writing the speech prefix, Ham. Dennis Klass notes how important a dead child's name is for many bereaved parents. As an example he quotes the end of one father's poem about his dead son, Orin: "He is real and shadow, was and is./Say Orin to me and say Orin again./He is my son and I love him as I always did. Say Orin." This is the reverse side of Leontes' wish never to hear his son's name again; for Leontes and for Orin's father the name touches their innermost feelings.[13]

Part of the appeal of the old play about Hamlet for Shakespeare, then, probably came from the coincidence of the hero's and his own son's name.

The Sadlers did not return the Shakespeares' compliment of naming a child after their friends for 13 years, although they had had at least four sons and two daughters christened between Hamnet's birth in 1585 and death in August 1596. Hamnet Shakespeare's death seems to have reminded the Sadlers belatedly of this omission, and that the most they could do for the mourning father was to suggest that, if Hamnet's name was gone forever, William's at least might survive. Even though Shakespeare had been living mainly in London for about 10 years, the Sadlers' next son, born in 1598, was christened William, and Shakespeare may have been his godfather. The Sadlers had lost children themselves, and this touching gesture suggests they knew that Shakespeare was still grieving for his boy. His fellow actor John Heminges' decision to christen a son William in 1603 may have been influenced by the same thought.[14]

Unpacking the Heart with Words

Another piece of evidence that the play's pervasive grief is linked to Hamnet's actual, as well as to John's impending, death is the recurrence of images of men trying, and failing, to avoid tears, which we saw in Chapter 1, is especially common with bereaved parents. Hamlet berates himself for this on several occasions, but revealingly he is not the only one to do so. Laertes also tries to "forbid" his tears when he learns of his sister Ophelia's death, but like Hamlet finds he cannot do so, and accuses himself of behaving like a woman (4.7.186). At the same time, there is a deep desire for the relief of weeping, as well as a social fear of it as unmanly. At the start of his first soliloquy, Hamlet, like many mourners, is thinking of suicide. Reiko Schwab reports more than a third of the bereaved parents in her study as stating that their pain was so extreme, and their desire to join their dead child so strong, that thoughts of suicide came into their minds, and "they would have welcomed death." She quotes one father: " 'Many times I wanted to go to sleep and never wake up.' "[15] Hamlet expresses the forlorn hope that his "flesh would melt,/Thaw, and resolve itself into a dew," before talking explicitly of "self-slaughter" (1.2.129–30, 132). The image is revealing. The nearest most of us come to melting in a literal sense is when we cry; that this is a strong connotation for Shakespeare is shown by the fact that he associates melting and tears on at least 20 occasions in his plays. And in *King John* Lewis says of the Earl of Salisbury's tears, "Let me wipe off this honorable *dew*/That silverly doth progress on thy cheeks" (5.2.45–6; my italics). I would argue, then, that Hamlet's language here reflects an unconscious desire to dissolve into tears, something his conscious mind cannot accept as manly, and that this probably reflects Shakespeare's own preoccupation with, and ambivalence about, tears.

A further feature linking the grief in *Hamlet* with both deaths comes from the sense of powerlessness linked with fatherhood. In *Henry the Fourth, Part 2*, this feeling provoked anger from both the King and Northumberland; here, the emphasis is on sorrow more than anger, and on paralysis. Hamlet's father is a ghost of a human being, confined to Purgatory, unable to prevent his wife's infidelity, and unable to act on his own behalf to gain his revenge.[16] This presentation probably reflects, among other things, Shakespeare's sense of his father's declining powers as he approaches death; but I think it likely that it also draws on Shakespeare's own sense of powerlessness as a father, now that his son and heir is dead. One of our few pieces of information about Shakespeare as an actor supports this. Nicholas Rowe reported in 1709, "though I have inquired, I could never meet with any further account of him this way, than that the top of his performance was the Ghost in his own *Hamlet*."[17] Why might this role have brought out the best in Shakespeare? Roland Kuhn discovered that often "mourners have the feeling that it is not the dead person but they themselves who have been ejected from the world hitherto familiar to them."[18] Shakespeare, then, might well have been able to identify with one of the living dead, a Ghost ejected from a normal life into a powerless, purgatorial existence, in which time passes in one sense but not in another, and the intense and detailed description of the Ghost's experiences suggests that for Shakespeare they might symbolize an aspect of his own: "Doom'd for a certain term to walk the night,/And for the day confin'd to fast in fires" (1.5.10–11). The Ghost is dependent on Hamlet to act decisively and restore his honor, but famously Hamlet finds himself unable to fulfill his father's needs, just as Hamnet can never fulfill *his* father's needs. As many commentators have noted, this sense of time as becalmed is anticipated in *Julius Caesar*, probably written within a year of the first version of *Hamlet*, when Brutus is pondering whether to join the conspiracy against Caesar: "Between the acting of a dreadful thing/And the first motion, all the interim is/Like a phantasma or a hideous dream," suggesting that this awareness of inertia is not just the product of a single play or dramatic situation (2.1.63–5).

But Shakespeare's own father had been more fortunate. His son had restored his social status. As we have seen, by 1596 Shakespeare had renewed his father's application for a family coat of arms, abandoned more than 20 years before. We do not know whether the application was made before or after Hamnet's death, but it was granted two months after that loss, a moment that must have been a bittersweet pleasure to Hamnet's father. We have also seen that he had started to acquire land and income from tithes that, in effect, replaced the land and income his father had lost from the late 1570s onward. What an irony this must have seemed to someone as aware of irony as Shakespeare was: he had been the dutiful son and had "avenged" his father's loss of honor and restored his father's status; but there was no son now to do it for him, should he fall on hard times, as his father had done, and no son to inherit the wealth he was amassing.

The need to maintain the family name and honor is one of the main themes in *Hamlet*, and the horror of being a father whose son cannot achieve this is emphasized by the fact that the play shows us not one but three sons who contrast with Hamlet. The first is the Prince of Norway, Fortinbras, who raises an army of mercenaries to try and recapture the land and status his father lost to Denmark 30 years before. When this plan is thwarted, he does not disband his army but keeps it intact by crossing Denmark to fight in Poland and so finds himself on hand to seize the Danish throne after the bloodbath at the end. Thus, the family name of Fortinbras is triumphant. The second active son is Laertes who, like Hamlet, has to restore his family honor by avenging his father's murder. But unlike Hamlet, he seems willing to go to any lengths to do this. To confirm he is truly his father's son in deeds *"More than in words"*—a pointed contrast with the wordy Hamlet—he would commit murder in church and "dare damnation" in pursuit of his revenge (4.7.126—my italics; 4.5.134).

But it is the third example that reveals the extent of Shakespeare's preoccupation with this contrast between action and inertia. This third son does not appear onstage; we only hear about him in a speech that is unnecessary in terms of the plot, and is usually shortened, or even omitted, in production. One of the traveling actors recites an account of the end of the Trojan War, when the Greek warrior Pyrrhus murders the elderly Trojan king, Priam—another powerless father figure. This murder is motivated by "A roused vengeance," and at least some of Shakespeare's audience would remember that Pyrrhus' father, Achilles, had died earlier in the war from a wound to his heel, and that this is the motive for Pyrrhus' revenge (2.2.488). And before Pyrrhus kills King Priam the play points to a similarity, but then a great difference, between Pyrrhus and Hamlet. Pyrrhus' sword seems to stick in the air, and the scene becomes motionless, like a painting, which anticipates Hamlet's later hesitation when he has the chance to kill his father's murderer when Claudius is apparently praying. But unlike Hamlet, who fails to kill Claudius because he stops to consider the implications of the situation, Pyrrhus swings into action and batters the old King to death like a blacksmith hammering metal into shape. This links Pyrrhus with Fortinbras and Laertes. And all three are linked with Shakespeare himself, who also acted to restore the family honor and name, albeit in a less violent way, and contrast with Hamlet/Hamnet.

I am suggesting, then, that Shakespeare's repeated contrasts between active and inactive sons reflect a sense of powerlessness following Hamnet's death and exacerbated by John's; and there is frustrated bitterness in many of Hamlet's comments (a feature taken even further in *Troilus and Cressida*, discussed in the next chapter). This leads to a manic inventiveness in Hamlet, to "wild and whirling words" (1.5.133). But this manic quality is not just in Hamlet the man, but in *Hamlet* the play as well. As many critics have noted, drawing on the work of Alfred Hart, there are more words new to Shakespeare in *Hamlet* than in any other play, and many of these he seems to have invented, as far as can be deduced from what has survived from the period.[19] The depth of emotion he is expressing requires a much wider vocabulary to present it, and the resulting linguistic inventiveness coincides with a breakthrough in the use of soliloquy and aside to present the disjointed and fragmentary rhythm and sentence structure of inner experience and reflection. For the first time in Shakespeare a character sounds *like a real man rather than a fictional invention agonizing to himself.* Hamlet is more self-conscious and has more soliloquies than any other Shakespearean protagonist. Further, there are more soliloquies than Shakespeare's company had time to present, and the two performance-based texts that survive from Shakespeare's period omit the final one, spoken as Hamlet watches Fortinbras taking his army to fight for a small piece of land "Which is not tomb enough and continent/To hide the slain"—another indication that Shakespeare is probably writing for himself as well as for public performance (4.4.64–5). I think Stephen Greenblatt is right that this technical development has come about in part from the pressure of deep personal pain linked to these family deaths, one actual, the second anticipated.[20] Indeed, the whole play has an improvisatory quality to it: the inherited plot provides a structure within which Shakespeare can explore inner feeling and character as he needs, rather than solely according to the demands of consistency, as we will see later.

In Hamlet's soliloquies the manic qualities we see in his encounters with other people, especially Polonius and Claudius, take second place, in the main, to a mood of melancholy and paralysis, what nowadays is sometimes called melancholic depression or, following Samuel Johnson and Winston Churchill, the black dog. This fits with the description of the Ghost, played by Shakespeare himself, who returns from the dead with a "countenance more/In sorrow than in anger," in contrast to the usual Revenge Tragedy Ghost of, for instance, *The Spanish Tragedy* and *Locrine*, who cares only for revenge (1.2.231–2). It also fits with the fact that the active, apparently desirable sons are not presented so as to attract the audience; it is the inactive, agonizing Hamlet who has been and probably still is Shakespeare's best known character, despite (or more probably, in part, because of) his manifest difficulties with life.

Many counselors and therapists working with melancholy caused by bereavement stress the importance of creativity in moving forward the journey through grief. For instance, Darian Leader, following Freud, uses the technical term melancholia to describe a state when the bereaved person is plunged into "a kind of wholesale identification with the dead, although the sufferer isn't generally conscious of this. It's as if they've died with the dead person, so they continue living but in this impossible situation of inhabiting the same space as the dead." Leader is not describing Hamlet, but how well it fits the man in black we see and hear at the beginning of the play. He continues, "In the therapies of melancholia, what matters is to help the person to find a new language to talk about the loss—it may be through writing or poetry."[21] Again this seems close to what Shakespeare unconsciously does in *Hamlet*—invents new words and a new kind of soliloquy under the pressure of a deep sense of loss and abandonment.

One peculiar feature of the play's inventive language that several commentators have commented on may be especially relevant to the loss of Hamnet—the use of what is technically called hendiadys, literally meaning one through two, when a single idea is conveyed by a couple of linked words. For instance, Hamlet tells his mother that the outwards features of his grief, such as his "inky cloak," are "but the *trappings and the suits* of woe" (1.2.77, 86; my italics). In logical terms one of "trappings" and "suits" would suffice, but the inclusion of both creates a rhythmic fluency, in addition to a variety of vocabulary, which appeals to the ear. "Angels and ministers of grace defend us," is another example (1.4.39). As James Shapiro indicates, it is a difficult way to write for any length of time—a writer had to have a brain attuned to synonyms as well as to rhythms, when there was no thesaurus to make it easier—yet he counts at least 66 examples in *Hamlet*, more than twice as many as in any of Shakespeare's other plays, and also registers a sudden growth in the use of the device in the plays just before *Hamlet*, from *Henry the Fifth*, probably written about three years after Hamnet's death, through to *Macbeth*, about 1606.[22] Eugene Mahon takes Shapiro's argument further in suggesting "a possible unconscious connection between lingering grief over a dead twin and this kind of ruminative linguistic doubling," producing phrases with twinned words. He also notes other doublings in the play, for instance the unusual amount of character pairing—Bernardo and Marcellus, Cornelius and Voltemand, Rosencrantz and Guildenstern—and an image that comes to Gertrude as she describes how Hamlet has fits of mad behavior, then suddenly becomes calm: "Anon, as patient as the female dove,/When that her *golden couplets* are disclosed/His silence will sit drooping" (5.1.286–8; my italics). This mother bird has a pair of baby birds, like twins.[23] And of course in *Twelfth Night*, written close in time to *Hamlet*, we have literal twins.

So we've seen much evidence that the mood of the play is connected with personal loss as well as with wider social unease. A further aspect to be considered is that Hamlet's supposed delay has, to some extent, to be forced onto the story Shakespeare has inherited, in defiance of the facts, to modify Eliot's comment. Why do we think that Hamlet delays unreasonably in acting against Claudius? Because he keeps telling us so. As several critics have remarked, the play would be very different without the soliloquies, for the underlying plot gives us clear reasons why Hamlet cannot act quickly. Firstly, he wants to be sure the Ghost is not a deceiving devil in disguise, a very real possibility for both Protestants and Catholics at this time; (the Witches prove to be just that in *Macbeth*). Secondly, Claudius is always with others, such as his Swiss Guards (famous for their efficiency), and/or his wife Gertrude, and the Ghost has told his son not to involve Gertrude in the revenge. The one exception to this is when Claudius is apparently praying, but then Hamlet fears the murderer may be repenting, and that if he kills him Claudius will not be damned for all eternity, as he needs to be for the revenge to be complete. This may appear a primitive attitude for someone who seems as sensitive to the complexities of life as Hamlet is, but this illustrates another disparity between the Hamlet we are presented with for much of the play and the world of Shakespeare's source materials—Scandanavian saga. There partial revenge is no revenge at all, and it is entirely fitting to that world that Hamlet should decide to wait until he can catch his father's murderer "about some act/That has no relish of salvation in't" since Claudius dispatched Hamlet's father "in the blossoms of my sin,/Unhous'led, disappointed, unanel'd/No reck'ning made" (3.3.91–2; 1.5.76–8).[24] Of course we know that Claudius has not repented because we hear his words at the end of the scene; but Hamlet does not. After this, Hamlet tries to kill Claudius, only to find he's killed Polonius, and then he's dispatched aboard ship for England. Hamlet is overcritical of his delay in my judgment because Shakespeare, like Viola in the extract in Chapter 2, needs a fictional outlet for the intensity of his inner turmoil in relation to loss, especially family death.

The strongest example of this inner turmoil affecting the play occurs at the end of Act 2, when Hamlet devises a plan to confirm Claudius' guilt by having the traveling actors perform a similar murder, so he can watch Claudius' reaction. It is a shrewd idea, and Hamlet is upbeat: "the play's the thing/Wherein I'll catch the conscience of the King" (2.2.604–5). We might expect the mood to last at least until the next evening, when the performance will take place, but before this can happen Hamlet is plunged into even deeper melancholy, in perhaps the best remembered speech in English drama, "To be, or not to be," which asks the fundamental question: is it worth being alive, having existence, at all? (3.1.55–87).

The position of this soliloquy is intriguing. In the (probably) pirated touring version of *Hamlet* it occurs much earlier, well before Hamlet conceives his plan to test Claudius' guilt. This could be a misremembrance by the pirating actors, although usually they recollect the order of scenes accurately; or Shakespeare may have revised the original structure, and moved the soliloquy to its present place. But in either case the question arises, why did the misremembrance or revision happen at all? The obvious answer is that the logical place for such a melancholy soliloquy is *before* Hamlet has invented his plan to test Claudius' guilt. Until then he does not know what to do, and is plunged into debilitating inertia; after it he has a plan to establish Claudius' guilt or innocence. In his 2009 production with David Tennant, Gregory Doran kept to this logic by placing "To be or not to be" before Hamlet conceives of his plan.

The strange position of "To be, or not to be," in the *Second Quarto* and *Folio* texts however, *after* Hamlet has devised his plan and so might be expected to be feeling more positive, supports Eliot's assessment that *Hamlet* is dealing with a depth of emotion "in excess of the facts" of the plot at this point in the play's development. But it is true to the experience of someone suffering from melancholic depression that even a sound plan cannot keep the black dog at bay, and so takes us more deeply into Hamlet's inner state. In addition, this soliloquy is significantly different from his other ones, which arise from the immediate circumstances he finds himself in; this one is a general account of the deep frustrations and fears of human life, some of which Hamlet the character has not experienced. For instance, he talks of "the law's delay," when he has never taken a case to law; but Shakespeare had recently been involved in a protracted and unsuccessful legal battle with the Lamberts to regain some of his mother's land mortgaged by his father, and knows "the law's delay" from experience (3.1.71). A further inconsistency is Hamlet's reflection that "No traveler returns" from "The undiscover'd country" of death, despite his having seen the Ghost (3.1.78–9).

Taken as a whole, these features suggest that the soliloquy might have been, in part, conceived away from its final context, and even from the play itself, because Shakespeare *needed to express* the sense of hopelessness within it. Its conclusion is unremittingly negative: we do not choose to stay alive for any positive reason, but because we fear what might happen to us in the next life if we kill ourselves. It reminds us that, when Polonius says he will take his leave of Hamlet, Hamlet replies, "You cannot take from me any thing that I will not more willingly part withal—except my life, except my life, except my life" (2.2.215–7). It may seem strange to say, but this intense consideration of negative thoughts and of suicide might have helped Shakespeare at this stage in his grieving: Susan Lendrum and Gabrielle Syme found that an acknowledgment of depression can be therapeutic, can help a mourner to survive.[25] A surprising example of this was broadcast at the end of 2009 on BBC Radio, when a former Welsh rugby captain, Gareth Thomas, said in public that he was homosexual—an incredibly brave thing for someone in the macho world of rugby, and sport in general, to acknowledge. Talking of the agony and depression of the years of disguise, he told how he used to go to the edge of the nearby cliffs and consider suicide. And the consideration of suicide in a setting where he could have enacted it helped him *not to take his life, to keep going*.[26] So it is possible that Shakespeare's writing down of intensely negative thoughts in this and other soliloquies helped him to place such thoughts at a distance, to gain some control over them, and experience a degree of catharsis.

Indeed I think the whole play, and the "To be" soliloquy in particular, is so famous and popular in part because it confronts taboo subjects society discourages us from discussing. That suicide and death might seem sometimes preferable to life is one such taboo, and in the final scene even God's law against suicide appears to be discarded. When Horatio proposes to join the dying Hamlet in the next life by committing suicide, Hamlet asks him to stay and tell Hamlet's story to the world: "Absent thee from felicity a while" (5.2.347). In other words, felicity, happiness, comes from leaving this world behind, and suicide is at this moment presented as a positive rather than a forbidden means of achieving this. But the other side of that taboo is also present: the horror of *not dying, of surviving, and being forced to endure* the "heart-ache and the thousand natural shocks/That flesh is *heir* to," (3.1.61–2—a telling image for a man who has lost his heir; my italics). This is what we all have to do after the loss of a loved one—to keep going, no matter how riven our hearts are. The speech almost envies the dead for having escaped this. (There is a similar emphasis in the funeral scene in *Cymbeline*, as we will see in Chapter 13, and interestingly the mourners there think they are speaking over the corpse of a young boy).

This sense of negativity and paralysis continues even in the apparently more positive fifth act, for at the end Hamlet does not bring about the situation in which he can enact his revenge, as do other avengers in Elizabethan tragedy. A revenge play had to end with the revenge enacted, but here it is as if this happens *in spite of Hamlet*, rather than because of him, as if Shakespeare was obliged to meet his audience's expectations, even though it did not really fit the rest of the play as he had written it.

Nor does the conclusion end the purgatory of the powerless Ghost, Shakespeare's own role. It indicates how engrossing *Hamlet* is that most theatergoers and readers do not notice the Ghost's bizarre disappearance. This is not how the Ghost behaves in *The Spanish Tragedy* or *Locrine*. There he returns to experience release and celebrate, indeed gloat over, the avenger's success. But I think Shakespeare's Ghost cannot return and be released from his suffering because his creator cannot yet be released from *his* inner purgatory.[27]

Man and Boy

So I would argue that one of the many things happening in *Hamlet*, as in some comedies, especially *Twelfth Night*, is that Shakespeare is doing what many mourners do, whether consciously or not: searching for his lost one. Colin Murray Parkes quotes an especially interesting example in the life of the artist Kathe Kollwitz, whose younger son was killed in October 1914. She wrote in her diary: "There's a drawing made, a mother letting her dead son slide into her arms. I could do a hundred similar drawings but still can't seem to come any closer to him. I'm still searching for him *as if it were in the very work itself that I had to find him*."[28] "In the very work itself" is also where I think Shakespeare is (unconsciously) searching for Hamnet, and now also for his father John, especially in the last act, where the separate identities of father and son, of Ghost and Hamlet, begin to merge. Eric Rayner summarizes the aspect of mourning involved here thus: "The mourner . . . has not necessarily been 'taken over' by the dead person, although this can happen. Rather an *internalization* has taken place."[29]

Dennis Klass reports the feelings of a father that exemplify this. His 17-year-old daughter used to go running with him before she died. After her death he continued running, and "Frequently, I sensed she was nearby, cruising at my elbow, listening."[30] Experiences like this are so common, indeed, that Phyllis Silverman and Steven Nickman conclude that "maintaining an inner representation of the deceased is *normal rather than abnormal*," and this links with Viola's behavior in disguising herself as her apparently dead twin brother.[31] Indeed, who would be more likely than a playwright, already experienced in creating characters within himself, to make such an "inner representation" of a lost one?

What form does this unconscious search take at the end of *Hamlet*? A change in the conception and attitude of the protagonist, which allows Shakespeare to attempt to move beyond the mood of dejection to an acceptance of the "thousand natural shocks" that life subjects us to. In the first four acts Hamlet is the student Hamlet from Wittenberg University, "young Hamlet;" but suddenly in Act 5 he turns out to be 30! Playgoers do not always realize this because we are not told it in so many words, but those who do are normally very surprised, since Hamlet's behavior and attitudes in the first four acts have seemed in the main those of a younger man, in his late teens or early twenties at the most.

In Act 5, however, Hamlet starts to sound like a mature 30-year-old, talking of death with acceptance rather than, as before, with anguish: "If it be now, 'tis not to come; if it be not to come, it will be now; if it be not now, yet it will come—the readiness is all" (5.2.220–2). The wording of the next sentence of this speech recalls Hamnet more than John: "Since no man, of aught he leaves, knows what is't to leave *betimes*, let be" (5.2.223–4; my italics). "Betimes" in Shakespeare is usually linked to the hours before daybreak, as in Sir Toby's "Not to be abed after midnight is to be up betimes," and here by analogy it means the early years of life (*Twelfth Night*, 2.3.1–2). Apparently Hamlet is trying to accept the fact that he might die in the early years of life; but 30 is hardly the early years even now, let alone in London in 1600, where the average lifespan has been estimated as between 22 and 23 years.[32] But 11 is. Shakespeare was 32 when Hamnet died, and one thing I suggest is happening at a deep level here is that, through Hamlet's resignation to death "betimes," Shakespeare is trying, as many mourners try, to accept this early death, and perhaps to believe that Hamnet himself accepted his death, as young Prince Arthur had done. And for John Shakespeare too the loss of his young grandson would have been a bitter blow he had had to learn to accept, and John's son would have been aware of this as well.

In other words, this older accepting Hamlet is a composite figure representing a father, John; a father/son, William; and a son, Hamnet. This compound figure is also present in the first scene of Act 5, in a graveyard. The early part of this scene has an elegiac, nostalgic quality, as 30-year-old Hamlet looks back over a lifetime (as we also heard Feste doing at the end of *Twelfth Night*, though in a different tone). When the Gravedigger hands him Yorick's skull Hamlet goes back "three and twenty years" to the lost happiness of his childhood, and to fond memories of this long-dead court jester bearing him on his back (5.1.173–4). Several critics have suggested that Shakespeare is thinking in part of Richard Tarleton, the most famous clown in London during the 1580s, who played at Stratford in 1587 and nearby Coventry in 1586, but who, by 1600, had been dead for 12 years. Interestingly, the *First Quarto* version has "this dozen year" at this point on page Ir, which may be a mistake, or may reflect an earlier thought of Shakespeare's before a change to "three and twenty years." Twelve years would make Hamlet about nineteen, much closer to the Hamlet of the first four acts. There is also the possibility that Shakespeare was in part remembering his own father: Thomas Plume in the mid-seventeenth century reports having heard that John "was a merry cheeked old man," who said, "Will was a good honest fellow, but he durst have cracked a jest with him at any time."[33]

The choice of the graveyard for Hamlet's musings about childhood and death is determined in plot terms by the funeral service for Ophelia, but we may remember from Chapter 3 that many people receive comfort after bereavement from the ritual of going to a graveyard and being close to the earth in which their loved one is buried. Perhaps Shakespeare did too when he had the opportunity, but because he was based in London, he would not have been able to visit his son's (probably unmarked) grave often, *except in his imagination*. Certainly this older Hamlet finds, momentarily, a more comforting calmness in musing on the universality of death in a place of skulls, and he abandons the agonized verse and bitter jibes of earlier acts for more reflective prose. There is another kind of comfort in the scene too. Humans have created thousands and thousands of jokes about death, for humor is one of the means we use to try and disarm the things that frighten us, and Hamlet certainly finds relief in exchanging corny jests with the Clown/Gravedigger, again perhaps in part a memory of Tarleton's famous jests and/or his father's. The fear of what might happen after death which paralyzes the will in the "To be or not to be" soliloquy here takes a more physical form, with the Clown/Gravedigger throwing up earth and skulls to make room for a new burial.

It was not uncommon for bones to be moved when a new grave was being dug; in most cases it seems that bones that were in the way were put to one side (thrown, in Shakespeare's version) while the new grave was being dug, and then reburied. How frequently were bones removed from their original grave? Unsurprisingly there are no records for the 1590s, but we do know that it was as frequent as six to nine months in the cities of London and Westminster 200 years later. Of course, the population of London had accelerated amazingly in the eighteenth century, but even at the end of Elizabeth's reign it was expanding considerably, and the pressure of burials from the regular outbreaks of sickness and plague must have meant that Londoners, including Shakespeare, were aware of a considerable turnover of graveplots. In Stratford in normal times there were about 50 burials a year, and a plot might be not be needed for many years, but in the year of Hamnet's death there were 81 burials, the main increase coming in the months after his death, and in 1597, 161 more than three times the average, and the worst year since 1564. Even allowing for the fact that some burials would be in a family grave, for instance a wife buried with her husband, clearly this would have increased pressure for used graveplots to be dug up. In 1598 the total goes down towards the norm, but is still 66. Shakespeare, probably writing his first draft in 1599 or 1600, would have had reason to fear that Hamnet's grave would be disturbed earlier than he hoped, and that, when his father died, his might suffer the same fate. Stratford too was unusual in the 1590s in having a functioning charnel-house where bones might be deposited/dumped when new grave plots were needed.[34] After the Reformation many charnel houses had been cleared, as the one in Norwich was in 1548, and put to more pragmatic use: this one became part of Norwich Grammar School. So here was another unpleasant fate awaiting his son's bones.[35]

But even the ignominious reality of what might happen to human bones after death doesn't disturb Hamlet as much as it would have done earlier in the play. The setting is assuaging his inner anguish, and he might well have mused with Horatio further, had Ophelia's funeral cortège not interrupted them. This leads to her brother Laertes and then Hamlet jumping into Ophelia's grave and wishing to hold her and be buried with her. But again, what is Shakespeare visualizing as he writes this scene? Onstage Ophelia's body, which Laertes and then this older Hamlet wish to embrace and be buried with, would have been represented by a young male. (The name Ophelia, like Hero in *Much Ado*, is sexually ambiguous: in one of the most popular sixteenth-century fictions, Sannazaro's *Arcadia*, Ofelia is male). It would have been possible for Shakespeare to imagine in Ophelia his own boy dead in the stage grave, just as he could imagine him as the (apparently) resurrected Hero. They are two sides of the same coin. Indeed, on page M4 verso in the *Second Quarto* draft version, Ophelia is merely referred to as the corpse rather than by name, as if the fact that a young corpse is carried onstage is what is important.

In modern productions Hamlet's jumping in the grave is often played satirically, as if *all* he is doing is mocking Laertes' extravagant language. Certainly this is a part of his response, but it is significant that the first *public action* that allows Hamlet to release his pent-up grief is a plunge into a grave, and an account of the first Hamlet—Richard Burbage—picks out this moment as one of deep emotion: "Oft have I seen him leap into the grave/Suiting the person that he seem'd to have/Of a sad lover, with so true an eye/That then I would have sworn *he meant to die*."[36] This suggests that Shakespeare's *primary* intention is for his audience to be moved by Hamlet's deep grief, so deep indeed that, if continued, he would have stayed in the grave for ever. It is an image of the search for the lost one *completed*, and draws much of its power from the feeling that many mourners have: that a part of them longs to be in the grave and embrace the lifeless body. It recalls what we saw in Chapter 3, where Alonso similarly needed to search for his apparently dead son Ferdinand, and to be "bedded" with him "i' th' ooze," to *become one with him* in his watery grave.

I would argue, therefore, that one of the many things going on in this wonderfully complex play is an act of catharsis, a release or, more accurately, a breaking out of emotions associated with grief that have been kept in check since Hamnet's death, a breaking out triggered by his father's anticipated death. This outpouring of the more negative and debilitating aspects of grief develops the process we saw in Chapters 5 and 6 by which Shakespeare can access his deepest feelings, no matter how disturbing, and can work towards a new relationship with his lost ones, especially Hamnet. But if at some level Shakespeare hoped that this was the end of such disturbed feelings and that, like his protagonist, he could become resigned to death "betimes," he was mistaken. The stoical philosophy that Hamlet espouses, "The readiness [for death] is all," is not enough, because underlying emotions still have not been dealt with *fully*, and resurface in the plays that follow.

Notes

Full publication details of every source are provided in the bibliography.

1. Kauffman, "Dissociative Functions in the Normal Mourning Process," p. 37. Francisco's unexplained melancholy recalls Antonio's at the beginning of *The Merchant of Venice*.

2. Rando, Parental Loss of a Child, pp. 223–4.

3. Eliot's essay on *Hamlet* is available in many collections of his prose writings.

4. Sigmund Freud developed Brandes' theory, and James Joyce's Stephen Dedalus elaborated on it in an insightful and creative way in *Ulysses*. More recently, Stephen Greenblatt has explored it in *Will in the World*.

5. Schiff, *The Bereaved Parent*, p. 58. Gordon Riches and Pam Dawson similarly found that "Bereaved parents and siblings often feel that their own sense of loss is unique," in *An Intimate Loneliness*, p. 53.

6. Greenblatt, *Will in the World*, pp. 312–22.

7. Clulow and Mattinson, *Marriage Inside Out*, p. 123.

8. Malan, *Individual Psychotherapy and the Science of Psychodynamics*, p. 139. Italics in the original.

9. Zisook and de Vaul, "Grief, Unresolved Grief and Depression," p. 253.

10. Rando's finding is presented in Vanderlyn R. Pine and Carolyn Brauer's "Parental Grief: A Synthesis of Theory, Research and Intervention," pp. 59–96, in Rando, *Parental Loss of a Child*. The finding is on p. 74.

11. Greenblatt, *Will in the World*, p. 311.

12. Rhodes, "Hamlet and Hamnet as Interchangeable Names," p. 395, and Eccles, *Shakespeare in Warwickshire*, p. 126. I am grateful also for an e-mail kindly sent by Mairi MacDonald at the Shakespeare Birthplace Trust.

13. Klass et al, *Continuing Bonds*, p. 210. Klass also quotes a mother who said that hearing her dead child's name brought tears to her eyes, but music to her ears.

14. Information about the Sadlers' children was kindly provided by Mairi MacDonald at the Shakespeare Birthplace Trust.

The intriguingly named Katherine Hamlett fell into a stream near Stratford and drowned in 1579, a year after the death of Shakespeare's younger sister Anne. Did Shakespeare know of this death? Unsurprisingly, there's no record of this, but similarities between this death and Gertrude's account of Ophelia's drowning provide at least circumstantial evidence that he did, and suggest that this death, and perhaps his sister Anne's the previous year, are also feeding into the outpouring of grief in the play.

It is intriguing too that there is so much reference in *Hamlet* to ears being assailed, done violence to, abused, subjected to leprous distilment, taken prisoner, cleaved, split, mildewed, subjected to daggers, infected, arraigned, made senseless, as well as, "I have words to speak in thine ear will make thee dumb" (4.6.23–24). These references are by no means confined to the poisoning of King Hamlet through the ear, a method of death that seems to be Shakespeare's own choice anyway, as far as we can tell from the surviving sources. If Shakespeare were not an eye witness to Hamnet's death, he must have received a letter or, more likely, have been told about it by a messenger: what "leprous distilment" that would have been. Certainly in *Hamlet* it is not good to have ears to hear.

15. Schwab, "Paternal and Maternal Coping with the Death of a Child," p. 416.

16. I'm grateful to my colleague, Katrin Wilhelm, for pointing out how King Hamlet's inability to control Gertrude's affections after his death adds to the sense of his powerlessness.

17. The only other role we know with reasonable certainty that Shakespeare played in his own dramas is the elderly Adam in *As You Like It*, according to an anecdote written down by George Steevens. Schoenbaum comments that both are "characters with either one or both feet in the grave," *William Shakespeare, A Compact Documentary Life*, p. 202. Perhaps the fact that Shakespeare was ageing was not the only reason that he was drawn to such parts; after all, Richard Burbage was only four years younger than Shakespeare, but could still play "young" Hamlet in this play.

18. In Parkes, *Bereavement*, p. 115. Kuhn's essay, "The Attempted Murder of a Prostitute," is in *Existence*, ed. Rollo May et al, pp. 365–427.

19. The language of *Hamlet* is examined in detail in Hart's "The growth of Shakespeare's vocabulary."

20. Greenblatt, "The Death of Hamnet and the Making of Hamlet," n.pag.

21. Both comments by Leader are from his interview with Pointon, p. 20.

22. Shapiro, *1599*, pp. 321–2.

23. Mahon, "The death of Hamnet," pp. 427 and 433–4.

24. Here Shakespeare uses Catholic vocabulary to express the Ghost's horror of dying without receiving the Eucharist, having the chance to make a confession, or receiving the last rites. At the very least, Shakespeare knows the technical terms of the old religion, and the Ghost he created, though ostensibly from a pagan world, thinks these rites essential.

25. Lendrum and Syme, *Gift of Tears*, p. 177.

26. BBC Radio 4 program *Today*, 22 December, 2009.

27. It is interesting too that Hamlet's main concern before he dies is that his story should be *told*–a recognition of the importance of retrospective narrative for making sense of traumatic and apparently chaotic events in our own lives.

28. From the catalogue to the 1967 London exhibition of Kathe Kollwitz's work, quoted in Parkes, *Bereavement*, p. 43. My italics.

29. Rayner et al, *Human Development*, p. 211.

30. Quoted in Klass et al, *Continuing Bonds*, p. 208.

31. Klass et al., p. 349. My italics.

32. Research by Vivien Brodsky Elliott, "Single Women in the London Marriage Market," in R. B. Outhwaite (ed.), *Marriage and Society: Studies in the Social History of Marriage* (New York: St. Martin's Press), pp. 81–100, referred to in Dubrow, *Shakespeare and Domestic Loss*, pp. 161, 226.

33. Schoenbaum, *William Shakespeare: A Compact Documentary Life*, pp. 30–1. There was no single number signifying manhood in sixteenth century England, but in several plays Shakespeare associates it with 23. This adds to other circumstantial evidence to suggest that the year he started to build his life in London was 1587, when he was that age.

34. I am grateful to Helen Rees, at the Shakespeare Centre Library and Archive in Stratford, for providing these statistics. The information in the rest of the paragraph comes from Julian Litten, *The English Way of Death*, p. 8, and an e-mail that he kindly sent me in answer to further questions.

35. Goody and Poppi, "Flowers and Bones," p. 161.

36. Fripp, *Shakespeare: Man and Artist*, volume 2, p. 847. My italics.

8

Grief and Chaos; And at That Time Bequeath You My Diseases

I would argue, then, that Shakespeare, like his protagonist, found himself at some level "too much in the son" in *Hamlet* (1.2.67).[1] The eruption of grief, wildness, and dejection there affected his writing profoundly. His comedies had always contained elements of potential tragedy, and his tragedies elements of comedy, but not so much as to create doubts about their genre. But after *Hamlet* several of Shakespeare's plays are harder to classify, none more so than the almost nihilistic *Troilus and Cressida*. It was entered in the Stationers' Register on 7 February 1603. The reference to "A prologue arm'd" seems to be a response to Jonson's "armed prologue" in *Poetaster*, penned during the 1601 "War of the Theaters," so probably the play was written close in time to *Hamlet* (Prologue, l.23).

To an extent the tone in this play reflects a change of style in the late 1590s, when satirical poems and plays started to become fashionable. In drama Ben Jonson in particular had begun writing comedies which were more caustic than Shakespeare's; he also implied that his plays were superior because he followed classical precedent. Shakespeare may have wished to show that he could more than match Jonson in savagery and may even have caricatured him in *Troilus and Cressida* as the slow-witted Ajax, pronounced a jakes (or toilet) in Shakespeare's period, perhaps a further arrow fired at Jonson. Another possibility is that this play was written for a specific audience, such as the law students at the Inns of Court. The English satire boom of the early 1960s began in universities and its first audiences were mainly students, who generally have a sharp eye for the failings of their elders. Some commentators have also suggested that Shakespeare's company needed to distance itself from the Earl of Essex's attempted coup in February 1601, involving as it did Shakespeare's former patron, the Earl of Southampton. Certain elements, such as the clearly homosexual relationship between Achilles and Patroclus, could be satirizing the two noblemen. We also saw in Chapter 7 an uncertain political and social situation feeding into the atmosphere of turn-of-the-century England.

But I think this breakdown of genre structure also links with the experience of counselors and therapists that one of the long-term effects of the loss of a child can be a parallel loss of belief in life as orderly and hierarchical. And for a clear reason: the death of a parent is profoundly distressing, but is still within the order of things as we perceive it; but when a child dies it is a turning upside-down of the natural order, and the universe seems frighteningly anarchic.

There is a sense of disorder for much of *Hamlet*, but we saw that Hamlet moves to an acceptance of his situation in Act 5, he manages to kill Claudius (albeit not till he himself is dying), and the fortuitous arrival of Fortinbras allows him to perform his royal duty and name his successor. In *Troilus and Cressida* no such release is provided, and the play faces the prospect that life is meaningless as no previous play by Shakespeare had done. Although it is now performed more than it used to be, it is still not one of Shakespeare's best-known plays—understandably, for it shows him at his most negative. He takes the most famous classical myth—the heroic story of the Trojan War—and debunks it with a vehemence well beyond *Hamlet*, and well beyond anything that can be accounted for by a desire to compete with Ben Jonson, by a possible student audience or by an attempt to distance his company from the taint of the Essex rebellion.

It's as if the mood of Hamlet's most sardonic jibes has taken over the whole play. Ulysses gives a famous speech about the need to restore rank and hierarchy in the dissolute Greek army; yet by the end of the play the Greeks have actually gained an advantage not because they have restored this hierarchy but because Achilles, stung by the death of his lover Patroclus, has used his private army to butcher the unarmed Hector and then claimed to have killed him honorably in single combat!

This sense of arbitrary events, disorder, and meaninglessness is everywhere. In Act 2 the Trojans debate whether it is worth continuing the war or whether they should return the abducted Queen Helen to the Greeks, and so end it. All logic is for handing her back because many thousands of Trojans have died during the seven long years of war, and every one of the dead "Hath been as dear as Helen" (2.2.20). And yet at the end of the debate they agree that because they would lose honor and face by handing her back, they should fight on, and thousands more should die. The senseless slaughter of the war could not be more emphasized. And many of the audience would know that the Trojan War lasted for 10 years, so is destined to drag on for another three.

Further, the play does not so much end as peter out. Prince Troilus vows revenge for the assassination of Hector; then, in one of Shakespeare's most startling changes to his source materials, we are suddenly transported from prehistoric Troy to seventeenth century London, and the speaker, Pandarus, addresses all the pimps and prostitutes in the seventeenth century audience, making bitter jokes about their, and his own, syphilis, the equivalent in 1600 of HIV. He thinks he will last another two months, and then will make his will: "Till then I'll sweat and seek about for eases,/And at that time bequeath you my diseases" (5.10.55–6). All Pandarus has to bequeath is syphilis. This ending is particularly savage and distasteful, unlike any in Shakespeare's other plays, and the final word "diseases" fits perfectly the sense of futility and decay in the rest of the play.[2]

In the midst of this meaningless world is the youngest of King Priam's 50 sons, Prince Troilus, a "youth" about the same age as the Hamlet of the first four acts of that play (4.5.110). Like both Hamlet and the younger Prince Arthur in *King John* he is a strangely passive young man, out of his depth in the brutal and dishonorable world around him, and again I would argue that, like them, he in part is a product of Shakespeare's need to represent certain emotions associated with loss and especially with his dead son. In Troilus' case his passivity comes from his love of Cressida, which makes him "weaker than a woman's tear"—another Shakespearean male who associates crying with unmanly weakness (1.1.9). By contrast Cressida is worldly wise and recognizes the need for a woman caught up in a war to have a survival strategy. She is aware that Troilus is much more naïve than she is and sees no alternative but to take advantage of this; she plays for time, fearing that he may be one of those men who discard a woman once they have slept with her. Left to Troilus, nothing would happen, but Pandarus persuades his niece to spend the night with the young man, and they swear eternal faithfulness. No sooner is their love consummated, however, than Cressida's father, who has deserted to the Greeks, arranges for her to be exchanged for a Trojan prisoner. Cressida has no choice but to go and, as a vulnerable woman in the Greek camp, agrees to accept protection from one of the Greek soldiers; the price is sharing his bed. Cressida's departure from Troy happens during a truce, and Troilus is able to follow her and witness her infidelity. As soon as the war resumes we have the cowardly assassination of Hector referred to above.

So even more than in *Hamlet* we have a green young man at the mercy of, and disillusioned by, a merciless, seemingly meaningless world. But Troilus does not respond to loss and grief as Hamlet did, by taking comfort in resignation to Providence, but by an outbreak of vengeful anger. He shouts across from the battlefield to Achilles, "thou great-siz'd coward,/No space of earth shall sunder our two hates." He dedicates himself to "hope of revenge," to hide his "inward woe" (5.10.26–7, 31).

Thus Troilus turns from passivity to a wild determination to seek revenge in a war shown to be futile, and most of Shakespeare's audience would know that the Greeks were going to win anyway by another deception—the apparent gift of the Trojan Horse. The sense of emptiness in *Troilus and Cressida*, then, extends beyond anything in *Hamlet*. Indeed, it is reasonable to consider the endings of these two plays, plus *Twelfth Night*, all written within a few years of each other, as being in dialogue: *Twelfth Night* gives us the hope of resurrection, *Hamlet* the importance of resignation to the slings and arrows of outrageous fortune, and *Troilus and Cressida* the fear that the whole thing has no purpose at all. But in Troilus' final fury and desire for slaughter the play also looks forward to *King Lear*, in which rage reaches a pitch unknown in earlier Shakespeare, and to Macbeth's frenzied and futile fight to the bitter end at Dunsinane. We'll see in Chapter 10 that delayed rage is another common response to bereavement. But before moving onto those plays we need to consider a nondramatic work that in my judgment bears marks of grief for Hamnet—the *Sonnets*.

Notes

Full publication details of every source are provided in the bibliography.

1. Most modern editions follow the *Folio* here and print "sun," but the *Second Quarto*, based on Shakespeare's draft version, has "sonne." Of course the line is a pun on both meanings, but the *Second Quarto* text suggests which part of the pun was uppermost in Shakespeare's mind.

2. It is possible that the frequent references to sexual disease in this and other plays Shakespeare wrote around this time reflect an author who, away from home for most of each year and working in a part of London where there were many brothels, either contracted syphilis, or feared he might. Katherine Duncan-Jones, among others, discusses the evidence in *Ungentle Shakespeare*, pp. 224–32. If true, it would give another obvious influence on the play's extreme bitterness.

9

Grief and a Young Man; He Was but One Hour Mine

Dating Shakespeare's *Sonnets* is extremely difficult, so some readers may wish to move to the less uncertain consideration of Shakespeare's later plays that begins in the next chapter. The *Sonnets* are not essential to my argument, but I do think them relevant to this exploration of grief.

The problem of dating is made complicated by the strong evidence that the *Sonnets* were written and revised over a period of years. In Sonnet 104 the speaker talks of three years passing since he first knew the young nobleman to whom Sonnets 1 to 126 are addressed. As Katherine Duncan-Jones notes, three years is not necessarily literally true because it was a conventional poetic way of stating that time has passed; but the general idea of time passing fits in with the retrospective tone and emphasis on the absence of the young man in many of the sonnets from 27 onward.[1] Secondly, four of the sonnets exist in more than one version, and at least some of the revisions seem to be authorial rather than mistakes made in copying or remembering the original, which suggests other sonnets may have been revised too. Thirdly, some of the later sonnets in the first sequence probably refer to events at the end of Elizabeth's and the beginning of James' reign, especially the "eclipse" of the "mortal moon" leading to a "crown" and "peace" (Sonnet 107:5–8)—one of James' first decisions was to make peace with Spain—and the "pyramids" (123:2) and "canopy" (125:1), which appear to link with the elaborate celebrations of James' accession and coronation. Duncan-Jones argues further that both internal stylistic and external evidence indicate "an intense period of writing (and perhaps revising)" in 1603–1604, when the theatres were closed because of the plague; and that is why this seems the best place in my account of Shakespeare's development to consider these enigmatic poems.[2] While differing over details, MacDonald Jackson and Colin Burrow agree that stylistic evidence suggests the *Sonnets* were probably begun in the mid- to late 1590s and revised with different degrees of intensity over many years.[3]

The *Sonnets* were not published in their entirety until 1609, but Meres refers to them in 1598, so some at least had been written by then. How much earlier might the first ones be? A promising clue is that the first 17 sonnets are addressed to a reluctant young nobleman, exhorting him to marry and produce a son and heir; for instance, in Sonnet 13, "You had a father, let your son say so" is presented as the only way to oppose the "barren rage of death's eternal cold" (13:12, 14). But from Sonnet 18 onward the focus changes to the close relationship between the speaker and the young man, and from 27 onward the intense anguish that separation causes the speaker. Number symbolism is common in Elizabethan poetry, and 17 in an unusual number for a series of linked poems, so it has been plausibly suggested that 17 reflects the young nobleman's age at the time of writing. Both the main candidates for the nobleman had refused marriages by 17: Henry Wriothesley, 17 in 1590 and Earl of Southampton, and William Herbert, 17 in 1597 and later to become Earl of Pembroke. A further intriguing detail is the first printer's dedication to Mr. W. H., which may or may not be based on being in the know, who is called the "only begetter" of the *Sonnets*. This fits William Herbert, not an Earl when the sequence started, allowing those in on the secret to recognize the young man, while hiding it from other readers who would not expect a nobleman to be addressed as a plain mister; but it could fit a further disguising of Henry Wriothesley, H. W., as W. H.

In a lengthy examination of the complex arguments for each candidate, Duncan-Jones provides strong evidence that William Herbert is the young nobleman—the man to whom, along with his brother, the *Folio* collection of Shakespeare's plays was dedicated in 1623, even though Henry Wriothesley was still alive then; or it might be more accurate to say the *principal* young nobleman because it is possible that features of Southampton and even other young men Shakespeare met have contributed to the appearance and behavior of the young man as the *Sonnets* present him.[4] If the first 17 sonnets were penned in the months before Herbert's birthday in April 1597, that is, after Hamnet's death the previous August, writing about the need for a son and heir would have been bittersweet for Shakespeare. Sonnet 3 might refer directly to Herbert's birthday, "Thou art thy mother's glass, and she in thee/Calls back the lovely April of her prime," although April was used traditionally as an obvious image of youth (3:9–10). But even if some of the *Sonnets* discussed below existed in the form we now have them before Hamnet's death, they would still be relevant to the exploration of Shakespeare's grief because a man so alert to double meanings would surely have been affected in his later revisions by the apparently ironical prophecy of lines like the following: "Even so my sun one early morn did shine/With all-triumphant splendor on my brow,/But out, alack, he was but one hour mine,/The region cloud hath mask'd him from me now" (33:9–12); and "As a decrepit father takes delight/To see his active child do deeds of youth,/So I, made lame by Fortune's dearest spite,/Take all my comfort of thy worth and truth" (37:1–4).

I am therefore arguing that, in the form we have them, at least some of the *Sonnets*, and possibly all of them, draw on two recent griefs: the conscious and foregrounded one is the deep pain caused by the young nobleman's absence from the speaker and involvement with rivals for his affection; but underneath is the grief for the young boy Shakespeare has lost for ever. In this reading the poems contain an *element* of autobiography: how far does that element go? Certainly the *Sonnets* are not directly autobiographical in the way that Wordsworth's *The Prelude* is, but there are clear indications in the second sequence of sonnets, starting from Sonnet 127 and addressed to a woman with unfashionably dark eyes and complexion, that the unidentified speaker is in fact named Will—a tremendous coincidence if Shakespeare is writing in *purely* fictional terms. The 1609 edition prints the word "will" without a capital in standard usage, but with a capital and in italics where a pun on the speaker's name is suggested, and the *Riverside Shakespeare* follows this usage. Sonnet 135 begins, "Whoever hath her wish, thou hast thy *Will*,/And *Will* to boot, and *Will* in overplus" (1–2). The surface meaning is of will as desire, especially sexual desire: other women gain their wishes, this woman has her will, her sexual fulfillment, and she has it to boot and in overplus, implying, as other sonnets do, that the woman is promiscuous. But this meaning would be conveyed by a lower case "w": "Will" with a capital suggests that the woman has her will by having Will "to boot," and the obvious inference is that a man named Will, Will Shakespeare, is one of the men she has had (and again other sonnets confirm the sexual relationship between them). Indeed, "Will in overplus" may suggest a second Will has had sex with the woman, perhaps Will(iam) Herbert. The first part of this deduction is supported by the pun at the end of the next sonnet, when the speaker is pleading not to be omitted from the woman's list of lovers, "Make but my name thy love, and love that still,/And then thou lovest me, for my name is *Will*" (136:13–14). I would argue therefore that there is an *element* of autobiography in the *Sonnets*, and that they draw in part, but not necessarily exclusively, on emotions Shakespeare has experienced in his own relationships.

Which features suggest that the loss of Hamnet as well as of the young nobleman is contributing to the pain in these poems? One is the change of focus that takes place from the need for the young man to marry and produce a legitimate male heir (something now impossible for Shakespeare) to the physical decay and emotional suffering of the older speaker of the *Sonnets* when the young man is *absent* from him. We have seen that in two plays written close in time to Hamnet's death—*King John* and *Henry the Fourth*, especially *Part 2*—it was the absence rather than the supposed death of a male child that was being explored. The absence of the beloved is of course a conventional sonnet theme, but again it is the intensity that separates these sonnets from, say, Sir Philip Sidney's, and that seems "in excess of the facts," to draw again on Eliot's famous comment about *Hamlet*.

This piercing agony is hard to illustrate by short quotation because it pervades so many sonnets, and is never answered by the young man's permanent return; the speaker is abandoned, cast aside. One strong example occurs in Sonnet 45. The young man is elsewhere and the older speaker's life "Sinks down to death, oppressed with melancholy," as Hamlet's does (45:8). There is no life without the young man, as there will be no life in *The Winter's Tale* for the old men of Leontes' court without Mamillius. In later sonnets this sense of the speaker as a weary, aging man of melancholy, as Belarius will be in *Cymbeline* when he thinks young Fidele has died, increases, especially in the section beginning with Sonnet 66, "Tir'd with all these, for restful death I cry." The next 11 lines list some of the horrors of life that have driven him to this state and are similar to Hamlet's catalog of life's woes in the "To be, or not to be," soliloquy and in the dirge, "Fear no more the heat o'th' sun," sung over what is thought to be Fidele's corpse. Other sonnets in this part of the sequence include, "No longer mourn for me when I am dead" (71:1) and "That time of year thou mayst in me behold/When yellow leaves, or none, or few, do hang/Upon those boughs which shake against the cold" (73:1–3).

True, the death-like state of the rejected lover is a common theme in many sonnet sequences, but again its pervasiveness, and the application of it to a beautiful young man rather than to a woman, is very unusual and goes far beyond the conventional sonnet relationship. The young man has "A woman's face," and is "the *master mistress* of my *passion*," (20:1–2; my italics). "Passion" has both its modern sense and its older sense of extreme suffering, as in Jesus' passion upon the cross and the Passion Sunday that preceded it. And "master mistress" recalls what we have seen in the comedies following Hamnet's death, with Portia/Balthasar, Rosalind/Ganymede and Viola/Cesario. Shakespeare's fascination with images that are twin-like, that are *simultaneously* male and female, may well have in part come from looking at beautiful young noblemen but also from the experience of looking from one face to the other and back again with his own twins and wanting both twins to look at again. I suggest therefore that the absence of the young man, like the anticipated death of his father, awoke in Shakespeare unresolved feelings for Hamnet. It should not be forgotten that William Herbert was less than five years older than Hamnet and the same age as Shakespeare's youngest brother, Edmund, and in the young nobleman Shakespeare may at some level have seen something of what his boy might have become.

In one of the later sonnets there is an unexpectedly direct address to the young man. The speaker has asked him, "What's new to speak, what now to register,/That may express my love, or thy dear merit?" and has answered himself, "Nothing, *sweet boy*; but yet *like prayers divine*,/I must each day say o'er the very same,/Counting no old thing old, thou mine, I thine,/Even as when first I *hallowed* thy fair name" (108:3–8; my italics). "Boy" covered a wider range of ages in Shakespeare's English than is usual in ours; nevertheless, this is the first time the young man is so addressed, and it has created unease in some editors, two having gone so far as to change it. It is a strange phrase to use to a young man well above the speaker in social rank, and reinforces the impression of a father-son relationship between the two men, at least from the speaker's point of view, and even the young man as a substitute son, as suggested by the quotation from the opening of Sonnet 37 above. "Hallowed" suggests someone calling out, hallo-ing the name of someone seen at a distance, but it also recalls the Our Father/Lord's Prayer's "Hallowed by thy name": the name is being revered as God's name is, or as a baby's might be at a baptismal ceremony.[5] This religious sense is reinforced by the image of "prayers divine."

If this reference to "boy" were single, we might leave it at that. But the last poem addressed to the young man, Sonnet 126, begins, "O thou my *lovely boy*" (my italics). This poem is a surprise because it comprises 12 lines, not the 14 expected in a sonnet, and these 12 lines are rhyming couplets, whereas the first 12 lines of the previous 125 sonnets rhyme alternately, as in the extracts quoted above. In general terms the poem fits the situation of the previous sonnets, but it hardly flows naturally from them. In the first published edition of 1609 the 12 lines are followed by

(   )
(   )

This could simply be the printer indicating that two lines are missing; but, as Duncan-Jones suggests, it could also be an image of the graves that will enclose the speaker and the young man, either now that the young man has abandoned the speaker or in the future after both have died.[6] Or if this poem has been *added* to the end of the sequence, and is not just about the young man, it could hint at another young grave as well. The cumulative evidence suggests an intertwining of the speaker's feelings for the young man with ones for a sweet, lovely boy. Perhaps, too, there is a similar deflection to the one in *Twelfth Night*, since it is easier to mourn the loss of a young nobleman than of a child.

A feature of the *Sonnets* that points forward to Shakespeare's last plays is the desperate search for something that will triumph over death and time. The conventional solution of the young man producing a male heir is replaced by the idea that art rather than fatherhood is the best defense against time's ravages—a view that might have been endorsed for Shakespeare if he were writing or revising this after the death of his son and heir. In Sonnet 18 Shakespeare presents the transience of the natural world, where "darling buds" are shaken, "summer's lease hath all too short a date," the sun's "gold complexion" is dimm'd, then says to his young nobleman: "So long as men can breathe or eyes can see,/So long lives this, and this *gives life* to thee," another image of resurrection (18:3, 4, 6, 13, 14; my italics). As some feminist critics have pointed out, the last line provides a very male consolation. In art a man can create a kind of life without the help of a woman, and further can create a life that does not die as a human's does.[7] This idea of art's power recalls *Twelfth Night*, where the dead twin is personated by the living one and then returned to her, and looks forward to the last plays, in which Prospero and Paulina (apparently) bring the dead back to eternal life onstage by the power of their art.

Notes

Full publication details of every source are in the bibliography.

1. Duncan-Jones, *Shakespeare's Sonnets*, p. 318.

2. Duncan-Jones, pp. 28, 324, 356, 360.

3. Burrow, *The Complete Sonnets and Poems*, pp. 103–10. MacDonald Jackson, "Vocabulary and Chronology: The Case of Shakespeare's *Sonnets*," pp. 59–75.

4. Duncan-Jones, especially pp. 49–64. I am grateful to Katherine Duncan-Jones for an e-mail updating me about her current thoughts concerning William Herbert and the young man of the *Sonnets*.

5. "Hallowed" is the translation of Luke 11:2 in both the *Geneva* and the *Bishop's Bible*.

6. Duncan-Jones, p. 366.

7. The difficulty which Hamlet has coming to terms with sexuality might be linked to this because sexual love produces beings born to die, at least in this life.

10

Grief, Rage, Guilt and Despair; Might I but Live to See Thee in My Touch

Heavenly Comforts of Despair

Before exploring the rack-like experience of *King Lear*, we need to consider another play that, like *Troilus and Cressida*, is difficult to classify in genre terms. *Measure for Measure* was probably performed at court on 26 December 1604, although the authenticity of the document recording this has been disputed. But in the unlikely event that it is a forgery, the links between James' dilemmas and behavior on becoming King of England and the Duke's in Vienna make it likely that the play was one of the first written after James' accession in 1603. As in *Twelfth Night* a sister, Isabella, thinks her brother Claudio is dead when we, and Shakespeare, know he is not, so again the grief in the play is deflected onto another. Claudio's apparent death, however, is potentially much more disturbing than Sebastian's—executed in prison on the orders of Angelo, despite Angelo's promise to release Claudio after, as he thinks, Isabella has slept with him.

As often, it's revealing to examine Shakespeare's alterations to his main sources. In the Italian play *Epitia* [= Isabella], the Captain of the Prison prevents Epitia's brother from being executed on Juriste's [= Angelo's] orders, but knows that he cannot reveal this until he can get the approval of the Emperor [= the Duke] for disobeying Juriste. In the final scene the

Captain explains the situation, and the Emperor gives his approval. In Shakespeare's other main source, *Promos and Cassandra* [= Angelo and Isabella], Cassandra's brother is again spared by a Jailer who dares not reveal what he has done. The brother flees to the woods for safety, and Cassandra does not learn that he is alive until he finds the courage to return to court and reveal his identity.[1]

Shakespeare's version is very different. The Duke pretends to leave Vienna in the hands of his Deputy, Angelo, then returns, disguised as a Friar, so he can see how well or badly his Deputy will adminster justice. Here it is the disguised Duke who saves Claudio from execution. Unlike the Prison Captain in *Epitia* or the Jailer in *Promos and Cassandra*, the disguised Duke has the authority to confide in Isabella that he has saved her brother, and then swear her to secrecy until the moment when he decides to make this public. But he chooses not to do this. He deliberately prolongs Isabella's suffering and grief, in plot terms to test whether she will be true to her beliefs and forgive Angelo; and of course this adds to the dramatic tension, but equally it runs the risk of alienating many of the audience from the Duke. Surprisingly, the reason he offers is not that he wishes to test her but one that anticipates the reason Edgar will give for a similar decision not to reveal his identity to his blind father in *King Lear*: "But I will keep her ignorant of her good,/To make her heavenly comforts of despair,/When it is least expected" (4.3.109–11). Prolonged, unresolved grief produces melancholy and despair, and we have seen Shakespeare battling with this in *Hamlet*; it needs the heavenly hope of resurrection to answer it. The Duke hopes that the "rebirth" of her seemingly dead brother Claudio, when it comes, will be all the more wonderful and comforting to Isabella because of the delay. As in *Twelfth Night*, fiction is, at some level, operating therapeutically, but in *Measure for Measure* is the beginning of a change: the focus is moving to *deliberately protracted* suffering, and we will find it even more protracted in the Gloucester plot in *King Lear* and in Shakespeare's final plays. (Indeed, the moment when the living Claudio is actually revealed to Isabella is perfunctory, suggesting Shakespeare's focus, for the moment, is elsewhere). I think there is an underlying reason why this change occurs. By the time of *Measure for Measure* the brother/son Hamnet has been dead for seven or more years. The deep need to move on in the process of mourning and arrive at a new relationship with the lost one is there; but it is taking longer and longer to happen, and I think Shakespeare needs the release of presenting this elongated waiting in fictional form. This becomes linked with the necessity to overcome another, nonliteral, death:

Shakespeare's going to London broke up the family group, and several of his plays from *King Lear* onward confront the need to restore family and, in particular, father-daughter relationships after a symbolic death.

His Father, That So Tenderly and Entirely Loves Him

King Lear is Janus-headed: for many playgoers and readers it is the pinnacle of Shakespeare's achievement in tragic drama (although not his last tragedy); but it also has many links with his final plays, especially *The Winter's Tale*, which similarly has a protagonist who destroys the world around him by an explosion of unjustified wrath, although, in the manner of romance, Leontes is spared some of the consequences that engulf Lear. In its willingness to encounter the depth of rage, and then of guilt, that two fathers feel against their children, *King Lear* takes Shakespeare further on in his journey through mourning.

Like *Hamlet*, it exists in a long draft version preserved in a *Quarto* text and a shorter revision (but with some additional lines) in the *Folio*. I think it significant that Shakespeare's two most famous and, I am arguing, most personal tragedies seem to have been the hardest to shape into a form acceptable for the time limits of the public theater, suggesting that more is involved in these dramas than writing a money-spinner for his company and himself as a sharer.

King Lear was acted at court on December the 26, 1606, and it is usually thought that the first version of the play was written in the previous year. "These late eclipses in the sun and moon" probably refers to the unusual occurrence of two eclipses in just over a fortnight in September and October 1605 (1.2.103). And Shakespeare's main source, the anonymous *King Leir*, although it probably dates from the previous decade, was published in 1605. But what about the second version? From stylistic evidence Gary Taylor, in *William Shakespeare: A Textual Companion*, concludes that the revised *Folio* version dates to 1610, close in time to *The Winter's Tale* and *Cymbeline*.[2] The presence of act divisions in the *Folio* but not the *Quarto* text supports Taylor's conclusion, suggesting that the *Folio* text was not written until Shakespeare's company started to use the indoor Blackfriars Theater in autumn 1609, where act divisions were probably introduced into the company's performances for the first time, replacing the fluidity of previous performances at the Globe and other outdoor theaters. This evidence adds to the idea of a dialogue between Shakespeare's late plays and *King Lear*, exploring different perspectives on life's traumas, as we have found already in the looser group of *Hamlet, Twelfth Night*, and *Troilus and Cressida*.

King Lear harrows its main characters and its audiences almost beyond endurance. Indeed, in the eighteenth century Samuel Johnson found the ending, and especially the death of Cordelia, so unbearable that he could not bring himself to read it again until he had to as editor of Shakespeare's plays. Many others shared his feelings. In 1681 Nahum Tate adapted the play to give it a happy ending, keeping Cordelia, King Lear, and the Earls of Gloucester and Kent alive and inventing a marriage between Cordelia and Gloucester's good son Edgar.[3] Adaptations of this version held the stage for more than 150 years. There are several reasons for these changes, but one was certainly the heartbreaking desolation of the ending, beyond anything in Shakespeare's other tragedies, and linked, I will argue, with unresolved feelings about Hamnet's death.

The intensity is there from the beginning. Shakespeare includes two main plots, something he does not do in any of his other major tragedies, and risks losing his audience because of the complexities that result from this decision. The opening acts are full of a rage and aggression unequalled elsewhere in Shakespeare, except in the unfinished collaborative venture, *Timon of Athens*, and stylistic features and the recurring theme of ingratitude indicate it was probably written close in time to the first version of *King Lear*. We've seen earlier moments of anger linked with children: Capulet's rage with his daughter when she does not wish to marry Count Paris; Henry the Fourth's sorrowful anger against his son for neglecting him and, he feared, wanting him dead; and Leonato's wrath against Hero for not dying after, he mistakenly believes, dishonoring him. But those moments were secondary elements in the plays as a whole. In *King Lear* repressed rage wells up, as repressed grief had in *Hamlet*, and drowns the cocks on the steeples.

Anger of course is common in life, and is not just linked to loss and grief; but it is significant that the torrent of rage in the opening scenes pours from *fathers who think (wrongly) the children they love have failed to return that love and have abandoned them to suffering*. Lear says of the apparently ungrateful Cordelia, "I loved her most, and thought to set my rest/On her kind nursery" (1.1.123–4). But now he cannot because she seems to have discarded him. And when Gloucester is deceived into believing that his only legitimate son Edgar plans to kill him—another image of a son killing a father—he exclaims, "He cannot be such a monster . . . To his father, that so tenderly and entirely loves him" (1.2.94, 96–7). These lines only occur in the earlier version of the play preserved in the *First Quarto*, and show that Shakespeare's first intention was to make the similarity between each father's sense of betrayal by a specially loved child as strong as possible. (Perhaps they were removed because they are repetitive and unnecessarily explicit about something already implied). Each father feels his love has been thrown back in his face, and I think this *in part* reflects Shakespeare's (probably unconscious) anger with Hamnet for having abandoned him by dying. This corresponds with what we saw in Chapter 6—that the pain of losing a child is sometimes so fierce as to provoke in the mourning parent irrational anger against the child. It is possible too that Shakespeare feels anger against himself for loving so intensely, for allowing himself to be vulnerable to so much heartache, again a not-uncommon response to bereavement.

But Lear and Gloucester are of course deceiving themselves. Cordelia and Edgar do love them dearly, and they feel deep guilt when they realize this—again a common consequence of violent rage. At the beginning of the play, indeed, neither Lear nor Gloucester really understands what love is, and each has to learn the nature of real love through extreme suffering. One of the things Shakespeare might have felt as he looked over his years away from Stratford, and particularly the years since Hamnet's death, was that it had taken the loss of his son for him to plumb the depths of what it means to really love a child.

Again the experiences of counselors and therapists are relevant here. In her 10 years of working with bereaved fathers Jean Scully found that "extreme anger, guilt and depression," were the most common paternal reactions, and these are the emotions that dominate this play, the first two primarily through Lear, the third primarily through Gloucester.[4] Here is one of the many benefits of having two main plots rather than one. To have a single father experience all three reactions equally would dilute the expression of, and impact of, each emotion: to split the emotions between two fathers for most of the play allows their full range and intensity to be presented. That the two fathers are in some ways facets of the same father is often shown through the imagery; for instance, Lear thinks of figuratively plucking his eyes out if they dare to cry again, but Gloucester literally has his eyes plucked out (1.4.301–3). We will find a similar splitting of the father figure's emotional experience in *Cymbeline* and *The Tempest*.

But a different kind of splitting is also present. Melanie Klein suggested that babies experience a good mother, who gives them sustenance from her breast, and a bad mother, who withdraws her breast. Of course there is only one mother, but there seem to be two to the baby, according to whether she fulfils or thwarts the baby's needs.[5] There is evidence that at times of intense pain in adult life we revert to this simplistic view of the world. Thus a father who feels deeply hurt by a loved good child—as Lear and Gloucester do—may suddenly experience that child as bad, as the baby did its mother when she was busy with other things. Certainly Lear and Gloucester see their children in this simplistic manner throughout, although which they see as the good child and which the bad varies as the play progresses. But the *pattern* in each case does not vary. In the opening scenes the children we know are good—Cordelia and Edgar—seem to their fathers to abandon them, so are seen as bad, and the children we know are self-centered—Goneril, Regan, and Edmund—ingratiate themselves with their father and are seen as good. By the middle of the play this evaluation has been reversed, with Cordelia and Edgar now seen as good, and Goneril, Regan, and Edmund as evil. What is really interesting is that there is no halfway house: each child becomes, to the father, *wholly good or wholly bad*. Indeed, at the deepest level good and bad are just different perceptions of the same child, according to the father's emotions at the time. I think that this dramatic situation allows the play, among many other things, to encounter the extremities of emotion Shakespeare had suffered in life, especially since Hamnet had seemed to discard him.

The first emotion Shakespeare explores is rage, first directed towards the loved, apparently abandoning child. When Lear's rage turns from Cordelia to Goneril and Regan, it can be expressed far more fully, without losing most playgoers' sympathy, because it is justified by his elder daughters' conspiracy against him, even unto death—yet another image of a child desiring to kill a parent. But it is the *same wrath* against ingratitude that was unleashed earlier against Cordelia. *King Lear* is brutally honest about the violence of a father's anger. Lear explodes at Cordelia: "Here I disclaim all my paternal care . . . /And as a stranger to my heart and me/Hold thee from this for ever" (1.1.113–6). This is frightening enough, but what is really revealing of Lear's inner state is the next image. "He that makes his generation messes/To gorge his appetite, shall to my bosom/Be as well neighbor'd, pitied, and reliev'd,/As thou my sometime daughter": a cannibal who eats his generation, that is those he has generated from his body, his own children, to slake his appetite, would be as welcome as Cordelia (1.1.117–20). The nearest equivalent Lear can find to express his pain and anger is a picture of a father who devours his own child; this says in effect to Cordelia that what she is doing in abandoning him is the equivalent of the most barbarous and aggressive act he as her father could do to her—that is how much she has hurt him. Later he adds, "Better thou/Hadst not been born than not t' have pleas'd me better" (1.1.233–4). A father can be so deeply wounded by being apparently discarded as to wish that he had never had this child who can do this to him—a horrifying truth that again recalls Leonato's rant against Hero.

It is significant too that this outburst follows Cordelia's perfectly reasonable comment that, when she marries, she will have responsibilities towards her husband as well as towards her father. This outrages Lear because he wants his daughter all to himself. Why should this desire to possess a child, specifically a daughter, be so strong in Shakespeare's thoughts in 1605 or 1606? His elder daughter Susanna had had her twenty-third birthday in May 1605 and was above the average age of 20 for Stratford brides (although she did not marry for another two years), and his younger daughter Judith had reached 20 in February 1605.[6] Shakespeare himself had been only 18 when he had married and may well have been thinking of the loss, including loss of control, he would suffer when his daughters became part of another family. Also Shakespeare has spent nearly half his life in the London theater and is perhaps beginning to think of, and to have (unconscious) fears about, what might await him when he retires to Stratford and grows old: will his daughters put their (future) husbands first? I would argue that Shakespeare endured a similar experience to the one he had had when writing *Hamlet*. There his father's approaching death reawakened unresolved emotions for his only son; but in that case they were primarily feelings of melancholic depression and emptiness. Here, another potential abandonment by one or both daughters, and the resultant sense of increased powerlessness and aging, reawakens other unresolved feelings towards Hamnet for leaving him. Rage has to be dealt with before a mourner can move onward, but as Marvin Krims indicates, rage can also become a means of deflecting deep mourning because it can push aside the need to admit vulnerability and hurt, the need to cry. Indeed, as Krims pertinently indicates, the Fool in some ways acts like a counselor for Lear, using indirect methods to try and help him move forward in his understanding of the injustice of his rage against Cordelia, and open himself to emotions that will help to heal him.[7]

But anger is not Lear's only response to what he sees as Cordelia's abandonment, even early on. At moments we hear, beneath the rage, the terrible hurt and sadness of a father parting, he thinks forever, from the child he still dearly loves. When the King of France still wishes to marry the dowerless Cordelia, her father says, "Thou hast her, France, let her be thine, for we/Have no such daughter, nor shall ever see/That face of hers again" (1.1.262–4). For Victoria Coren the last line has "perhaps the saddest rhythm in all literature," and we shall find its falling cadence recurring at other crucial moments in the play.[8] Therese Rando quotes

many bereaved parents as saying that one of the stages of their grief was a
time of "angry sadness," and those words encapsulate much of Lear's
response in the early part of the play, as well as recalling the tone of
Henry the Fourth's speeches to his neglectful son.[9] Indeed, the combination of love and aggression we find in Lear is common in cases of unresolved emotional trauma, as David Malan observes:

> As has been mentioned above, this mixture of love and hate for the same per-
> son is one of the deepest and most painful conflicts that human beings suffer
> from ... It needs to be emphasized throughout all this that the love is as
> genuine as the aggression; but at the same time it is *not* genuine if it
> is expressed *without* the aggression, and the only way of making it genuine
> is for the two opposite feelings to be expressed together.[10]

Malan's conclusion complements the play's intuition about the conflicting
emotions arising in Lear when he feels discarded by his child. Other counselors and therapists confirm that anger is a normal part of the grief process
for someone we dearly love. Colin Murray Parkes devotes a whole chapter
to it in *Bereavement* and uses Lear's wild "Blow, winds" speech, quoted
below, as its epigraph, showing the connection in his mind between Lear's
rage and his grief at his sense of abandonment. Another feature Parkes
records in a study of widows could also be applied to Lear, particularly when
he has been shut out of Gloucester Castle by Goneril and Regan and is rest-
lessly wandering in the storm. Parkes notes that the commonest form of
anger "was a general irritability and bitterness ... Anger was closely associated with restlessness and tension."[11] Indeed Shakespeare finds the perfect
actions and setting—wandering about and raging on a heath in a thunder-
storm—to convey the purgatorial experience of Lear's inner pain, pain so
piercing that it eventually makes him mad and makes him desire the
destruction of the whole world:

> Blow, winds, and crack your cheeks! rage, blow,
> You cataracts and hurricanoes, spout
> Till you have drench'd our steeples, drown'd the cocks! ...
> And thou, all-shaking thunder,
> Strike flat the thick rotundity o' th' world!
> Crack nature's moulds, all germains spill at once
> That makes ingrateful man! (3.2.1–3, 6–9)

There is nothing like this rage in Shakespeare's main dramatic source, *The
True Chronicle History of King Leir*. The image recalls the Biblical flood

and God's destruction of all humans for their wickedness except for Noah and his family. Specifically, Lear wants all fertility destroyed: cocks, in various meanings, have long been associated with fertility, and it is the germains, or the germinating seeds of life, that Lear wants spilt.[12]

But the image also reminds us of the thing many of Shakespeare's males, Lear being a prime example, cannot cope with—a flood of tears—and might reflect at some level Shakespeare's need to produce that flood, to cry and cry for the losses of his life, above all the loss of Hamnet. Indeed *King Lear*, like *Hamlet*, returns several times to the social horror of a man weeping. Lear feels ashamed that his eldest daughter Goneril can "shake my manhood" by forcing from him "hot tears" (1.4.297–8). Even more strongly, when chastising Goneril and Regan in Act 2, he feels the danger of hysterical passion possessing him, hysteria being, in a tradition that went back to the Ancient Greeks, a weakness women display, not men; in other words, he feels the danger of *turning into a woman*. Lear prays for

> noble anger,
> And let not women's weapons, water-drops,
> Stain my man's cheeks! . . .
> You think I'll weep:
> No I'll not weep.
> I have full cause of weeping, but this heart
> Shall break into a hundred thousand flaws
> Or e'er I'll weep. O Fool, I shall go mad! (2.2.276–8, 282–6).

In Chapter 6 we saw that Northumberland's loss of his son in *Henry the Fourth, Part 2* provoked a similar desire for the world to be flooded and buried in darkness. And shortly after *King Lear* comes *Macbeth*, in which the protagonist is much concerned that he has no heir, and demands to know the future from the Witches, even though, "the treasure/Of nature's germains tumble all together,/Even till destruction sicken" (4.1.58–60). His image is almost identical to Lear's in the "Blow, winds" speech quoted previously, again enacting the obliteration of life and fertility. Shakespeare goes far beyond his sources in expressing Macbeth's horror at the Witches' prediction that Banquo's descendants will inherit the crown:

> They hail'd him father to a line of kings.
> Upon my head they plac'd a fruitless crown,
> And put a barren sceptre in my gripe,
> Thence to be wrench'd with an unlineal hand,
> *No son of mine succeeding.* (3.1.59–63; my italics)

Macbeth returns obsessively to these ideas—"For Banquo's issue have
I fil'd my mind . . . To make them kings—the seeds of Banquo kings!"
(3.1.64, 69). The repetition emphasizes Macbeth's horror that he will
not be able to pass the kingdom to a son, and leads to his attempt to murder Banquo and his only son Fleance. Later he has Macduff's family
destroyed and becomes an indiscriminate butcher of those who do or
might have children—"Each new morn/New widows howl, new orphans
cry" (4.3.4–5). Many commentators have noted that the language of
Macbeth is full of children, such as the apparitions of "a bloody Child"
and "a Child crowned, with a tree in his hand" in Act 4 Scene 1, and
the picture of pity "like a naked new-born babe" (1.7.21).[13] In both
Macbeth and *King Lear*, then, children are prominent in person or in fig-
urative language, and the protagonists feel an angry desire to annihilate
life because, in one case, of the way children have abandoned their father,
and in the other because of the absence of a son and heir, fictional repre-
sentations with connections to Shakespeare's own situation.

But irrational anger frequently gives way to guilt and remorse, as it does
in *King Lear*. Lear finds it difficult to express his feelings directly, but they
are conveyed through the imagery he uses. For instance, when he starts to
recover from his madness to find that Cordelia has returned from France
and is watching over him, his first words are, "You do me wrong to take
me out o' th' grave:/Thou art a soul in bliss, but I am bound/Upon a wheel
of fire, that mine own tears/Do scald like molten lead" (4.6.38–41). The
image links tears with feelings of guilt and resultant punishment. Lear sees
himself as one of the living dead, like the Ghost of Hamlet's father, who
was by day "confined to fast in fires," or like Ixion in Greek mythology,
bound to a wheel of fire as a punishment by Zeus. Such a picture is strange
to us, and we need to remember how common visualizations of hellish
punishment for sin were in Shakespeare's period. Robert Burton tells the
story of a suicidal painter's wife, "that was melancholy for her son's death,
and for melancholy became desperate; she thought God would not pardon her sins, 'and for months still raved that she was in hell-fire, already
damned.' "[14] From a psychological point of view, these feelings of punishment are an indirect representation of guilt feelings. Lear imagines he has
died and is being punished in Hell, whereas Cordelia, whose death he
imagines he has caused, has been rewarded by the bliss of Heaven.
Revealingly, the closest the father can come to a direct admission of guilt
is by an action, not by words, when he tries to kneel to her. This would
have been even more striking on the Jacobean stage than on ours because
at this time a daughter would be expected to kneel to receive her father's

blessing, not the other way round. Shakespeare here is taking another step on his journey by beginning to explore a father's feelings of deep guilt toward a loved and lost child—one of the dominant themes in his final group of plays.

But there is another strong paternal response to a sense of abandonment by a child, which is not shown through Lear but through Gloucester. Like Lear, Gloucester exploded in rage when he thought Edgar had turned against him and sent his servants to "dispatch" Edgar, an ambiguous word, often meaning to kill (2.1.58). But even before he discovers that Edmund has deceived him and that Edgar really loves him, his anger has given way to feelings mainly absent in Lear until much later in the play—depression and despair—as in these lines to Kent:

Thou sayest the King grows mad, I'll tell thee, friend,
I am almost mad myself. I had a son,
Now outlaw'd from my blood; he sought my life,
But lately, very late. I lov'd him, friend;
No father his son dearer; true to tell thee,
The grief hath craz'd my wits. (3.4.165–70)

The speech has a series of dying falls, emphasized by the pause in the middle of each line, and recalls the falling rhythm of Lear's "nor ever shall see/That face of hers again." This is a countenance more in sorrow than in anger, and Gloucester is much more rational than Lear in analyzing his state of mind. Despite his reference to his "craz'd" wits, he does not follow Lear into madness. Rather he has already started his heartsick journey towards attempted suicide, and it is significant that this begins even before he has been blinded for trying to help his king.

When it comes, the blinding is the most savage onstage act in Shakespeare, if we except his early gore-filled *Titus Andronicus*. It results in Gloucester almost losing all hope and to some extent acts as a physical manifestation of that inner state, since Gloucester has to be led like a help-less child. Catherine Sanders records how most of the bereaved parents she encountered "gave the appearance of individuals who had just suffered a physical blow and that left them with no strength or will to fight, hence totally vulnerable."[15] We may recall that at the end of the scene when Leonato realizes he has falsely accused Hero of infidelity and caused her to collapse and almost to die, he too becomes helpless, saying, "Being that I flow in grief,/The smallest twine may lead me" (*Much Ado*, 4.1.249–50). And the similarly named Leontes gives himself over to Paulina's direction after he has caused his wife's apparent and his young son's actual death. In all three cases the depression and paralysis is linked to feelings of guilt.

Here is another of the play's intuitions that has been confirmed by therapists and counselors: burning anger and its extension beyond "normal" sanity and into seeming madness, as in the case of Lear, can be a positive element in coping with loss, in the sense that it takes the mourner out of normal consciousness and keeps him from taking his own life. Gail Ashton reports a bereaved mother as saying, "They say that anger is not good, but in some forms anger is better than the place where I was in wanting to die and wanting to be with him."[16] The raging Lear avoids thoughts of suicide; rather he imagines the opposite, an army creeping up on his enemies, then "kill, kill, kill, kill, kill, kill!" (4.6.187). But once Gloucester knows that he has falsely sought the life of his loved son and heir, he exclaims, "O my follies! then Edgar was abus'd./Kind gods, forgive me that, and prosper him!" (3.7.91–2). Now the way to Dover Cliff and to suicide seems all that is left. And this is frighteningly logical, for what is there to live for? Everything he valued has been destroyed, and the one person who might make life bearable he thinks is lost for ever. The blind Gloucester's yearning for Edgar and sense of guilt for his apparent death is emphasized in the scene that follows his blinding: "O dear son Edgar,/The *food* of thy abused father's wrath!/Might I but live to see thee in my touch,/I'ld say I had eyes again" (4.1.21–4; my italics). The image in the second line links with Lear's picture of cannibals eating their children in Scene 1, to show the horrifying destructiveness of irrational anger. Now all Gloucester wishes is to fall into the sea, anticipating Alonso's similarly rational wish to join, at the bottom of the ocean, the son whose death he views as a punishment for his sins. It is hard to believe that the reaction of these fathers does not draw at some level on feelings of despair and guilt after Hamnet's death, which may have happened when Shakespeare was away from home, and that he did not at moments wonder whether it was worth being at all, whether it would not be better just to die, as we heard other bereaved parents admit in Chapter 3.

Alas for Gloucester that he is so rational: he cannot find the relief in madness that Lear does, although he does desire it after his failed attempt at suicide, "Better I were distract,/So should my thoughts be sever'd from my griefs" (4.6.281–2). We may remember Constance expressing similar sentiments when she knows she will never see again her Arthur. The pain of the loss of a child is presented as unbearable to a sane mind.

Never (O Fault!) Reveal'd Myself unto Him

Both sanity and insanity, then, lead a distraught father into terrifying pain, but each survives, and is reluctantly brought back to the world of the living. This release clearly could be seen in terms of Christian resurrection. Yet brought back for what? Further suffering, it appears, which is what Shakespeare himself is still enduring nearly 10 years after Hamnet's death. But here it is worth noting a pattern that occurs in both plots, although it is more usually associated with a comic or romance structure like that of Shakespeare's final plays than a tragic one. It involves characters, usually in disguise, trying to protect (in this case) the two fathers and guide events to a happy ending: Rosalind in *As You Like It* and Portia in *The Merchant of Venice* are examples considered previously.

In each plot it is relevant that the father does not know he is being protected, but Shakespeare and the audience do. This allows Shakespeare to enact the feeling of abandonment, but also of hope that, somehow, the father is still being watched over. Kent disguises himself to try and protect Lear from Goneril and Regan, until Cordelia returns from France to take over this role. But much stranger are the scenes in which Edgar watches over the blind, suicidal Gloucester while adopting a whole series of disguises. And there is a very curious element to this guardianship: Edgar takes over the protection of his father near the beginning of Act 4, but does not reveal his identity during the long journey from the heath outside Gloucester Castle to the cliffs of Dover; nor does he try to persuade his father against committing suicide. There is nothing like this in the source story of Leonatus and Plexirtus in Sidney's *Arcadia*. Indeed, the nearest anticipation is, as Lawrence Danson points out, in Act 2 Scene 2 of *The Merchant of Venice*, in which Launcelot pretends to his blind father that he is someone else and that Launcelot is dead. The incident is short and the tone comic, but the father's momentary pain is clear. This is perhaps another way in which *The Merchant of Venice* acknowledges, albeit briefly, what it is like to feel you have lost a child.[17]

Why does Edgar not reveal himself to his blind father? Of course it adds to the dramatic tension but again takes the same risk as the Duke's behavior toward Isabella did of alienating many in the audience. Edgar's explanation is that he wishes to save his father from the sin of despair; and when this (at first) fails, he allows Gloucester to think he has attempted suicide so that he will believe he has been miraculously preserved by the gods when actually he has been preserved by his son. Life as presented in this play is so cruel that only disguise and deception can restore the father's faith. We might have thought that telling his father he [Edgar] was alive and would look after him would be a less hazardous way of saving him from despair and that not telling him might *increase* his despair, but Shakespeare does not allow Edgar to consider this. Instead Edgar pretends to take his father to the edge of Dover Cliff, while really keeping him on safe ground. Yet he is aware that he is taking the ultimate risk in following this course of action. When Gloucester falls forward in an attempt at suicide, Edgar acknowledges to himself that this action might be enough to kill him. A real-life loving son would be very unlikely to take this gamble; it is Shakespeare's inner need that is making Edgar do this.

At moments, indeed, Shakespeare seems aware that he is forcing Edgar to act unconvincingly. Before Gloucester's suicide attempt Edgar had been almost unable to continue deceiving his father about his identity, saying, "I cannot daub it further," but the revised *Folio* text has an addition in which he rebukes himself, "And yet I must" (4.1.52–3). That this addition was thought necessary in a rewriting primarily aimed at shortening the play suggests unease with the behavior required of Edgar. R. A. Foakes' note in the Arden edition of the play is worth quoting: "it is hard to see why he still *must* conceal himself from his father, except in terms of the needs of the plot."[18] And it certainly is "hard to see" why later, when Edgar does manage to cure his father of despair, and Gloucester exclaims, "Henceforth I'll bear/Affliction till it do cry out itself 'Enough, enough,' and die," Edgar still does not identify himself (4.6.75–7).

Shakespeare continues to prevent Edgar from revealing his identity until almost the end of the play. When Edgar finally does so, he himself cannot understand why he has continued this deception for so long: "Never (*O fault!*) reveal'd myself unto him/Until some half hour past" (5.3.193–4; my italics). This again illustrates Shakespeare's need to *lengthen* the purgatorial suffering of this grieving, despairing father, which at some level echoes his own; but at the same time he needs to include the hope that, *unbeknown to the father, his son is still present and watching over him*. What a wonderful metaphor the blind father and the disguised son is for capturing what many a bereaved parent has felt: terrifying, suicidal despair, but also the hope that cannot be relinquished that somehow, although unseen, my child is still present like a good angel, protecting me. There is a movement toward acknowledgment of Hamnet's death, as the mourner is a father rather than the sister of *Twelfth Night* and *Measure for Measure*; but also a dissociation, as the knowledge of the absence of the loved son is replaced by an image of his physical presence. This recalls Jeffrey Kauffman's suggestion that integration and dissociation take place *simultaneously* as mourning progresses. In Shakespeare's final plays the need to lengthen the pain of the apparently bereaved parent is even stronger: Pericles, Leontes, and Cymbeline are separated from their apparently dead children for 14, 16, and 20 years, respectively, before the miraculous restorations occur.

When it comes to Gloucester's death, Shakespeare finds a marvelous way to combine the simultaneous hope-and-despair experienced by a father exhausted by pain. Gloucester, on hearing Edgar finally disclose his identity, is " 'Twixt two extremes of passion, joy and grief," before his heart "Burst smilingly" (5.3.199–200). At the very, very, very last, this blind father learns that his loving son is indeed present and has been his guardian angel. But Gloucester is so utterly weary that this at-last restoration causes his battered heart to cease beating. Does Gloucester die happy? There is "smilingly;" but his heart "burst," unable to cope any longer. We have moved beyond happiness and unhappiness, to as moving an evocation as possible of how a racked father subjected to unendurable suffering might feel on believing his dead son is actually alive. Indeed *one* of the functions of both the extreme age of Gloucester and Lear and the physical and mental violence to which they are subjected is to find a way of representing unendurable paternal suffering. Lawrence Danson makes a revealing contrast between the successful and ultimately celebratory reunions between father and daughter in *King Lear* and later plays, and the "strong avoidance of the father-son reunion—a reunion he [Shakespeare] is nonetheless drawn repeatedly to attempting."[19] Again, this mirrors Shakespeare's own situation: his hope of reestablishing successful relationships with his two daughters when he eventually retires from London to Stratford, his desire for such a relationship with his son, and his knowledge that that is impossible.

By the last scene of this excoriating play Shakespeare is finally ready to face more fully than ever before a bereaved father's agony, something he has avoided since *Henry the Fourth, Part 2*. Agony like this: "If I ever really truly believed this really happened, and he's never coming home . . . I think I will go crazy. I have enough pills on hand. I can do it."[20] (Compare the similar cadence and vocabulary in Gloucester's "true to tell thee,/The grief hath crazed my wits.") This mother *knows* her son is dead, but cannot *believe* it; if the rational were to triumph here, it would, as we have seen for Gloucester and Alonso, lead to attempted suicide. Shakespeare knows his son is dead; but can he accept it yet?

This Feather Stirs, She Lives!

There are many versions of the Lear story prior to Shakespeare's, and in all of them Lear's enemies are defeated, and he is restored to his throne. His daughter Cordelia succeeds him when he dies, her sisters' sons rebel against her and put her in prison, and usually she commits suicide, although in some versions she is murdered. Shakespeare often uses his sources very freely, but even by his standards the ending here is a startling change, for in no other version does Cordelia *predecease her father*.

As we have seen, Lear's entry carrying the dead Cordelia was for Samuel Johnson the most unbearable moment in Shakespeare. John Joughin describes it as a " '*pietà*-like' image of Lear holding the dead Cordelia in his arms, a scene of 'pity and hope' which has continued to haunt critics, editors and spectators alike."[21] "This image links Lear's suffering with the traditional epitome of mourning: the Virgin Mary holding the body of her dead *son* Jesus. It recalls Laertes' desire to hold Ophelia in his arms and be buried with her, and Hamlet following Laertes into the grave and claiming the same right, and anticipates images in later plays, especially in *Cymbeline*.

This image is one reason why Johnson's difficulty with the ending of *King Lear* is not so strange as it may appear to us now. This ending is past endurance: a father who howls, howls, howls, unable to find language to express his anguish at the loss of his innocent child. And when he recovers language his words emphasize his separation from everyone else present: "O, you are men of stones!/Had I your tongues and eyes, I'd use them so/That heaven's vault should crack" (5.3.258–60). He asks the unanswerable questions all bereaved parents ask—"Why should a dog, a horse, a rat, have life,/And thou no breath at all?" (5.3.307–8). Earlier in the play Edgar kept thinking that he had encountered the worst that life can throw at him, only to find "the worst is not/So long as we can say, 'This is the worst' " (4.1.27–8). But this scene is the worst: a parent oblivious to everything but his attempt to face the fact that his child will return "never." In *King John* when Constance thought her son was gone for ever, she said, "never, never/Must I behold my pretty Arthur more." In the earlier *Quarto* version of this play Lear says that Cordelia will come, "Never, never, never." In the revised *Folio* text it is, "Never, never, never, never, never," a whole line of verse repeating one heart-tearing word that encapsulates the father's aloneness (5.3.309).[22] And there is a significant addition in the revised text. The worn-out father still cannot let go of hope even at the bitter end: he dies sensing breath on the dead Cordelia's lips,

"Do you see this? Look on her! Look her lips,/Look there, look there!"
(5.3.311–2). Lear is going back to an earlier moment, when he held a
feather to her lips, "This feather stirs, she lives! If it be so,/It is a chance
which does *redeem all sorrows/ That ever I have felt*" (5.3.266–8; my italics).
As John Pitcher notes, this in turn takes up the image of the "happy smilets/
That play'd on her ripe lip" (4.3.19–20).[23] How well Shakespeare understands the difficulty for a bereaved parent of letting go; how many bereaved
parents must have said similar "if only" words.

So in the *Quarto* text Shakespeare goes further than ever before in facing the desolation of loss and the possibility that there is nothing—a key
word in the play—to hope for. In the *Folio* revision he perhaps pulls back
slightly from this bleakness, allowing Lear one final hope; but how we take
the addition is left up to us. For more than half the twentieth century
Christian readings predominated, seeing Cordelia as a Christ-like sacrifi-
cial victim, and the image of something (movement?) on her lips as a
premonition of the afterlife; in the latter part of the century materialistic
readings became more common, seeing Lear as deluding himself with
false hope even in his last breath. For those who take this latter view, the
ending may be even more devastating than in the *Quarto*. But more
recently there has been a realization that it is not necessarily an either/or
situation: throughout *King Lear*, Shakespeare seems to be exploring the
heights of hope and the depths of despair *simultaneously*, rather than
deciding that one response is more accurate to life than the other.
Certainly in both versions Shakespeare plunges his old men into the
whirlwind of contradictory and overlapping emotions that follow the loss
of a child: love, anger, guilt, suicidal despair, desolation, (unrelinquish-
able?) hope.

Shakespeare still cannot approach an end to his mourning journey,
however, because there is still a deflection of grief. He makes the good
daughter die, not the good *son*, almost the copy of his child that died,
not the copy itself, suggesting that intense suffering caused by the thought
of a daughter's death is still easier to contemplate than that caused by a
son's, just as a sister's mourning for a brother in *Twelfth Night* and
Measure for Measure was easier to present than a father's. Because we know
what happens at the end of *King Lear* we forget that Edgar could die as
well as Cordelia, making the desolation complete.

But although Shakespeare can sacrifice Cordelia, Edgar is special. Early
in the play, when Gloucester believes that Edgar has plotted to kill him,
Regan exclaims, "What, did my father's godson seek your life?/He whom
my father nam'd, your Edgar?" (2.2.91–2). As Michael Hays points out,

this is the only time "godson" occurs in Shakespeare's plays.[24] It is one of those strange moments when we seem to be looking into Shakespeare's private thoughts, to be seeing something very important to *him*, but not to the *play* as a narrative, for the idea is not taken up and developed but was not removed in the revised *Folio* text. R. A. Foakes' note in the Arden edition is helpful again: "Lear invokes only pagan gods in Act 1, but this reference to his acting as a godfather to Edgar links them in Christian terms and also hints that Edgar is the son Lear might have wished for." So Edgar is in one sense a substitute son, a motif of increasing importance in Shakespeare's final plays.[25] And instead of dying, the substitute son becomes a hero, saving his real father from being murdered and then defeating his wicked half-brother Edmund, like a chivalric knight, as Hays suggests. After Lear's death Edgar is regarded by the Duke of Albany as a potential ruler. Albany is actually heir to the throne by marriage, and usually in a Shakespearean tragedy the figure with the best claim has no hesitation in seizing the crown (as Fortinbras did in *Hamlet*). But Albany is so devastated by the horror he has seen that he cannot imagine becoming king himself, so he offers the throne jointly to the Earl of Kent and to Edgar, now Earl of Gloucester. But the ever-loyal Kent is not going to outlive King Lear, and gently tells Albany so.

This leaves Edgar. In the earlier *Quarto* version the play's last words are spoken by Albany, the man of highest status, as we would expect at the end of a Shakespearean tragedy, and Edgar does not reply to the offer of the crown.[26] In the revised *Folio* text it is Edgar who gives the last speech and reluctantly accepts the crown, making him the character of highest status. I think there is still a dissociation from grief for Shakespeare here because it is a male heir, Lear's godson, his wished-for son, who will be the next monarch, rather than the daughter who succeeds Lear in all previous versions of the story. We may remember that Shakespeare's will showed his determination to ensure that his wealth and property, after passing unavoidably to his elder daughter, should go to her male heirs; this male inheritance could not be assured in real life, but it could be in fiction.

We are now approaching the last stage of Shakespeare's career, and it is the reunions in *King Lear* between guilty, pain-racked fathers and their children that most point the way to his final plays. There, though, his fathers are treated more hopefully than here. But that is only possible after the heights and depths of this play.

Notes

Full publication details of every source sources are in the bibliography.

1. *Epitia* and *Promos and Cassandra* are in Bullough, *Narrative and Dramatic Sources of Shakespeare*, Volume 2.

2. Wells and Taylor, *William Shakespeare: A Textual Companion*, pp. 131, 529– 32. Clearly some of the differences between the *Quarto* and *Folio* texts reflect mistakes and changes made in the printing process, but a substantial number seem to have been by Shakespeare or another member of The King's Men, and reflect changes of focus.

3. I certainly would not defend Tate's change of the tone of the ending, but it is not quite so hard to understand as it might at first appear. The source play, *King Leir*, ends with the Gallian King and the still-alive Cordella triumphing over the still-alive Leir's enemies, and in all versions of the story prior to Shakespeare's Cordelia lives beyond her father's death. Further, Tate would know that *The Winter's Tale* and other Shakespearean romances take tragic plots and bring them to less desolate endings.

4. Scully, "Men and Grieving," p. 97. In *An Intimate Loneliness* Gordon Riches and Pam Dawson comment, when comparing paternal and maternal grief, "Emotionally, fathers are more likely to feel anger and a need to blame someone," p. 62. Melancholic depression has, of course, already been explored in *Hamlet*, but here Shakespeare is probing further, for it is a father feeling it, and a father who tries to kill himself, rather than just thinking about it as Hamlet does.

5. Klein writes often about the early defense mechanism of splitting, for instance in "On the Theory of Anxiety and Guilt," in *Envy and Gratitude and Other Works*, pp. 25–42.

6. Palliser, *The Age of Elizabeth*, p. 48. Shakespeare probably wrote *Othello* in the year before *King Lear*, and there a daughter openly flouts her father's authority in her choice of husband (and is punished for it when her husband murders her).

7. Krims, *The Mind According to Shakespeare*, pp. 133 and 132.

8. Coren, programme note, "Gilded Butterflies," for the Royal Shakespeare Company, 2004. I am grateful to Kiernan Ryan for alerting me to this note in response to an e-mail.

9. Rando, *Parental Loss of a Child*, p. 14.

10. Malan, *Individual Psychotherapy and the Science of Psychodynamics*, pp. 152 and 168. Italics in the original.

11. Parkes, *Bereavement*, p. 81.

12. The True Chronicle History of King Leir is in Bullough, *Narrative and Dramatic Sources of Shakespeare*, Volume 7, pp. 337–402.

13. For instance, Weis, *Shakespeare Unbound*, pp. 351–6, and *Shakespeare Revealed*, pp. 311–4. I am grateful also to Carol Rutter for an e-mail about the

child imagery in *Macbeth* that helped me to crystallize my own thoughts on the relevance of these moments to *King Lear*.

14. Burton, *The Anatomy of Melancholy*, partition 3, p. 396.

15. Sanders, "A Comparison of Adult Bereavement," p. 317.

16. Ashton, "Pebble on my wing," p. 9.

17. The story of Leonatus and Plexirtus is in Bullough, *Narrative and Dramatic Sources of Shakespeare*, Volume 7, pp. 402–14. Danson, "Shakespeare and the Misrecognition of Fathers and Sons," in Spaas, *Paternity and Fatherhood*, pp. 236–45; the quotation is on p. 243. I am grateful to John Drakakis, editor of the Arden *The Merchant of Venice*, for an e-mail confirming that this moment has no known source.

18. Foakes, *King Lear*, p. 307. Italics in the original.

19. Danson, "Shakespeare and the Misrecognition of Fathers and Sons," in Spaas, *Paternity and Fatherhood*, p. 245.

20. Quoted in Rosenblatt, *Parent Grief*, p. 85.

21. Joughin, "Lear's Afterlife," in Holland, *Shakespeare Survey 55*, pp. 67–81. The quotation is from p. 68.

22. Many commentators emphasize the fact that these words were written almost a decade after Hamnet's death, and about Cordelia, not Hamnet. Clearly this is true in a literal sense, but the argument that Shakespeare could be at some level recollecting the loss of Hamnet if they had been written within a few years of that death, and if it were a son carried onstage by a howling father but not a daughter, seems naïve to me. It underestimates the length of time the loss of a child stays with most bereaved parents as evidenced by many counselors and therapists. It is further evidenced by the fact that much mourning takes place below the level of consciousness, Shakespeare's need to present experiences via transformations, and his fondness for androgynous and twin-like images. And of course in rehearsal and performance Shakespeare would have seen a young male in Richard Burbage's arms.

23. John Pitcher, *The Winter's Tale*, p. 22. This description only occurs in the earlier *Quarto* text and was perhaps rejected as unnecessarily saying something about to be shown and as holding up the frenetic forward movement of the plot.

24. Michael Hays kindly sent me a copy of an unpublished paper that discusses the use of "godson," since published in *Shakespearean Tragedy as Chivalric Romance*. It is not widely known that Shakespeare was a godfather at least once, to William Walker, to whom he left 20 shillings in gold in his will—a substantial amount. Almost certainly this is the William Walker baptized on 16 October, 1608, who became Stratford's high bailiff in 1649, and who was probably named after William Shakespeare. I am grateful to Robert Bearman at the Shakespeare Birthplace Trust for these details. Shakespeare may have already been a godfather at the time he was writing *King Lear*, although there is no proof of this. We may recall that the Sadlers named their son born in 1598 William, and the Heminges their son in 1603; the taking of Shakespeare's own name may mean that

Shakespeare was invited to be godfather. There is also a story that he was godfather to one of Ben Jonson's children. Even more interesting from the viewpoint of *King Lear* is the possibility that he might have had an illegitimate child in March 1606, a month of fearsome storms, which might also have influenced the play if the storm scenes were not yet written—William Davenant, who became a playwright. There is strong evidence that Shakespeare stayed at the Davenants' inn at Oxford on his journeys between London and Stratford, and the choice of the name William for the boy suggests that Shakespeare may also have been his godfather and that one or both of the parents were fond of the playwright. Thus, Shakespeare might have been writing or revising the part of Edmund in *Lear* when he knew he was to become, or had already become, the father of an illegitimate child. Edmund leaves his father to be tortured (and murdered, for all he knows) by the Earl of Cornwall and Regan. If Shakespeare did have a sexual relationship with Jane Davenant, this punishment of the adulterous father, who enjoyed "good sport" with Edmund's "fair" mother, could be an expression of Shakespeare's guilt over the relationship (1.1.23). Shakespeare did not remember him in his will, as he did William Walker, but there is an obvious reason why he may not have wished to make a gift to an unacknowledged, illegitimate child. Katherine Duncan-Jones, in *Ungentle Shakespeare*, and René Weis, in *Shakespeare Unbound/Shakespeare Revealed*, discuss this possibility in further detail.

25. Foakes, *King Lear*, p. 222. In connection with the idea of Edgar as Lear's substitute son, it is also worth noting that when Lear shows concern for another human being for the first time, it is a fatherly concern for the Fool in the storm scenes: "Come on, my boy. How dost, my boy? Art cold?" (3.2.68), and, "In boy, go first . . . /Nay, get thee in" (3.4.26–7). The last example is especially interesting because it only occurs in the revised *Folio* text, suggesting that this sense of fatherly concern had increased in importance for Shakespeare. In some ways, too, the Fool is protective towards Lear once Cordelia has been banished, and his bizarre term for Lear, "nuncle," which seems to be either a contraction of mine uncle or of not uncle, further hints at (symbolic) kinship. Of course "boy" is a more flexible term in Shakespeare's English than in ours, and a king could use the term to his jester regardless of the jester's age; it is apparent, however, that Lear regards the Fool in a paternal way that goes beyond his role as father to his people, a role that the lines which follow "In boy; go first" show he realizes he has neglected, until pity for this "boy" recalls its importance. It is also worth remembering that when Lear, after disowning Cordelia, offers her portion of the country to be divided between his elder daughters, he offers it to Albany and Cornwell, calling them "Beloved sons," not sons-in-law, as he calls them later when they have incurred his wrath (1.1.138). So Edgar is not the only substitute son in the play; but he is the most prominent one.

26. Of course, it is possible that Albany as the last speaker in the *Quarto* version is a mistake by the compositor and that Edgar was always intended as the last speaker. Either way, it does not affect the argument I am putting forward.

11

Grief and New Life; To Mourn Thy Crosses . . . Give Them Repetition to the Life

The emotional exhaustion at the end of *King Lear*, then, is in my judgment not just Gloucester's and Lear's, but Shakespeare's as well. He has been able to access the terrible sense of abandonment that a parent can feel but also the guilt that follows the recognition that the child has not really abandoned the parent. He has also acknowledged the absolute desolation of a father looking at a dead child, albeit still a daughter rather than a son, and having acknowledged it, he can now move further on. Four of his final plays journey towards a similar tragic despair, but they do not close with it as *King Lear* does. These plays are usually termed romances, in the sense of the Greek romances (or novels) from the first centuries after the birth of Jesus, in which characters are buffeted by wild, improbable, and potentially tragic adventures, with interventions by supernatural forces, before eventually reaching a generally happy ending. These four plays have more in common than any other group in Shakespeare's later career, and they return obsessively to the same situation—a family sundered by tragedy, then wholly or partially reunited—and explore variants of this theme in a way that recalls David Malan's observation about the need, in cases of unresolved grief, for the mourner to keep returning to the basic situation and to explore every aspect of it. Shakespeare's last three sole-authored plays offer more evidence than any we have considered so far of continuing grief for Hamnet, linked with a wider guilt in relation to the splitting apart of a family, and the need to ask for forgiveness.

But as usual with Shakespeare, these plays do not present a break with his previous work, but rather a further outgrowth of his career as a whole, from his earliest comedies to his most recent tragedies. And there are hints of a change before the first of these romances. *Macbeth* ends in celebration of Macbeth's defeat and the return of order and harmony to Scotland rather than in the desolation of *King Lear*. Even more striking is *Antony and Cleopatra*. Because it is set in a pagan world, and because the afterlife Cleopatra ecstatically anticipates at the end of the play is a pagan one in which none, or few, of an audience are likely to believe, the resurrective tone of the ending has been underplayed by most commentators until recent decades. But Cleopatra has faith (albeit a pagan one), just as Leontes has to have at the end of *The Winter's Tale*; and Shakespeare seems much concerned with the need to believe to achieve redemption in his final plays.[1]

But it is *All's Well That Ends Well* that most predicts these final plays. On the surface it is closest to *Measure for Measure*, but stylistic analysis suggests it might be a slightly later play, perhaps written near in time to *King Lear*.[2] At its beginning the King of France is fatally ill—another near-dead father figure—and all medical cures have failed. Lord Lafew, however, knows that a physician's daughter, Helena, has a touch powerful enough to "araise" the long-dead King Charlemagne, anticipating the healing powers of Cerimon in *Pericles*, Paulina (apparently) in *The Winter's Tale* and Prospero in *The Tempest* (2.1.76). The King is skeptical and has to gain faith in Helena before he can be miraculously healed. Helena loves a count called Bertram but is spurned by him, even after the King forces him to marry her as a reward for his cure; Bertram leaves court for Florence, where he falls for Diana. Helena then has herself reported dead, although the audience knows she is not; as Sean Benson comments, Giletta [Helena] does not enact such a deception in the source story, a translation of a tale by Boccaccio. Helena then pretends to be Diana, sleeps with Bertram and becomes pregnant by him.[3] In the final scene the French court experiences a moment of apparent resurrection when Helena reappears from the dead, and Bertram has to ask for forgiveness, as many of Shakespeare's later males need to in the plays from *King Lear* onwards. She is introduced by a riddle showing Shakespeare's fascination with death and life as *simultaneous* states: "Dead though she be, she feels her young one quick./So there's my riddle: one that's quick is dead" (5.3.302–3). Literally, of course, Helena is pregnant, but the symbolic associations of the quick-dead will reverberate through Shakespeare's later plays.

But this sequence of romances begins with a paradox: *Pericles* is a collaboration. The first two acts are primarily by someone else, almost certainly George Wilkins, and the rest primarily by Shakespeare. The style of the opening scenes does not sound like Shakespeare, whereas the later scenes do, and more detailed stylistic analysis of features of language use has confirmed this intuition.[4] The play is absent from the *Folio* collection, perhaps because Shakespeare had collaborated with a man of dubious reputation and behavior rather than a respectable playwright like John Fletcher, and/or because of difficulties over gaining the copyright, and/or because there are two acts of (principally) Wilkins before Shakespeare's main contribution starts. The surviving *Quarto* text is in very poor condition. It was certainly written by 20 May 1608, when it is mentioned in the Stationers' Register, and the Venetian and French ambassadors saw a performance at some point after May 1606. The theaters were closed because of plague from July to December 1606, for all but a week in 1607, until April in 1608 and then after mid-July. There is a reference to it being "lately presented" in the novel Wilkins made out of the play that was published in late 1608 and this, together with stylistic considerations, make it likely it was written late 1607 or early 1608.[5]

At this stage in his career, why should London's most successful playwright engage in collaboration? Firstly, it was common practice among Shakespeare's contemporaries, and evidence exists of Shakespeare collaborating in his early years in London (for instance, on *Henry the Sixth, Part One*), and in the years before *Pericles*, on the unfinished *Timon of Athens*. Secondly, Shakespeare may have been having further thoughts about retirement by 1607—he had had a financially successful but very exhausting career, and was now in his early forties, nearly twice the age that the average Londoner reached at this time. He had bought land and tithe income in and around Stratford, and probably had enough now to retire on. Further, the theater closure from July 1606 and for all but a week of 1607 because of the plague was yet another reminder of the precariousness of theatrical performance, and may have been an added incentive to quit the tiring and unpredictable existence of company playwright. Why should he commit himself to the effort involved in writing a long play that might never be performed if the plague did not abate?

Collaboration allowed Shakespeare to keep his options open: half a play was less of a commitment than a whole one but meant he was still around, should he decide a permanent return to Stratford was not yet desirable. Indeed, as we saw in the previous chapter, the prospect of returning permanently to a family he had left about 20 years before and whose surviving members he had probably not seen frequently during that time, and who had managed to run the household and take important decisions without his input, might well have been viewed with apprehension as well as with hope, so it is likely that he wished to avoid committing himself for now either way.

It is impossible to be certain whether Wilkins or Shakespeare initiated the collaboration, but the fact that Wilkins wrote most of the first two acts and Shakespeare most of the last three suggests, if it were not a joint venture from the start, Wilkins as the more likely initiator. Wilkins had had a hit with *The Miseries of Enforced Marriage*, acted by Shakespeare's company, probably in early 1606, and perhaps wanted to have something ready for when the theaters reopened. Shakespeare may even have been called in by his fellow sharers to rescue a play where Wilkins was struggling. But if Wilkins were the instigator, he managed to choose a plot that had much to interest Shakespeare. The main source is a Greek romance, *Apollonius of Tyre* [Pericles].[6] As Suzanne Gossett notes, a fashion for romance was sufficiently established by 1607 for it to be parodied in Francis Beaumont's *The Knight of the Burning Pestle*, so there was likely to be a ready audience for such a play—indeed, it was an instant success.[7]

One aspect of the story that might have struck Shakespeare at this point in his life was its focus on a father: as David Bevington notes, Shakespeare is increasingly drawn to stories that focus on a father severed from some or all of his family and who wants, and needs, reunion.[8] In this story there is an emphasis on restlessness: Apollonius never settles in one place before circumstances drive him elsewhere, and on his voyages he loses his wife and has to leave behind his baby daughter. For many years he thinks they are dead—and death is a metaphor likely to resonate with a man living apart from his family for much of 20 years—but they are eventually restored to him. This sense of rootlessness, and grief for what is lost in life's travels, might have been psychologically compelling to Shakespeare.

Apollonius' spirit is *almost* broken by his losses, and so is Pericles'. Near the end of the play, with his wife and daughter lost for 14 years and apparently for ever, Helicanus tells us that Pericles—face unwashed, hair uncut, attired in sackcloth—has spoken to no one for three months and only takes sustenance to "prorogue" [prolong] his grief—in other words, he takes no interest in living (5.1.26). As for Gloucester, death would be a relief. Indeed, Pericles at this late point in the play might seem bound to the same wheel; but his reunion with his daughter Marina does not end, like Lear and Cordelia's, in death, but in new life—again a typically Shakespearean exploration of different possibilities inherent in the same situation. Marina (now 14, the age of Susanna in the year following Hamnet's death) returns her father to life, gives him the strength to carry on. Shortly before the probable beginning of the collaboration, Susanna had married Dr. John Hall and become pregnant, and she gave birth to the only grandchild Shakespeare knew in February 1608, probably close in time to the completion of the play. The prospect of becoming a grandfather probably gave him, as it does many, a new hope in life. So it is likely that this change of direction away from tragedy feeds on, among other things, hopes invested in his elder daughter and new son-in-law—a healer, like Cerimon. But also on fears: Suzanne Gossett argues that the dangers of childbirth in *Pericles*, apparently costing Thaisa's life, and in other late plays—Posthumus' mother dies as soon as he is born in *Cymbeline*, and in *The Winter's Tale* Hermione apparently dies shortly after giving birth to Perdita—reflect in part Shakespeare's awareness of the hazards of childbirth and anxiety for Susanna and her unborn child, and any future children. He had the memory of the death of his brother Edmund's illegitimate baby in August 1607 and then Edmund's own death in December as recent reminders of mortality.[9]

But there is a strangeness about the events leading to Pericles' reunion with his daughter that Shakespeare's version emphasizes. The opening part of the play, written mainly by Wilkins, had shown the terrible danger of a too-close, incestuous relationship between a father and daughter; now Pericles seems to go to the other extreme. He has been unavoidably separated from his wife and daughter and does not search for his wife because he believes she is drowned; but he also does not go to find his daughter for 14 years, even though he knows he left her to be cared for at Tarsus. Why it takes him so long to seek Marina is not explained in the various versions of the source story or in the play, and this may have been another element that appealed to Shakespeare: Jonathan Bate, amongst others, has drawn attention to the fact that, as Shakespeare's dramatic writing develops, he shows less interest in clear motivation and more in presenting character as unfolding through action.[10] We have already seen in the case of Edgar and Gloucester another example of Shakespeare's attraction to prolonged, barely motivated, inaction in a parent-child relationship, but there it was a son not revealing himself to a father, allowing the father's suffering to be stretched taut. This time it is a father neglectful of his daughter, and suggests an awareness at some level of a falling-short on Shakespeare's own part as a father.

When the two do finally meet, by accident rather than because Pericles has started to search for Marina, we have one of Shakespeare's most moving recognition and resurrection scenes. In keeping with the above, it is the daughter who restores the father; he can do nothing without her generosity of spirit, shown, for instance, in not rebuking him once for failing to return to find her. As in *Twelfth Night*, time almost stands still as Pericles gradually allows himself to believe that this is indeed his daughter. He has to give himself over to belief, to faith, before he can accept the miraculous truth. Finally, he speaks one of Shakespeare's most memorably paradoxical lines to Marina, "Thou that beget'st him that did thee beget"—she has given new life to the father who first gave her life (5.1.195). Movingly, she kneels to him for his paternal blessing, recalling the restoration scene between Cordelia and Lear. Pericles' heart almost bursts, as Gloucester's actually had when Edgar revealed himself to him:

> O Helicanus, strike me, honored sir,
> Give me a gash, put me to present pain,
> Lest this great sea of joys rushing upon me
> O'erbear the shores of my mortality,
> And drown me with their sweetness (5.1.190–4).

We shall hear similar words from another father reunited with lost children in *Cymbeline*. This sense of overwhelming joy through a miraculous restoration is something Shakespeare is strongly drawn towards. It implies a hope that his daughters, especially Susanna, soon to provide him with a grandchild, would welcome him with open arms if he did decide to live permanently in Stratford, and would help him into a new life as Marina had Pericles—the reverse of the fears expressed about daughters' behavior in *Othello* and for most of *King Lear*.

Interestingly, in the early part of the recognition scene, Pericles thinks, "This cannot be/My daughter—*buried*!" (5.1.162–3; my italics). At no point has there been anything to suggest to Pericles that his daughter has died and been buried (although, as the *Quarto* text is in poor condition, it is possible that a relevant comment has been lost); so it is possible that the image of a *buried* child returning to life is at some level recalling Hamnet as well as, more straightforwardly, the metaphorically dead Susanna and Judith. And as Sean Benson notes, when Pericles is reunited with his wife Thaisa, she faints. For a moment he thinks she "dies," and when she recovers and speaks he exclaims, "The voice of dead Thaisa!" (5.3.15; 34). Then he holds his arms open to her, saying, "O, come, be *buried*/A second time within these arms," again suggesting that perhaps not Anne alone is present in Shakespeare's unconscious (5.3.43–4; my italics).[11]

Overall, however, the reunion with Thaisa is a much more perfunctory affair, even allowing for the fact that some lines may have been lost in the poor *Quarto* text. It is the child who keeps the father/husband going here and at other points in these late plays, with the partial exception of *The Winter's Tale*. Here, the focus is on the daughter, and it is Marina's marriage to Lysimachus, mirroring Susanna's to John Hall, that leads to the likely restoration of the line of inheritance, which we have seen was of great concern to Shakespeare. When Thaisa's father, the King of Pentapolis, suddenly dies, the inheritance is conveniently expanded. This, of course, would appeal to a court audience, which would hope for similar alliances of love and property/territory from royal marriages; but the personal is present as well. Pericles and Thaisa can now reign in Pentapolis and give Pericles' kingdom of Tyre to "Our son and daughter" (5.3.82). This wording is revealing: the male comes first, despite the fact that he is not Pericles' child and is called son, not son-in-law, although the latter occurs 13 times in other plays by Shakespeare. It is as if Pericles is adopting his future son-in-law as his substitute son, a pattern we saw starting to emerge in *King Lear* and which we will find emphasized more strongly in *The Winter's Tale* and *The Tempest*. And in contrast to the partial restoration in *Twelfth Night*, this story brings the *whole family* together, a whole family that echoes Shakespeare's own: a family with a wife, daughter, son-in-law, and with the prospect of a grandchild; but no son.

The fact that *Pericles* concentrates on a father-daughter relationship might suggest at first that Shakespeare has now come to terms with the loss of his son but, as the following plays will show, this limited reunion proves insufficient. Indeed, in them Shakespeare seems to follow the advice of the goddess Diana, who appears to Pericles in a dream-vision, after he has been eased into sleep by "heavenly music" (5.1.233). The ability to accept the truth of what comes to you in a dream-vision is akin to having faith and is also important in other late plays. Diana tells him:

> To mourn thy *crosses*, with thy daughter's, call
> And give them *repetition to the life.*
> *Or perform my bidding, or thou livest in woe;*
> Do't, and happy, by my silver bow!
> Awake, and tell thy dream. (5.1.245–9; my italics)

Here "crosses" recalls Jesus' agonizing crucifixion, even though the words are spoken by a pagan Goddess; we will find a similar reference in *Cymbeline*.

Indeed in these late plays Shakespeare mixes pagan and Christian ideas of the supernatural with apparent ease. The 1606 Act of Parliament introducing heavy fines for blasphemy in plays may have encouraged Shakespeare to limit direct references to the Christian God in his later plays, but it also seems that he wants to be inclusive and present similarities between aspects of pagan religion and Christianity, rather than stressing, as many preachers did, the irreconcilable differences between the two.

I do not know whether Sigmund Freud ever read Diana's lines above, but if he did they might well have struck him as an anticipation of the "talking cure" of psychoanalysis, in which *telling and repeating one's traumatic experiences, one's crosses, "to the life," often via disguised and transformed images*, is a way of coming to terms with them. Or in traditional religious terms, it has clear links with the process of confession from the old religion. In this and subsequent plays Shakespeare follows the Goddess' advice, which of course is his own.

A final interest in *Pericles* is the hero's name. Why was it changed from Apollonius, and by whom? Perhaps it was a joint decision, made partly because of the difficulty of fitting a five-syllable name into lines of verse.[12] But if George Wilkins made it alone, he must have been a good reader of Shakespeare's state of mind, or have made an inspired guess, for the name has associations dear to Shakespeare's heart. The most famous Pericles lived in ancient Athens. Plutarch's *Life of Pericles* praises him for his equitable, mild, and patient temper in the face of life's perils—his name indeed is almost an anagram of perils. Certainly Pericles in the play has to show great patience and powers of endurance. Shakespeare might have been particularly attracted to him at some level because, after more than 30 years in public affairs, he lost many relations to the plague, and finally his only remaining (legitimate) son. Pericles was not seen to mourn until this last death, when, as he put a garland of flowers on the head of the corpse, he broke down weeping. (We shall see the importance of flowers for corpses in both *The Winter's Tale* and *Cymbeline*. Shakespeare may of course not have been there to lay any on Hamnet's coffin; indeed, there is no evidence that flowers were regularly laid on graves in sixteenth and early seventeenth century life, as opposed to in the literature of the period). Following this blow Pericles was invited to command the Athenian defences against the Spartans but was so grief-stricken and depressed by the loss of his son that he stayed at home, leaving this to others. Eventually, he was persuaded back into public life, and what he did next might especially have touched Shakespeare. Earlier in his career he had introduced a statute whereby illegitimate children could not have the rank of citizen and could not inherit their father's property; now he requested that the statute be suspended, and that one of his own illegitimate sons be named as his successor, so important was it to him to have an heir. The Athenians took pity on him and granted it. We have seen Shakespeare similarly concerned with inheritance, so there was much to attract Shakespeare, at some level, in the name and history of the most famous Pericles.

Notes

Full publication details of each source are in the bibliography.

1. Shakespeare's last tragedy is probably *Coriolanus*. Apparent allusions to the social unrest in the Midlands in 1607 and 1608 suggest the former year at the earliest, and it may have followed *Pericles* rather than preceded it. Again a personal element could have contributed at some level here. Shakespeare's plays are noticeable for the relative scarcity of strong mother figures, but Volumnia in *Coriolanus* is a conspicuous exception. One of Shakespeare's longest plays, *Coriolanus* presents a man who needs to impress his mother by his manliness, suppressing tender emotions—again there is a horror of tears—for most of the play but who finds he cannot when his mother appeals to him to show mercy toward Rome at the end of the play. His wife and young son are also present, but it is the appeal from his mother that allows his tender emotions to triumph. Shakespeare's mother died in September 1608. There may be a repetition of what happened with *Hamlet*: a parent's impending death took Shakespeare first to thoughts about that parent figure, and then at some level to earlier losses, particularly that of his son. This could be one factor causing the change from Pericles, who has no son, to the later romances in which Leontes, Cymbeline, and Alonso do have sons who they lose either for ever or apparently so.

2. Wells and Taylor, *William Shakespeare: A Textual Companion*, pp.126–7.

3. Benson, *Shakespearean Resurrection*, p. 59. The source story for *All's Well That Ends Well* is in Bullough, *Narrative and Dramatic Sources of Shakespeare*, Volume 2, pp. 389–96. A possible minor attraction in the original for Shakespeare is the fact that Giletta [Helena], when made pregnant, bears twin sons. This perhaps recalled, in a bittersweet way, Shakespeare's own twins, as well as the possible desire which Richard Wheeler discusses that his surviving twin, Judith, had been a boy.

4. Gossett, *Pericles*, pp. 68–70. Persuasive evidence for links between Wilkins and Shakespeare is given in Katherine Duncan-Jones' *Ungentle Shakespeare*, pages 203–13.

5. Gossett, *Pericles*, pp. 54–5.

6. Two versions of the story which the playwrights knew, by John Gower and Laurence Twine, are in Bullough, *Narrative and Dramatic Sources of Shakespeare*, Volume 6, pp. 375–482.

7. Gossett, *Pericles*, pp. 79 and 2–3.

8. Bevington, *Shakespeare's Ideas*, p. 188. This may not seem to be the case at first sight in *Cymbeline* and *The Tempest*, but in both plays, as in *King Lear*, the exploration of fatherhood is split between two characters, Cymbeline and Belarius (the latter thought of as father by Cymbeline's abducted sons), and Prospero and Alonso.

9. Gossett, *Pericles*, p. 159. René Weis suggests that, at Edmund's funeral, Shakespeare might have seen the monument to John Gower in the Church, *Shakespeare Unbound*, p. 362, and *Shakespeare Revealed*, p. 322. As Gower is used as Chorus in *Pericles*, this is a plausible suggestion. As someone associated with the King's Men, Wilkins might have been there as well.

10. Bate, *The Genius of Shakespeare*, pp.146–7. Sean Benson makes the same point about the apparent resurrection scenes: rational explanation is sometimes offered for those who want it, but often it is put to one side in the wonder of the moment, *Shakespearean Resurrection*, p. 140.

11. Benson, *Shakespearean Resurrection*, pp. 133–4.

12. Gossett, *Pericles*, p. 73.

Grief and Deeper Guilt; He Dies to Me Again When Talk'd of

Would They Else Be Content to Die?

Probably the three plays similar in many of their concerns to *Pericles*—*The Winter's Tale, Cymbeline*, and *The Tempest*—did not immediately follow it. In summer 1608 plague closed the theaters yet again, and they were kept closed for most of 1609 and parts of 1610. Katherine Duncan-Jones argues that this closure, which of course deprived Shakespeare of income both as writer and sharer, allowed and encouraged him to return to his *Sonnets* and to make some final revisions before agreeing to their publication in 1609.[1] We also know that the King's Men spent some of the time on tour and that Ben Jonson's new play *The Alchemist* was performed in Oxford in September 1610 while the London theaters were still closed; but the Shakespeare play recorded as performed in Oxford at the same time is *Othello*, which is partial, but not conclusive, evidence that no new Shakespeare play was yet available.

What is the relationship between these three plays? John Pitcher makes a case for saying Shakespeare wrote them over a period of 12 to 15 months in 1610–11 and "conceived and wrote the plays as a group."[2] External and internal features indicate that *The Tempest* is the final one, but it is unclear whether *The Winter's Tale* preceded *Cymbeline* or vice versa, or even whether they overlapped in composition, as Mozart's final symphonies did. It does not affect my argument as to which of the two came first or whether all three were conceived as a group or not, but I do wish to suggest that, in terms of certain themes, they do at least *become* a group, that *The Winter's Tale* and *Cymbeline* encounter matters that previously Shakespeare has pushed to one side, and that he could not have written *The Tempest* as we have it without at some level confronting these issues first. I would agree with Stanley Wells' judgment that, as Shakespeare grew older, he "became less inclined to consider the needs and interests of the traditional audience. The plays became less theatrical, more introverted."[3]

But Shakespeare still retains his alertness to theatrical fashion. In all three plays there is a sense of the older generation making way for a new one, and Shakespeare would have been aware that tragicomic romances were becoming the vogue; after all, he and George Wilkins had contributed to this with *Pericles*. Two young playwrights, Francis Beaumont and John Fletcher, were writing tragicomic romances, which although unsuccessful at first, would soon develop and extend the fashion, and Fletcher linked his own approach to the Italian tradition of pastoral tragicomedy, derived from Giovanni Guarini, in which, although characters come near to death, no one actually dies.[4] Shakespeare may also have been aware of a cult following for *Don Quixote*, with its mixture of antiromantic main plot and inserted romantic tales: Valerie Wayne has shown that Cervantes' very successful novel was referred to by a variety of dramatists and writers, including George Wilkins, from 1606 onwards, well before the first published English translation. One inserted tale in particular, known as 'The Curious Impertinent,' may have contributed to Shakespeare's interest in the presentation of the jealous then penitent husbands, Leontes and Posthumus.[5]

But typically Shakespeare adapts the vogue to his own purposes. In contrast to the tradition of Guarini, *The Winter's Tale* and *Cymbeline* contain deaths. Further, Beaumont and Fletcher's plays are clearly young men's plays influenced by Sidney's *Arcadia*, and offer representative and often idealized characters: Shakespeare gives us some idealizations, especially of children, but in the main he continues an older man's sense of flawed but not irredeemable (in the main) individuals. The similarities with some of the inserted tales within *Don Quixote* are stronger, but Shakespeare's settings (two pagan, one on an enchanted island), more complex characterization, and extended, magical reunions suggest he is, as usual, using the fashion in a very selective manner.

The Winter's Tale was seen by Simon Forman on 15 May 1611. This may or may not have been a first or early performance. It includes a dance of satyrs staged in Ben Jonson's court masque *Oberon* on New Year's Day

1611, so on the face of it would seem to have been written after that performance; but Shakespeare's company was involved in the court celebrations and would have known about the masque a few months in advance. Indeed, a minority of critics, including Wells and Taylor, think that the dance was interpolated into *The Winter's Tale* after it was written, so it seems best to say that the play was probably written in 1610 or some time in early 1611.[6]

In this play Shakespeare returns to the grief associated with the loss of a daughter and a wife in *Pericles*, but now includes a son as well, giving us his most developed and tender picture of a young boy so far—King Leontes' son and heir Mamillius. In Leontes' feelings for his son we will find Shakespeare coming closer than ever before to presenting and facing the experiences and emotions of a bereaved father. Possibly two of his final tragedies contributed to this movement forward: in both *Macbeth* and *Coriolanus* a young son is presented onstage, and the image during rehearsals and performance, and in Shakespeare's imagination when writing, may have further recalled his own lost boy, especially as in the later play Coriolanus' son is active and survives the tragic events, unlike Macduff's son in *Macbeth*.

But it is not just in the main father-son relationship that Shakespeare—now in his mid-forties—seems to be looking back over life in *The Winter's Tale*. Indeed, the very title suggests a world that has been through the other seasons and is now in danger of being mired forever in the final one. Leontes' explosive anger that (almost) kills all the things he loves recalls Lear's and is later reenacted on a smaller scale by King Polixenes of Bohemia. At several points in the play, most strongly in the exceptionally long scene at the sheep-shearing festival in a Bohemia that seems very like rural Warwickshire, Shakespeare chooses imagery that takes us through the cycle of the agricultural year. Sheep-shearing is traditionally early June, but Perdita is linked to April at the beginning of the scene, later speaks of flowers associated with spring, midsummer, and early autumn, then talks of "blasts of January" (to Camillo) and of one of the oldest stories of how the seasons arose—the myth of Proserpina (4.4.2–3, 73–108, 111, 116–8).

This mood of retrospection and awareness of seasonal, and human, cycles seems to have been with Shakespeare even before he started writing. He chose as his source story *Pandosto or the Triumph of Time* by Robert Greene. As we saw in Chapter 2, when the rookie Shakespeare started to establish himself in London he attracted the ire of Greene, who had been to university, and regarded himself as superior to this yokel from Warwickshire. In the posthumously published *Greene's Groatsworth of Wit, bought with a million of Repentance*, Shakespeare was called, "an upstart crow, beautified with our feathers . . . in his own conceit the only Shake-scene in a country"—an accusation of plagiarism, social climbing, arrogance and aggression.[7]

Since this savage attack, Shakespeare had had a kind of dialogue with the dead Greene, for, as Stephen Greenblatt has argued, he may be one of the sources for Shakespeare's most successful comic creation—Sir John Falstaff—and perhaps also for Sir Toby Belch.[8] Now, 17 or so years after the attack, Shakespeare returns to thoughts of this man who was a very popular writer when Shakespeare first came to London and decides to use Greene's tragic tale of *Pandosto* for his own purposes. Its subtitle—*The Triumph of Time*—must have seemed ironical to Shakespeare because he had survived Greene's hostility to become the most successful playwright in London; but Shakespeare was also aware of a generation replacing him, as he had replaced Greene.

Like *Pericles*, *Pandosto* deals with a family separation, this one lasting 16 years; but in contrast to *Pericles*, it is not the result of misfortune but of the irrational jealousy of the husband/father, King Pandosto [Leontes], which leads to the deaths of his wife Queen Bellaria [Hermione] and of his young son and heir Prince Garinter [Mamillius], and to the abandonment of his baby daughter [Perdita] on a hillside. Sixteen years later Pandosto desires an unknown (to him) young woman and imprisons her lover; she is revealed as his daughter, and his guilt over this incestuous desire leads to his suicide—a tragic tale indeed, recalling the opening act of *Pericles*, except that the father there felt no shame.[9] By contrast, in Shakespeare's version, what factually happens to Hermione is ambiguous: as John Pitcher puts it, "Hermione, in romance, is and isn't dead," although she is certainly restored to Leontes.[10] Further, the idea of incestuous desire between Leontes and his unrecognized daughter Perdita is played down, and Leontes celebrates rather than opposes the betrothal between this young woman and Prince Florizel, heir to the throne of Bohemia. As in *Pericles*, the celebration of this peaceful uniting of two kingdoms clearly reflects hopes for successful dynastic marriages for James the First's children, but I would argue that the return to life of Hermione's "statue," the discovery of the lost daughter Perdita, and her marriage, also mirror, as in *Pericles*, Shakespeare's hope that his relationship with his wife Anne would revive after 20 or so years of virtual separation and that his elder daughter's actual marriage, and any future marriage of his younger daughter would be a source of family unity rather than division. Also there may be hopes for his young granddaughter Elizabeth in the growth of Perdita to a mature, able, and hospitable young woman.

But although Shakespeare spares Leontes and Hermione the tragedy that engulfs their prototypes in *Pandosto*, he does not spare Leontes' son and heir Mamillius. He dies as Garinter did in Greene's story, horrified by his father's mistaken jealousy and condemnation of his mother, and I think this is another feature that drew Shakespeare to Greene's story. He is now ready at some level to face the worst of all possible parental experiences directly, not through the disguise of a daughter, as in *King Lear*, but through the loss of a young son; and the plot of Leontes' jealousy allows him to explore the feelings of guilt the loss of a child creates even more than he had in *King Lear*. But despite their similar fate, there is a world of difference between Greene's Garinter and Shakespeare's Mamillius. There are five brief mentions of Garinter, none of them developing any individuality of character. Mamillius' appearances in *The Winter's Tale* are much fuller and are foregrounded and developed in such a way as to place him at the heart of the drama, as a physical presence in the first scenes of the play, and thereafter as a ghostly absence.

We hear of Mamillius before we see him and, like other children in Shakespeare's late plays, he is idealized. This no doubt draws on the hopes placed in James the First's elder son Henry, but is also a common parental response to bereavement; here, as often, we see the wide-ranging nature of Shakespeare's response to life, in this case creating a situation that his court audience would enjoy but that also met a need of his own. Mamillius' qualities are so important that they are made the climax of the short first scene. A Bohemian lord, Archidamus, is told that Mamillius is "one that, indeed, physics the subject [restores the King's subjects], makes old hearts fresh. They that went on crutches ere he was born desire yet their life to see him a man" (1.1.38–41). Archidamus asks, "Would they else be content to die?" The reply is, "Yes; if there were no other excuse why they should desire to live" (1.1.42–4). In other words, Mamillius' simple vitality keeps the old and infirm alive; without the prospect of seeing him become a man they would answer Hamlet's crucial question, "To be, or not to be," by not being, by dying (as Sicilius does in *Cymbeline*). This anticipates the devastating effect Mamillius' death will have on the kingdom and on his father (and ironically anticipates the effect of Prince Henry's sudden death in 1612).

This eulogy prepares us for Mamillius' first appearance in scene 2, where he watches his father sink into the quicksand of jealousy. Hermione is pregnant, and Leontes is wrongly starting to believe that the father is their guest, Polixenes. Leontes asks his son, "Mamillius/Art thou my boy?" Mamillius responds to this unexpected and frightening question confidently by trying to reassure his father, as befits the prince described in the previous scene, "Ay, my good lord" (1.2.119–20). There follows a loving domestic picture unlike anything in *Pandosto*. Leontes notices his young son has "smutch'd" his nose, and goes to wipe it, so his son should look "neat." But, like his creator, Leontes cannot escape the hidden meaning of words, and "neat" sets him thinking about animals like steers, heckfers [heifers] and calves, called "neat" because they have horns, the traditional image of a cuckolded husband (1.2.121–6).

If Mamillius hears his father's mutterings about steers and heckfers, he is certainly too young to understand them fully. Yet he does notice what children are expert at noticing—a parent's mood. So when his father turns to him and resumes, "How now, you *wanton calf,*/Art thou my calf?" Mamillius' reply is more diffident: "Yes, *if you will,* my lord" (1.2.126–7; my italics). Leontes' second question is noticeably more crude, linking sexual activity with animal instinct and lust. The boy's "*if you will*" suggests he recognizes, as children do, that the parent is asking a rhetorical question, that the answer lies within the adult's will, that the adult will produce the answer he has already decided on, regardless of anything the child might assert. After all, hasn't Mamillius' first confident reply been dismissed by his father?

By now Leontes is tiring of his son's presence—something again a child senses quickly—and he repeatedly tells Mamillius to go away and play, but again the word 'play' makes him think of his wife's apparent playing with Polixenes, and of his own role as a cuckold. That the boy does not go suggests he is hurt and wants the reassurance that a child needs—that his father's disturbing mood will pass. Leontes' final question to him, "How now, boy?" elicits the response, "I am like you say," taking up the "if you will" from earlier, and meaning, I am whatever you say I am, your will decides what I am (the *Folio* wording).[11] Leontes turns quickly to speak to Camillo, then delivers a further peremptory "Go play, Mamillius," which finally does drive his son away (1.2.207–11). He is too preoccupied with himself to consider his son properly, something Shakespeare may have felt as he looked back at himself and his determination to leave his young family behind while he searched for success in London.

There is much sympathy and love in the portrait of Mamillius here, together with a sense of how a parent's self-focus can make a child feel unwanted. This sympathy and love is continued in the picture of Mamillius with his mother and her ladies at the beginning of Act 2 before Leontes bursts in accusing his wife of adultery and tears domestic peace to pieces. Mamillius is highlighted here partly because it is he who names the play. When he asks his mother what kind of tale she would like to hear, Hermione answers, "As merry as you will." But like many young lads he needs to be independent of his mother and contradicts her, "A sad tale's best for winter" (2.1.24–5). There is more to it than being a typical boy, however: he seems to have picked up on the wintry chill emanating from his father, and to be aware that it has already entered his own life.

How old is this young boy? When Leontes looks at him he thinks of "myself unbreech'd" (1.2.155). Breeching was one of the rites of passage in a boy's life in Shakespeare's period. Very young boys and girls were dressed similarly, and being put in breeches was the first sign, in terms of clothing, that a boy was growing into a young man rather than remaining an asexual being. In other words, Mamillius is presented to us at an age when Hamnet and Judith would, because of their dress, have looked most like a single being, recalling the fact that the older Viola deliberately "imitate[s]" the dress of her twin brother in *Twelfth Night*. There was no regulation as to when exactly breeching should occur—nowadays there no doubt would be—but most commonly it seems to have happened around the age of seven.[12] A Mamillius aged about seven would fit well with the need to be independent of his mother noted above, with the awareness of women's beauty aids that he shows in the same scene, and with his offended rebuke of one of his mother's ladies-in-waiting, who will "kiss me hard, and speak to me as if/I were a baby still" (2.1.6–7). He is soon to die, and when he does he will fit into a grave three feet long, like Prince Arthur. It is hard to believe that Shakespeare did not recall the earlier prince as he wrote of the later one, or that he did not remember the real-life equivalent of both of them when Hamnet was about this age.

The beginning of Act 2, where we see Mamillius with his mother and her ladies, is the last time we see him onstage, but not the last time we are aware of him. After Leontes imprisons the pregnant Hermione, Mamillius falls ill. According to Leontes, "Conceiving the dishonor of his mother!/He straight declin'd, droop'd, took it deeply,/Fasten'd and fix'd the shame on't in himself" (2.3.13–15). This again demonstrates Shakespeare's psychological acuity—children do blame themselves for problems in the family. But it is also a clear example of the accuracy of Mamillius' earlier words to his father, "if you will." Leontes wills an interpretation of Mamillius' behavior that suits his suspicion of his wife, despite a more obvious explanation: that Mamillius' decline results from his intuition that his mother has been unjustly accused. Leontes then says to his servant, "See how he fares. [*Exit First Servant.*] Fie, fie, no thought of him" (2.3.18). The sequence is crucial here: the first "he" is Mamillius, then the servant leaves, and Leontes' thoughts move to his supposed betrayer, Polixenes, the "him." This kind of transition is one of those things that make Shakespeare's characters so believable, for in the midst of tormented thoughts our minds do lurch from one subject to another.

But the line is also an unconscious prediction of the rest of the play. Soon Leontes puts his wife on trial, finds her guilty, and threatens to execute her, and Mamillius dies from mere anticipation of this last action. After Mamillius' death, Leontes has ostensibly "no thought of him," no thought of his son. He apparently disappears from the play. Yet his absence will be a presence, as Hamnet's is for Shakespeare.

Might I a Son and Daughter Now Have Looked On

But before examining that in detail, we need to consider the contrast between Mamillius' death and that of his prototype in *Pandosto*. Garinter's death occupies one sentence and *follows* Pandosto accepting the truth of an oracle that proclaims his wife's innocence. Pandosto then repents and asks Bellaria's forgiveness, but she dies later after hearing that Garinter has died. Shakespeare alters the order of events. The oracle asserting Hermione's innocence is announced but, unlike Pandosto, Leontes does not accept its truth; instead he reaches the height of blasphemy with a display of hubris worthy of Greek tragedy—indeed, the mention of oracle at Delphi reminds us that we are in the world of Greek tragedy: "There is no truth at all i' th' oracle," that is tantamount to saying, "There is no truth in the pronouncements of the Gods" (3.2.140). Leontes does not believe the oracle *until he hears that Mamillius has died*. In Shakespeare's version the death of the son is put at the center of the scene by being the *cause* of Leontes' change of heart and repentance, for he now swings to the opposite extreme, seeing the Gods as punishing him by taking the life of his son. Guilt for the boy's death is strongly emphasized here, in contrast to *Pandosto*. As Pitcher notes, "This is a cruel fable of childhood, in which the father sacrifices the son."[13] Then Hermione apparently dies on the news of Mamillius' death, further highlighting the devastating effect on a parent of the loss of a child. Indeed, she has not only lost her son, but earlier Leontes has given instruction that their newborn daughter, which he thinks is Polixenes' bastard, be abandoned to die far away from Sicily. Husband and wife are seemingly childless, and it is all Leontes' fault. The rest of the play focuses on his guilt for breaking the domestic harmony of his family; (Hermione was probably pronounced Harmonie at this time, which emphasizes further what she has given to the play so far).[14]

Once Leontes believes the oracle's pronouncement of Hermione's innocence, he decrees that they should be buried together in a chapel and,

promising to visit it every day, dedicates himself to mourning and repentance. When we see him again 16 years later, his memories seem to be
solely of Hermione "and her virtues," not of Mamillius (5.1.7). Why does
he not think of his son and his virtues, which we heard about in the opening scene, as well? He certainly celebrates when he realizes his lost daughter is not lost and has returned, betrothed to Florizel, so a child and heir is
important to him. Again Shakespeare's own situation with a daughter and
son-in-law, is mirrored.

As Perdita and Florizel approach Leontes' court we learn the reason for
the absence of mourning for Mamillius; the father's grief and guilt are so
lacerating that his mind has repressed all conscious memory of his boy,
and this insight supports the view that much of the catharsis we have been
exploring in Shakespeare's plays is not at a fully conscious level. Paulina
has dared to refer to Mamillius, although even she dare not speak his name:

> Had our prince,
> Jewel of children, seen this hour, he had pair'd
> Well with this lord [Florizel]; there was not full a month
> Between their births.
> *Leontes*. Prithee no more; cease. Thou know'st
> *He dies to me again when talk'd of.* Sure
> When I shall see this gentleman, thy speeches
> Will bring me to consider that which may
> *Unfurnish me of reason* (5.1.115–23; my italics).

Even an indirect reference to Mamillius is enough to make Leontes feel he
will lose his reason and go mad if he lets himself think about the boy, again
recalling the frenzied grief of Constance for Prince Arthur and Gloucester's
desire to be distract [*sic*], so his thoughts and his griefs could be severed. By
contrast, Leontes can manage to hear talk about Hermione, even though he
is as guilty of her apparent death as he is of Mamillius'. Significantly, she
does not "die again" when "talked of." The truth then is that Leontes can
speak about and enact penance for the death of Hermione because,
although with difficulty, it can be endured; he cannot talk of and enact penance for Mamillius' death because the searing pain of this loss is *beyond
endurance*. Shakespeare has created a man who has repressed conscious grief
for his son as a way of surviving it, but has found that the grief is still there.

So Shakespeare seems at last to have found the courage and strength,
through Leontes, to express the unending agony and sense of guilt caused
by the loss of a son. The acknowledgment that the pain cannot be forgotten
recalls the words of one of the bereaved fathers Jean Scully counseled:

In response to the question, "How long did it take you to get over the death?" one father told me, "If you mean how long did it take me to resume a normal life, a year or two. But if you mean how long did it take . . . to not miss him, then I'll never be over it."[15]

Bill Merrington quotes the similar experience of another bereaved parent: "If final acceptance is getting over it, then I never will! But if acceptance is missing him, then I am there now."[16]

Shakespeare too is not "over it," for although he is taking another step in his journey by acknowledging the forever loss of Mamillius, and through Mamillius of Hamnet, the end of the play is not as simple as that suggests. Shakespeare clearly links Mamillius and Florizel—they are almost twins, born within a month of each other, as Paulina told us. Indeed, beginning in Act 4 of this play, set in Bohemia, Shakespeare presents Florizel as Leontes' *substitute son*, a replacement for Mamillius. This is done through a partial reenactment of the events of the first three acts; Leontes' angry destruction of his family in Sicily is echoed in Bohemia by Polixenes' rage against Florizel for wanting to marry against his father's wishes. Camillo advises Florizel to escape his father's anger by fleeing with Perdita to Sicily and throwing himself on the mercy of Leontes. Camillo then imagines Leontes desiring to atone for his earlier suspicion that Polixenes had betrayed him with Hermione, and that Florizel's arrival will give him the opportunity to do so. He pictures Leontes saying to Florizel, "*Son*, forgiveness!" and continues, "As 'twere i' th' father's person," meaning that Leontes is really asking Polixenes to forgive him, but as Polixenes is not there, he has to ask Polixenes' son Florizel instead (4.4.549–50; my italics). But as often in Shakespeare, the actual wording is revealing: Leontes is not presented as saying, "For your father's sake, forgive me," or, "Oh, I wronged your father—forgive me". Rather the contrived situation leads him to say, "*Son*, forgiveness." It is as if in reality Florizel would not be there primarily as a substitute for his father Polixenes, but as *a substitute for Leontes' dead son Mamillius*; as if Leontes needs to ask *his own son* to forgive him because of his deep sense of guilt for Mamillius' death. This develops a motif in *King Lear*, in which Lear asks Cordelia for forgiveness. But Cordelia forgives Lear easily; here, Shakespeare gets closer to facing the bitter truth that the person who needs to say he forgives him is gone for good and that the father will have to carry this guilt without absolution.

This is perhaps another reason why Robert Greene is still in Shakespeare's thoughts; his *Groatsworth of Wit*, in which he had caricatured

Shakespeare as an "upstart crow," had been *bought with a million of Repentance*—the latter phrase could be a summary of Leontes' 16 long years of penance and of the agony Shakespeare is still suffering 14 or so years since Hamnet's death. Similarly, in *The Tempest* Alonso has to ask "my child forgiveness" (5.1.198). Ostensibly, he means his future daughter-in-law Miranda, but he has just been in conversation with his son Ferdinand. Paternal guilt is ocean-deep in several of the plays from *King Lear* onward.

When Perdita and Florizel appear at the Sicilian court, Leontes, not knowing yet that Perdita is his daughter, can at last refer to both his apparently dead children, although still he can only do so by a euphemism:

I *lost* a couple, that 'twixt heaven and earth
Might thus have stood, begetting wonder, as
You, gracious couple, do . . .
                    What might I have been,
Might I a *son and daughter* now have look'd on,
Such goodly things as you? (5.1.132–4; 176–8; my italics).

There is a happy irony for the audience *and for Shakespeare*, for we know Perdita is that lost daughter, that Leontes' daughter is standing before him; but equally significant is the image of a father longing to see together a "son and daughter," an impossibility now for Shakespeare, as Leontes thinks it is for him. Interestingly, Florizel, *well before* Leontes knows he will become his son-in-law, is brought into this fantasy family as a substitute son, as Lysimachus was in *Pericles*, again presenting the possibility of a partial fulfillment through a daughter and son-in-law.[17]

Yet as Florizel is almost the copy of Mamillius that's dead, he does not escape entirely the imagery of death associated with the boy. In the previous act, before his father's anger had forced him to flee Bohemia, Florizel, disguised as a shepherd, went to the sheep-shearing festival to be with Perdita. She clearly loves him deeply and wishes she had the flowers of springtime with which to adorn him. It is a wonderful moment of innocent, youthful fantasy. Yet Florizel inexplicably destroys it by responding, "What? like a corse?" (4.4.129). Certainly flowers could be strewn over corpses, but they were also associated with lovers courting in the natural world and were spread over bridal beds. It is the latter image you would expect to occur to Florizel here, given the clear demonstration of Perdita's undying love. Why does Shakespeare make him think of a corpse at such a moment? Perdita's anxious response reflects this change of mood, "No, like a bank, for love to lie and play on;/Not like a corse;

or if—not to be buried,/But quick and in mine arms" (4.4.130–32, recalling "one that's dead is quick" in *All's Well*; my italics). This plays on the double meaning of 'cor[p]se' in Shakespeare's English as a living as well as a dead person. The moment recalls *Hamlet*, when Gertrude says, as she scatters flowers on Ophelia's coffin, "I thought thy bride-bed to have deck'd, sweet maid,/And not have strew'd thy grave." We may remember that Laertes then jumps into the grave in his desperate desire to hold his sister's dead body in his arms, "Now pile your dust upon the *quick* and dead," and then Hamlet follows him (5.1.245–51). In these examples Laertes/Hamlet and Perdita are two sides of the same coin. Laertes/Hamlet wants to be buried with the corpse he cannot revive; Perdita wants to go a stage further and revive the corpse. I think both instances enact at some level Shakespeare's yearning to be with Hamnet again, and the later example shows that the need to raise the lost one has not been banished by Mamillius' offstage death.

The approximate ages of Mamillius and Leontes are further clues to Shakespeare's personal involvement in his subject matter. We have seen that Mamillius was about seven when he died. Sixteen years have passed since then, so that would make Mamillius (had he lived) and Florizel about 23. Hamnet, had he lived, would have been 23 in 1608, so Leontes' substitute son is about Hamnet's age. Many bereaved parents report that, as the years go by, they imagine what their child would be like had he reached 15, 20, and so on. Greene's Pandosto is about 50, which Shakespeare would not be until 1614. At the beginning of the play, however, when Leontes looked at Mamillius he remembered "myself unbreech'd," and this took him back "twenty-three years" (1.2.155). As breeching took place about the age of seven, this would make Leontes about 30 at the start of the play. Plus 16 years, and he is about 46 at the end, Shakespeare's own age in 1610.[18] I am not arguing for an exact correlation here: Shakespeare is not a mathematician. But the general *similarity* of age between Mamillius/Florizel and Hamnet and between Leontes and Shakespeare is striking; the more so when we shall find that the restored son and heir Guiderius in *Cymbeline* is also 23 at the end of that play. We have seen that this age is associated by Shakespeare with the coming of manhood here and in other plays, so it could be that part of the inner appeal for Shakespeare in presenting Mamillius/Florizel and then Guiderius as 23-year-olds is that he can imagine what Hamnet might have been like had he come to manhood.

It is not only the princes who are twinned; so are the kings. One of the first things we learn is that, as boys, Leontes and Polixenes were "twinn'd lambs" (1.2.67). Of course, a major function of linking them is to make

Leontes' suspicion that Polixenes has slept with his wife as horrifying as possible, twin brother turning against twin brother; but it is not the only function. We have seen that Polixenes reenacts Leontes' angry possessiveness, spying on his son and Perdita, as Leontes had spied on Hermione and Polixenes; and when he forbids Florizel to marry Perdita, he comes near to losing his heir, something that has already happened to Leontes. Florizel's response to the threat of disinheritance is to imagine himself saying to his father, "From my succession wipe me, father, I/Am heir to my affection" (4.4.480–1). The father's rage is in marked contrast to his prototype in Shakespeare's source story, who is "half dead for sorrow . . . conceiving such secret grief for his son's reckless folly."[19] In other words, Polixenes' reenactment of Leontes' wrath is Shakespeare's own invention. Why does he do it?

Of course, one reason may be that intense anger is theatrically effective; but we have seen that a father "more in sorrow than in anger" can be theatrically effective too. Another reason is that this change allows the second father to escape the tragedy of the first one. Although Polixenes reenacts Leontes' destructive possessiveness, he *does not lose his son as a punishment for it.* So, as the substitute son Florizel replaces the dead Mamillius, so the substitute father Polixenes escapes the consequences that befell Leontes. In the opening half of the play, through Mamillius, Shakespeare has looked into the abyss of his own irreparable loss, but it is still too unbearable to view for more than a moment, so has to be replaced, if only by the provision of a substitute son for Leontes, and by a destructive father saved from his own destructiveness. Indeed, visions and magical acts of resurrection dominate Shakespeare's last plays: for instance, Cerimon's revival of the coffined Thaisa (3.2.78ff); Pericles' "dream" of the seemingly dead Marina (5.1.161); Alonso's "vision" of his apparently lost son Ferdinand (5.1.176). Their creator needs to believe in this magic and, in his final play, to make his protagonist a magician so powerful that he can open graves and bring the dead to life, before he can finally let go.

The equivalent in *The Winter's Tale* is Paulina's "lawful" magic in apparently bringing Hermione's statue to life (5.3.111). For members of the first audience who knew Greene's popular *Pandosto*, this must have been an amazing experience; Hermione's equivalent Bellaria has been buried in *Pandosto*, and Shakespeare leads us to believe that Hermione is also dead and buried. A number of Shakespeare's characters practice deception for good purposes, but the audience is normally in on the secret; here, very unusually, Shakespeare deceives his audience. The "proofs" of death are strong: when he first realizes the extent of his wrongdoing, Leontes says that he is going to see the dead bodies of his queen and son, and that they shall be buried in "one grave" (3.2.234–6); Antigonus has a vision of Hermione as a spirit of the dead, who names her baby daughter Perdita, as she is "counted lost *for ever*" (3.3.16; 31–3); and while the oracle has hinted that Perdita might not be lost for ever, it makes no mention of a possible change of fate for Hermione (3.2.135–6). So what do we make of this deception?

As in the tragedy most like *The Winter's Tale*, *King Lear*, we are given two possibilities: skepticism and faith. But in *King Lear* the balance is in favor of skepticism, an absence of resurrection, definitely in the earlier *Quarto* version, more uncertainly in the *Folio* text. Here, the balance is the other way, an exploring of different possibilities in the same situation that we have seen is typical of unresolved grief. A brief rational explanation is provided for those who want it: Paulina has hidden Hermione away for 16 years while they waited to see if the lost one would be found. But Shakespeare's interest in this seems minimal; how Paulina prevented Hermione being buried with Mamillius in "one grave," and how she managed to take food and water to Hermione without anyone noticing, is not considered. Rather, the scene is presented to us as if a magical resurrection is taking place, so that, in Pitcher's words, it is not "reason that is overwhelmed, but corrosive doubt."[20]

As Sean Benson points out, Shakespeare prepares us in the long, restorative scene at the sheep-shearing when Camillo suggests to Florizel how he can escape from his father's wrath and control, and marry Perdita; it would be "almost a miracle," says Florizel.[21] And it is "almost a miracle" we see at the end of the play, a ceremonial miracle. The reunion of Hermione and Leontes, and Hermione and Perdita, is presented ritualistically, in contrast to the destruction of ritual enacted by Leontes at the beginning of the play; and, very interestingly, it is a female semi-priestly figure who conducts the ceremony. Of course, this can be explained by the pagan setting, but it certainly adds a radical element to the (apparent? actual?) resurrection. As Pitcher notes, the scene, set in a private chapel, also has remembrances of Catholicism, with an apparent statue curtained off as in some Catholic churches, a statue carved by Giulio Romano, associated with Rome and the world of the papacy; and, most daringly, Perdita kneeling before the "statue," as a Catholic might. Shakespeare is aware of the controversial nature of this last example, Perdita asserting, "do not say 'tis superstition," as many Protestants would (5.3.43).[22] Paulina offers Leontes and Perdita the chance to leave the chapel; if they are to stay, "It is requir'd/You do *awake your faith*" (5.3.94–5; my italics). Shakespeare is again aware of a possible hostile audience response, and Paulina says she is afraid Leontes will think her "assisted/By wicked powers" (5.3.90–1). They do awake their faith, and Paulina performs the almost-miracle of making the statue move.

Among many things happening here, Shakespeare is creating *his own ritual*, something we will also find him doing in *Cymbeline*. This takes us back to Stephen Greenblatt's argument that *Hamlet* expresses dissatisfaction with the truncated burial ceremony of Protestantism, and that Shakespeare recognized that theater could fill some of the emotional void that the colder, more rational approach of some Protestant reformers had created. It also recalls the debate about art and nature near the beginning of the sheep-shearing festival, another kind of ceremony Shakespeare clearly remembers with fondness, when Polixenes argues that art can "mend Nature—change it rather; but/The art itself is Nature" (4.4.96–7). In other words, to use art to heal the things that go wrong in the world we live in, as Shakespeare is doing, is a natural thing to do.

Here the "resurrection" of the wife is emphasized much more than in *Pericles* (even allowing for the loss of some lines from the latter). Most obviously, this relates to the "death" of Shakespeare's relationship with Anne during his long years in London and a hope that she will accept him back, forgive him for those things that need to be forgiven, and that they can reestablish real love between them. But is that all that is happening here? Geoffrey Bullough provides convincing evidence that Shakespeare knew *The Rare Triumphs of Love and Fortune*, author unknown, published in 1589, at a time when Shakespeare was probably starting to write plays and may well have been reading examples in print as well as watching plays in performance. Its influence is seen most strongly in *Cymbeline* and *The Tempest*, but I think it is present in *The Winter's Tale* as well.[23] Perhaps Shakespeare remembered *The Rare Triumphs* clearly, or (re)read it around this time; we have already seen him go back to *Pandosto* for his source story. Or it may have been revived on stage because of the fashion for romance (as we know *Mucedorus*, probably dating from the 1590s, was, from the notice accompanying the *Third Quarto*). Interestingly, the Hermione in *The Rare Triumphs* is the *son* of Bomelio, (a hermit magician like Prospero in *The Tempest*), and has been separated from his father for many years. In terms of its origin, the name Hermione is linked to Hermes—another male figure—which in turn seems to come from the piles of stones used originally to mark the boundary between territories. This association is taken up when the apparent statue of Hermione seems to come to life at the end of *The Winter's Tale*. It is certainly Leontes' wife who is seemingly being returned to life, albeit played by a male; but the sexual ambiguity of the name Hermione suggests that once again at some level in Shakespeare's imagination the "resurrection" might not be the only one present. As Hans Urs von Balthasar wrote about Shakespeare's romances, "In these self-contained plays the Christian resurrection from the dead becomes the reappearance of those believed dead." Balthasar also calls these plays "a pure gift to those in mourning," because of the accuracy with which they present, and the hope with which they invest, the mourning process.[24]

And Hermione is not the only ambiguous name in this play: Mamillius, Shakespeare's invention, is a second one. Again, Shakespeare seems to have been thinking back to Robert Greene, whose *Mamillia* is the story of a *woman* duped by her (false) lover. Greene's choice of name is quintessentially feminine, referring to the mamma, the breast and/or nipple, a basic difference between a woman and a man; and yet Shakespeare makes the name masculine. Why does he do this? A possible explanation is suggested by the dialogue from Scene 1 quoted earlier. Mamillius "physics the subject, makes old hearts fresh;" his growth to manhood is the reason why those "on crutches ... desire to live." So Mamillius is like the mother's breast, sustaining life; and the loss of the son is like the loss of the mother's breast to a baby.[25] Shakespeare has now traveled further than ever before in allowing emotions associated with loss, especially the loss of his son, strongly linked now to the wider sense of his separation from his wife and daughters, to be invoked in his fiction.

Notes

Full publication details of every source are in the bibliography.

1. Duncan-Jones, *Shakespeare's Sonnets*, p. 13. Some commentators think the publication of the *Sonnets* in 1609 was without Shakespeare's agreement, and that it was, in effect, a pirated edition.

2. Pitcher, *The Winter's Tale*, pp. 87–8.

3. Quoted in Bryson, *Shakespeare*, p. 148.

4. Gurr, *Philaster*, pp. xlv-l.

5. Valerie Wayne kindly sent me her paper, "*Don Quixote* and Shakespeare's Collaborative Turn to Romance," before its publication in *The Quest for Shakespeare's Cardenio*, edited by David Carnegie and Gary Taylor.

6. Wells and Taylor, *William Shakespeare, A Textual Companion*, p. 131.

7. Schoeenbaum, *William Shakespeare: A Compact Documentary Life*, p. 151. There are indications that Shakespeare was, understandably, hurt by Greene's attack, and remembered it at various points in his career. For instance, Polonius comments on the word "beautified" in Hamlet's letter to Ophelia, "That's an ill phrase, a vile phrase, 'beautified' is a vile phrase" (2.2.111–2). This is at least seven years after the *Groatsworth of Wit*, and is further evidence of a characteristic

we have seen in Shakespeare: that things which pierce him deeply remain with him for a long time.

8. Greenblatt, *Will in the World*, pp. 216–25.

9. *Pandosto*, is in Bullough, *Narrative and Dramatic Sources of Shakespeare*, Volume 8, pp.156–99. He also prints extracts from *The Rare Triumphs of Love and Fortune*, discussed later in this and subsequent chapters, on pp. 90–103.

10. Pitcher, *The Winter's Tale* p. 6.

11. The *Folio* reading of Mamillius' final words to his father, "I am like you say," is usually changed to "I am like you, they say," which also suggests the child's confusion and sense of being at the mercy of other people's definitions but perhaps carries a desire to reassure his father as well. The change may be correct, and is more regular rhythmically; but the broken rhythm of the *Folio* reading would certainly fit with Mamillius' defeated resignation to his father's inability to listen to him. In "Mamillius and Leontes: Their Final Exchange," Susan Bruce argues as I do that the *Folio* words make sense, but punctuates them very differently: "I am like you. Say." There are strong arguments for both changes, but I still think that the original text and punctuation make sense and do not need emendation.

12. Pitcher, *The Winter's Tale*, p. 140.

13. Pitcher, p. 38.

14. Pitcher, p. 141.

15. Scully, "Men and Grieving," p. 100.

16. Merrington, *Suffering Love*, p. 59.

17. When Leontes discovers that Perdita is his daughter, she can, to some extent, take the place of Mamillius in his affection. In *Shakespeare*, Peter Ackroyd suggests that this may have been represented physically on Shakespeare's stage, with the boy who took the part of Mamillius also playing Perdita (p. 287, Anchor edition, p. 270 Chatto and Windus). This would be a powerful visualization of twins and more acceptable on the Jacobean stage when audiences came under less social pressure to be literal-minded. On the modern stage it would be more difficult to have a young male present convincingly a seven-year-old boy and a 16-year-old young woman.

18. Pitcher, *The Winter's Tale*, p. 140.

19. Bullough, Narrative and Dramatic Sources of Shakespeare, Volume 8, p. 191.

20. Pitcher, p. 72.

21. Benson, Shakespearean Resurrection, p. 163.

22. Pitcher, pp. 46 and 66.

23. Bullough, *Narrative and Dramatic Sources of Shakespeare*, Volume 8, pp. 21–3, 26, 27, 34, 37, and 251. It is possibly a memory of *The Rare Triumphs* that underlies Malvolio's memorable line in *Twelfth Night*, "My masters, are you mad?" (2.3.86). In the earlier play Vulcan asks, "Are ye mad, my masters?" (*The Rare Triumphs* online, image 5 right hand column).

24. Balthasar, *Theo-Drama*, Volume 1, p. 384, quoted in Benson, *Shakespearean Resurrection*, pp. 1 and 160.

25. Katherine Duncan-Jones points out that Greene is visited by the spirits of Chaucer and Gower in *Mamillia*, and this may have been an influence on *Pericles*. She also notes that Autolycus' tricks have been influenced by Greene's *The Second Part of Conny-Catching*, showing the extent to which Greene is still in Shakespeare's mind.

13

Grief, Ceremony, and Repeated Restoration: Behold Divineness/ No Elder Than a Boy

The Winter's Tale acknowledged that a bereaved father might find it unbearable to think about and hear his son "talked of," although many years had passed since the death, but equally that the child needed to be thought about and "talked of." *Cymbeline*, probably written shortly before or shortly after *The Winter's Tale* (or even overlapping with it), was seen by Simon Forman towards the end of April 1611; again this may have been a first or early performance. In it Shakespeare recognizes more than ever before that a dead child needs to be mourned *ritualistically*, and that the ritual might have to be of the mourner's invention.

Set in a Britain under the threat of Roman invasion in the years before the birth of Christ, *Cymbeline* is not well-known or popular, and it is easy to see why: the play is one of Shakespeare's longest and contains his most complicated plot—convoluted might be a better word—at times proving hard to follow even for theatergoers familiar with his works. Why did he, with 20 years and more theatrical experience, write such a difficult-to-follow and lengthy play? The answer is complex, involving such political matters as the wish to set part of the play in Wales in honor of the investiture of Henry as Prince of Wales in June 1610; but the aspect I will concentrate on lies in the need to contrive a situation where ceremonial mourning can be introduced into the plot.[1] James Nosworthy sensed something of this personal element when he wrote that *Cymbeline* "has the appearance of being the outcome of some peculiar, and perhaps decisive, turning point in Shakespeare's private or personal life."[2] Roger Warren wrote more specifically of the mourning scene (Act 4, Scene 2) as "so extraordinary that one feels it must have been Shakespeare's starting-point, that it was, so to speak, *what he wrote the play for.*" He adds that there is nothing in the source stories to suggest it, "and yet Shakespeare prepares for this climactic episode from much earlier in the play."[3]

The build-up to Act 4 Scene 2 is extremely complicated. King Cymbeline's two young sons and heirs, Guiderius and Arviragus, were stolen by Belarius 20 years before the start of the play, and he has brought them up as his own children, so Cymbeline, in a now-familiar pattern, has a daughter, Imogen, for his heir.[4] In the middle of the play Imogen flees from her husband Posthumus' jealousy and disguises herself as a young male, calling herself Fidele, the faithful one. This reminds us of Portia, Rosalind, and Viola—three such disguises within four to five years—but also of the fact that Shakespeare has not presented such a disguise for nine or so years, perhaps having felt he had exhausted its potential by the end of *Twelfth Night*. Wandering in the mountains near Milford Haven, Imogen/Fidele stumbles upon the cave where Belarius has brought up Guiderius, now 23, and Arviragus, 22. Belarius' motive in stealing the young boys is telling. Banished unjustly by Cymbeline, he thought "to *bar thee* [= Cymbeline] *of succession*" (3.3.102; my italics). We may recall this motif in *Macbeth*, and it recurs in all the late plays: the fear of having no son and heir. Here, it is explored through a pair of father figures, as it was in *King Lear* and will be in *The Tempest*.

As soon as the father-figure Belarius meets (what he thinks is) the boy Fidele he loves him, and praises him in terms that recall Mamillius in *The Winter's Tale*: "By Jupiter, an angel! or if not/An earthly paragon! Behold *divineness*/No elder than a *boy*" (3.6.42–4; my italics). Shakespeare is again idealizing almost the copy of his child that's dead. Immediately Guiderius and Arviragus also fall in love with him. Arviragus says, "I'll love him as my brother" and later imagines that if either his father or this young boy had to die, "I'd say/'My father, not this youth'" (3.6.71; 4.2.23–4). Suddenly Shakespeare introduces the frightening possibility that this divine boy Fidele might meet the fate of Prince Arthur, Prince Mamillius and Hamnet himself, and be carried to his grave. Once more Shakespeare is giving his own experience "repetition to the life."

Arviragus' words certainly relate to the political themes of *Cymbeline*, suggesting that as a child of royal birth he intuitively responds to a kinswoman, even if she is in disguise and he has never met her! A further implication is that Arviragus also senses that Belarius is not his real father. But these are not the only levels operating here. How many bereaved parents must have wished that in fact they had died rather than their child, the wish put in disguised form into Arviragus' mouth? Many therapists and counselors report parents saying things like, "It should have been me" who died.[5] And this anguished wish occurs in some of mankind's earliest writings, such as King David's desire that he had died instead of his rebellious son Absalom—a story Shakespeare would certainly have known.[6]

By the time of *The Tempest* Shakespeare can express this desire more directly. When Alonso learns that Prospero too has apparently lost his child, he exclaims, "O heavens, that they were living both in Naples,/The King and Queen there! That they were, I wish/Myself were mudded in that oozy bed/Where my son lies" (5.1.149–52). Alonso wishes he had died instead of his son—evidence of Shakespeare's continuing agony over the loss of Hamnet. And now Arviragus' strange fantasy of Fidele dying happens, and Shakespeare reenacts, albeit still in disguised form, the devastating loss of his boy. Although we know that it is Imogen, and that, like Juliet, she is only in a drugged sleep, for the characters onstage the divine Fidele appears to die, and this leads into the longest scene of mourning in Shakespeare, its length unnecessary in terms of plot, but I would argue necessary emotionally.[7]

Shakespeare prepares us for this death in the early part of the scene, creating an imaginative world of death and grief before the apparently-dead apparently-boy is carried in. At its beginning, Fidele, feeling very sick, talks of "clay" and "dust," words that suggest mortality and, "dust" in particular, the burial service (4.2.4–5). It is the "ninth hour" (4.2.30); this is the time, according to the gospels of Matthew and Mark, when Jesus cried out, "My God, my God, why hast thou forsaken me?" and then died.[8] And Belarius reminds his "sons" of the need to go and hunt by saying, "It is great morning," meaning broad daylight (4.2.61). But it is also great *mourning* that we are to experience when Fidele is carried in. Indeed, Shakespeare has prepared us for this moment even earlier, when in Act 2 we saw Iachimo in Imogen's bedchamber as she slept, and he wished her to lie senseless and still "as a monument,/Thus in a chapel lying," that is as a carved effigy on a tomb (2.2.32–3).

The great mourning begins when Arviragus is heard offstage playing an instrument that has not been played since the death of his (supposed) mother, Belarius' wife Euriphile. Guiderius, not knowing what he is about to see, is horrified that his brother is playing it and exclaims, "Triumphs for nothing, and lamenting toys,/Is jollity for apes, and grief for boys" (4.2.193–4). Literally, he means that fools enjoy making triumphs out of things of no importance, and that boys lament the loss of trivial things. But again the phrasing hides a second meaning, for deep grief for the "boy" Fidele is what Shakespeare is about to present.

Then Arviragus enters with, Guiderius and Belarius suppose, Fidele, "*dead*" in his arms, according to the stage direction in the *Folio*. One editor, not surprisingly, changed this to the more literally accurate "as dead" because Fidele is only in a drugged sleep.[9] But "dead" is really better because it indicates how Shakespeare wants us to experience the scene. As Roger Warren comments, the intensity of the moment encourages us to forget that this is Imogen in disguise, not Fidele, and that she is only sleeping: "And yet the reaction of an audience, in all the productions I have seen or been involved in has been the same: a hushed, tense stillness in which, so to speak, they seem to suppress that factual knowledge."[10] That is, Shakespeare creates a scene where, in the short term, most of the audience react as if the boy has indeed died, and can feel something of the agony that Shakespeare himself might still be feeling, while having, in the long term, the reassurance that he is not really a he but a she, and is not really dead. This effect illustrates one of the attractions of the romance play for Shakespeare: it allows him to separate family members, become involved, and make his audience involved, in their unendurable sufferings, even apparent deaths, within a structure that promises that they will eventually be at least partially reunited. In other words, it allows both great involvement *in*, and distance *from*, these agonies *simultaneously*, and as such carries further the cathartic process. Terrifying sufferings, such as the seeming death of an innocent young boy, can be enacted and *controlled* within this structure.

Shakespeare may have been remembering an earlier scene as he wrote this one, for the moment recalls the pietà-like image of Lear carrying the truly dead body of Cordelia, perhaps firmly in Shakespeare's mind if he had been revising the earlier version of *King Lear* recently. Arviragus' language reinforces this connection, recalling Lear's earlier words before he and Cordelia are taken to prison: "We two alone will sing like birds i' th' cage" (*King Lear*, 5.3.9). Arviragus' words are, "The bird is dead/That we have made so much on" (4.2.197–8).

Tellingly, however, the main expression of grief at this point comes not from Arviragus, but from the father figure Belarius. Although still in disguise, the play contrives a situation where we can have an agonized enactment of a "father's" grief at the loss of his "son". It was also Belarius' own "ingenious instrument" that provided the solemn music preceding Arviragus' entry carrying Fidele, so the father figure is given a crucial role in the mourning process (4.2.186). Belarius exclaims:

> O melancholy,
> Who ever yet could sound thy bottom? find
> The ooze to show what coast thy sluggish crare [small boat]
> Might easil'est harbor in? Thou blessed thing,
> Jove knows what man thou mightst have made; but I,
> Thou diedst, a most rare boy, of melancholy (4.2.203–8).

We may remember that in *The Tempest* Alonso responds with a similar image when he thinks his "trespass" has resulted in his son drowning: he wishes to "lie *mudded*" with Ferdinand "deeper than e'er plummet sounded ... *i' th' ooze*" (my italics). In *King Lear* Gloucester also wishes to fall from Dover Cliff into the sea when he knows that his folly has led to the persecution of his loving son Edgar. Shakespeare seems to associate a father's grief with sinking to the bottom of a sea or ocean and on into the mud, as if it were quicksand. And Belarius, again like Gloucester and Alonso, is made a man of melancholy, of depression and despair, by his grief.

But do the references to melancholy that open and close Belarius' speech just refer to himself, the father figure, or does the second one refer to the boy as well? Did Fidele die of melancholy, or is it the father whose overwhelming melancholy begins and ends his exclamation? I think the ambiguity of the speech's structure allows "father" and "son" to merge in a single image of melancholy that encloses the whole speech, just as father and son merge in the last act of *Hamlet*, and Alonso wishes to merge with Ferdinand in *The Tempest*. The convoluted nature of the utterance, indeed of the play as a whole, enacts the protracted search for a new relationship with the dead person, which we have seen is common after bereavement. We might expect "Thou diest a most rare boy" for someone who has only just died, but "diedst" is a very definite past tense and occurs nowhere else in Shakespeare (whereas "diest" occurs 22 times), as if the event being commemorated happened some time ago. And when we come to the end of this long scene of mourning, it is also Belarius who is given the final words over Fidele's body. One purpose of this funeral scene is to show the civilized behavior of Guiderius and Arviragus, really royal princes of course, and behaving as princes should even though they had been brought up in the wild Welsh mountains; but that could have been shown without the apparent death of Fidele. Indeed, if that is its only purpose, it is strange that the father figure Belarius is given such an important role. To show a father's mourning for a divine boy is clearly important to Shakespeare as well.

Returning to the earlier part of the scene, Arviragus describes how he found Fidele "Thus smiling, as some fly had tickled slumber/ . . . his right cheek/Reposing on a cushion" (4.2.210–2). If Fidele is dead, it is a painless, smiling end—what a parent would wish for a child who has to die. When Guiderius speaks about Fidele, we hear Shakespeare's typical exploration of all the possibilities of the situation. Guiderius sets hope against the father figure's despairing picture of melancholy: "Why, he but sleeps!/If he be gone he'll make his grave a *bed*," again anticipating Alonso's "my son i'th' ooze is *bedded*," and "I wish/Myself were mudded in that oozy *bed*" (4.2.216–7; my italics). Guiderius' image is gentle and tender, and he goes on to imagine female fairies protecting Fidele's body from something that repeatedly troubled Shakespeare—being eaten by worms. (If a man's body lasts about eight years in the ground before it rots, as the First Gravedigger states in *Hamlet*, Hamnet's body, and even Shakespeare's father's, will have been consumed by now, in 1610, unless they have received such protection).

Indeed, Shakespeare seems to feel the absence of, and need of, a female presence to complete the funeral ceremony he is inventing, for he allocates to Arviragus a catalogue of appropriate flowers, a role normally given to a woman like Ophelia or Perdita. One of the list, the delicate "azur'd harebell, like thy veins," is not mentioned elsewhere in Shakespeare (4.2.232). It normally starts flowering in July or August, and perhaps was new on the ground when Hamnet died. Arviragus also imagines that, when winter comes, the raddock [robin] will cover the grave with flowers. That Shakespeare is uneasy with Arviragus speaking in this way is shown when Guiderius rebukes his younger brother: "And do not play in wench-like words with that/Which is so serious" (4.2.230–1). Yet Shakespeare feels the need to include these "wench-like words," even though they do not exactly fit any of the characters onstage, recalling Stanley Wells' comment about the introspection of these last plays. Arviragus had begun, "With fairest flowers/ *Whilst summer lasts* and I live here, Fidele,/I'll sweeten thy sad grave" (4.2.219–21; my italics). This recalls Marina laying a carpet of flowers on her nurse's tomb, "*While summer days doth last*," and Perdita's flower catalogue in *The Winter's Tale*, when "the year growing ancient,/*Not yet on summer's death*, nor on the birth/Of trembling winter" (*Pericles*, 4.1.18; *The Winter's Tale*, 4.4.79–81; my italics).[11]

It is hard to believe it a coincidence that all three instances in plays written within a few years associate late summer and death, especially when we remember that the major losses of Shakespeare's life happened at this time of year: his father and mother died in early September 1601 and 1608, respectively (his mother after *Pericles* was written), and Hamnet in early August 1596. In addition the James Shakespeare who was born in the same year as Hamnet and who died in September 1589 could have been Shakespeare's Uncle Henry's child; if so this may also have affected Shakespeare deeply.[12] The example from *The Winter's Tale* is especially revealing, since it is spoken at a sheep shearing festival, customarily in June, and yet "the year growing ancient/Not yet on summer's death" suggests late summer. In other words, Shakespeare actually has to distort the time scheme to produce the image he requires. Further on in the scene is Florizel's image of Perdita strewing flowers over his corpse that was discussed in the previous chapter, which links it even more strongly with the other examples.

When we come to the funeral dirge for Fidele, "Fear no more the heat o' th' sun," features that do not fit the dramatic context and suggest that Shakespeare is not just writing out of the needs of the play increase (4.2.258–81). Arviragus tells his brother that they should "use like note and words" as they did for the funeral of their "mother ... Save that Euriphile must be Fidele" (4.2.237–8). This leads us to expect Fidele's name in the lament, or at least words appropriate to a mother's and an adopted brother's situation. Neither happens: the dirge is written in general rather than particular terms, and this is one reason why, like the equally general "To be, or not to be" soliloquy, it has become so successful as an anthology piece; and in both cases this generality suggests they may have been composed *in part* independently of their respective plays, and as a response to intense feelings in Shakespeare's own life. Take the couplet at the end of the first stanza: "Golden lads and girls all must,/As chimney-sweepers, come to dust" (4.2.262–3). Even allowing for Shakespeare's famously cavalier attitude to historical accuracy, it is bizarre to find two young men who have lived in a cave in prehistoric Wales since they were babies referring to chimney-sweepers; but if we think of Shakespeare in part conceiving the dirge outside of its immediate context, the difficulty disappears. From a poetic viewpoint, it is obvious why chimney-sweepers: the black faces contrast with the golden health of the lads and girls of the previous line. At the beginning of the seventeenth century, "An average flue measured nine inches by four inches or eight inches square, and could only be climbed by children."[13] So soot-blackened children, whose faces looked to be turning to dust—a clear symbol of mortality recalling the "dust to dust" of the burial service—as flakes of soot fell off them, would have been a familiar sight to Shakespeare in London.

In other words, the horror of a boy's early death, a death betimes, conjures up for Shakespeare a group of children whose life expectancy was especially low. That this is a very personal image for Shakespeare is supported by Roger Warren's comment that, in Warwickshire dialect, "chimney-sweepers is a name for the spiky heads of plantain," which spectacularly "*come to dust.*"[14]

In the main, however, as Valerie Wayne notes, the dirge, rather than concentrating on the dead boy, emphasizes "what death relieves one from . . . the conditions the mourner must still endure."[15] Like "To be, or not to be," it is in part about the horrors faced by those who *remain alive*, who have to keep going, and it envies those who have escaped this wearisome struggle. For instance, "Fear no more the lightning-flash,/Nor th' all-dreaded thunder-stone./Fear not slander, censure rash./Thou hast finish'd joy and moan" (4.2.270–3).[16] The final stanza prays for protection against such forces as witches and ghosts, which materialize, of course, in other Shakespearean plays. Dirges, the name derived from the opening antiphon in the traditional matins before a burial, had been prohibited by Protestant reformers for involving excessive emotion and superstitious prayer so, as at the end of *The Winter's Tale*, Shakespeare is again developing a *private ritual* that finds features of the Catholic tradition crucial to the range of emotion that needs to be expressed. The force of the lament hoodwinks many of those watching, as Wayne notes: "The song's effect is so moving that audiences do not question the absence of any actual burial" of Fidele. The dramatic context makes burial impossible, since Fidele must come back to life later in the scene, but Shakespeare writes *as if the burial of the "most rare boy" is actually taking place*. It is another instance of the clash between Shakespeare's inner need and the dramatic situation he has created.

Shortly after this Belarius and his "sons" depart to pray elsewhere, and we have an even more contrived situation. Fidele, really Imogen in disguise of course, comes back to consciousness beside a headless body, dressed in her husband Posthumus' clothes. We know the corpse is the villainous Cloten (laid to rest there by Belarius), but Imogen naturally thinks it is her husband and that he has been murdered, and so we enter yet another scene of mourning; but after the calm and dignified sorrow of the men, Imogen's mourning is impassioned, horrified, frantic, broken, as if Shakespeare needs to express this other side of grief as well. For example,

> Murther in heaven? How? 'Tis gone. Pisanio,
> All curses madded Hecuba gave the Greeks,
> And mine to boot, be darted on thee! Thou,

Conspir'd with that irregulous devil Cloten,
Hath here cut off my lord . . .
                                    O Posthumus, alas,
Where is thy head? Where's that? Ay me! where's that? (4.2.312–6; 320–1).

The two scenes of mourning allow Shakespeare to perform a wide range of reactions to loss, while maintaining the pretence that it is only women who need to lament in such "wild and whirling words" (*Hamlet*, 1.5.133). Imogen's horrified grief reaches its climax when she embraces all she thinks remains of her husband, and in doing so smears her cheek with his blood, then faints onto the corpse, again seemingly dead.

An intriguing feature of Imogen's disguise as Fidele is worth exploring here. Imogen becomes more inert as Fidele than she had been as herself. And there is evidence that Shakespeare's first intention was a more active Fidele. When Imogen was preparing to disguise herself as a boy, she was advised to show "waggish courage" and to "present" herself to the invading Roman General, Lucius, and "desire his service" (3.4.157; 173). But this plan was abandoned and replaced by Lucius coming upon an apparently dead body. Further, Fidele is more passive than the disguised heroines in Shakespeare's source stories, and than Shakespeare's own earlier disguised heroines, especially Portia and Rosalind. Rather Fidele seems to come from the same mould as the princes Arthur, Hamlet, and Troilus—young men whose inertia I am arguing goes back in part to feelings connected with Hamnet.

Through this long scene of mourning Shakespeare is moving forward on his journey, approaching the point at which he will be able to leave behind his need to present his disguised child onstage; but how hard it is for Shakespeare to let go is shown by the way images of father-son and substitute father-substitute son separations and magical reunions recur in *Cymbeline* as never before in his plays, often independently of the requirements of the plot.

Your Low-Laid Son Our Godhead Will Uplift

The play begins with another idealized son, Leonatus. He is matchless: looking for his like "there would be something failing/In him that should compare" (1.1.21–2). He is *Posthumus* Leonatus, Shakespeare's choice of name rather than one found in the stories of Cymbeline's reign, and is the subject of the first father-son separation we encounter. When Posthumus' father lost his two elder sons in war, we are told that he "took such sorrow/That he *quit being*" (1.1.37–8; my italics). This father's answer to Hamlet's question, "To be, or not to be," was that it is not worth being without his sons, and so he gave up the ghost, even though his wife was pregnant. Posthumus' mother survived only long enough for Posthumus to be born. So as a young man Leonatus had a doubly post-humous life, a life after both his parents have been laid under the humus. Many years before the start of the play Cymbeline adopted the orphan and named him, as Lear had named Edgar, perhaps in part as a substitute for his own baby boys abducted by Belarius—a further father-son separa-tion. We hear that in his "spring [he] became a harvest," meaning that Posthumus, although still young, ripened; but again there might be unconscious associations for Shakespeare of a young lad in the spring-time of his life who did indeed become a harvest, dying at harvest-time (1.1.46).

Near the beginning of the play, Posthumus' secret marriage to Imogen angers the King, and like Cordelia he is banished for ever, so he loses his adoptive father as well—a third father-son separation. He continues in this orphaned state until the penultimate scene, by which time he is a prisoner-of-war in one of Cymbeline's stockades, resigned to execution. Here he has a vision of his dead family—father, mother, and two brothers. The scene is one of the most criticized in Shakespeare because it seems to come out of nothing that has gone before, because the writing is below Shakespeare's usual standard, and because it is only loosely tied to the rest of the plot by a patriotic prophecy tagged on at the end. If Shakespeare's main purpose were that prophecy, why did he bother with the long vision presenting the dead family?

I think the main reason is that this vision again fulfills an emotional need, presenting an image of a reunited family, and of parents needing to berate God for their loss and for His failure to protect their son. Father further complains that he will be deprived of an heir when Posthumus is executed. As the play is set in pre-Christian times, the God berated is Jupiter, but clearly similar complaints could be made against the Christian God. Jupiter appears and counsels patience promising to raise Posthumus' fortunes and to increase his happiness *because* of his affliction, "Whom best I love I *cross*; to make my gift,/ *The more delay'd, delight'd*. Be content,/Your *low-laid* son our godhead will uplift" (5.4.101–3; my italics). "The more delay'd, delight'd,"—as we have seen, this could be an epigraph for several plays from *Measure for Measure* onward, as Shakespeare holds onto the hope of future delight ending long pain.[17] The phrase "low-laid son" is unexpected, however: Posthumus is not literally low-laid in a grave, (which is what the word means in its only other use in Shakespeare, by Prince Arthur). Certainly he is in the lowest of social circumstances as a prisoner condemned to death; but it is as if Jupiter is speaking *after* Posthumus has been killed and laid in the earth and that He is going to raise the dead son out of the tomb as God did Jesus. Indeed, despite the fact that Jupiter is a pagan deity, there are obvious Christian associations: God loved His only son "best," and yet He allowed him to be nailed to a *cross* then *low-laid* in a tomb, before *uplifting* him in resurrection.

But for now there is further delay. Posthumus' vision, like the one Prospero will create in *The Tempest*, proves insubstantial: the visionary figures "went hence so soon as they were born" (5.4.216). But if the son cannot be reunited with his natural family except in a vision, Shakespeare is going to allow him to be reunited with his adoptive father, Cymbeline, his two abducted brothers and his sister/wife, Princess Imogen. The prophecy that follows the vision confirms that Jupiter has marked Posthumus out as someone special. Part of the prophecy relates to the political and patriotic themes in the play, and King James' presentation of himself as a man of peace and plenty; but part of it hints that the soon-to-be-uplifted Posthumus will find his true home when Cymbeline's fragmented family is restored, "when from a stately cedar shall be lopp'd branches which, *being dead many years, shall after revive, be jointed to the old stock, and freshly grow*; then shall Posthumus end his miseries" (5.4.140-3; my italics). Posthumus does not understand the prediction (and nor does an audience fully at this point), but he senses, "The action of my life is like it" (5.4.149). He has faith, as Leontes and Pericles have faith, and the final scene justifies this. All these plays emphasize the importance of *hope through believing the impossible.*

This final scene also continues the idealization of Imogen, but significantly still in the guise of Fidele, not as herself. We left Fidele collapsed on the ground, apparently dead, and there he is found by the leader of the Roman invaders, General Lucius. Like Belarius, Guiderius, and Arviragus, Lucius is immediately entranced by Fidele, and when the boy revives the General wishes to adopt him as his page and *substitute son*, saying to Fidele he would "rather *father* thee than master thee" (4.2.395; my italics). So we have yet another father-son relationship set up, which leads to yet another separation in the final scene, after the Romans have been defeated by the Britains. Lucius is brought before Cymbeline, and his love for his surrogate son makes him plead for the boy's life above his own, as a real father might, reminding us of Arviragus' earlier wish for the father to die instead of the son, "This one thing only/I will entreat: my boy, a Britain born,/Let him be ransom'd. Never master had/A page so kind, so duteous, diligent" (5.5.83–6). Cymbeline's reply shows he hardly needed Lucius' prompt. He has been surprised by joy, also finding himself enraptured by Fidele. Of course, this is his disguised daughter, so we may expect an intuitive response to her, but it is significant that it is as a *boy* that the father is drawn to the figure before him, "Boy,/Thou hast look'd thyself into my grace,/And art mine own. I know not why, wherefore,/To say 'Live, boy,'" (5.5.93-6; my italics). 'Live, boy'—what bereaved father, as Cymbeline thinks he is, would not die to speak those words? What might Shakespeare have felt as he wrote them? They recall Jupiter's promise to Posthumus' parents, "Your low-laid son our godhead will uplift," and in fiction the writer has the godlike power to do just that. But in the context of Imogen's disguise as Fidele, it also recalls Richard Wheeler's suggestion about Portia, Rosalind and Viola—that at a deep level Shakespeare might wish he could replace his surviving twin Judith with Hamnet, even though he may love both of them dearly. As David Malan noted, such contradictory emotions are often present simultaneously after the devastation of grief. Further, we have seen that it is not just Fidele's blood relations but Belarius and Lucius as well who are attracted to this "divineness/No elder than a boy." Fidele is the boy of boys, and everyone who sees him falls in love with him—an idealized picture of a boy who does not exist, except in Shakespeare's imagination.

Bill Merrington reports one bereaved parent as saying, "I think about him daily, in fact more so now he's dead than when he was alive. *You don't need to think about them if they are alive*."[18] From the parents he interviewed, Merrington found that more than half had not come through their anguish after five years, and that as many as three out of every five said they still had problems to resolve relating to their child's death after 10 years.[19] And we saw in Chapter 3 that bereaved parents were ringing the Child Death Helpline as much as 50 years after their loss. So Shakespeare's continuing deep preoccupation with characters who are, in part, fictional versions of his boy is neither unusual nor surprising.

Having been spared death, however, Fidele does not return his substitute father's favor and beg for Lucius' life, and the General becomes disillusioned, "The boy disdains me./He leaves me, scorns me. Briefly *die their joys*/That place them on the truth of girls and boys" (5.5.105–7; my italics). The play is given to these general couplets about children, especially boys: "Triumphs for nothing, and lamenting toys,/Is jollity for apes, and grief for boys," and "Golden lads and girls all must,/As chimney-sweepers, come to dust." We've already noticed the awkwardness of chimney-sweepers in prehistoric Wales. Similarly, Lucius' generalization here is hardly justified by the dramatic circumstance; which other girls and boys have let him down? True, the phrase is proverbial; but why does *this* proverb occur to Lucius, or rather to Shakespeare, at this moment? It suggests there are strong associations between children, especially boys, and grief and death in Shakespeare's mind, and that he found himself inventing couplets that enact these associations, perhaps independently of the dramatic context. This is not the only play in which boys and grief are associated: the Fool in *King Lear* tells us, "He's mad that trusts in the tameness of a wolf, a horse's health, a boy's love, or a whore's oath" (3.6.18–19). Lucius' couplet that we started with emphasizes yet another separation between a father figure and a (substitute) son.

Belarius and his "sons" Guiderius and Arviragus, now in Cymbeline's army, hear this dialogue and are of course amazed to see Fidele alive; and through their reactions, Shakespeare presents again the wonder of imagined resurrection:

> *Belarius.* Is not this boy reviv'd from death?
> *Arviragus.* One sand another
> Not more resembles that sweet rosy lad
> Who died, and was Fidele. What think you?
> *Guiderius.* The same dead thing alive . . .
> *But we see him dead* (5.5.120–3, 126—the last line in the *Folio* wording;
> my italics).

True, "see" could mean "saw" in Shakespeare's English; but why not use "saw," which occurs more than 270 times elsewhere in Shakespeare, if a definite past tense is meant? The phrase as it stands recalls the disciples' amazement at Jesus' resurrection, and its continuous present tense recalls Don Pedro's "The former Hero! Hero that is dead!" in Shakespeare's first tentative resurrection of a seemingly dead child in *Much Ado*.

Typically, however, Shakespeare prolongs his characters' wait for reunion and not merely for dramatic effect; indeed, the prolonged nature of the ending is one of the features that contributes to the infrequent productions of *Cymbeline*. Now he brings Posthumus, released from prison, back into the plot. Posthumus fails to recognize the disguised Imogen and, when she tries to speak to him, strikes what he thinks is Fidele, who falls down, seemingly dead, yet another enactment of apparent death for the "most rare boy." But Posthumus' servant has recognized Imogen and speaks her name. The focus now switches to her father, Cymbeline. On hearing the name "Imogen" he starts to speak like other Shakespearean fathers reunited with their lost ones after so very, very long; for instance, Gloucester, whose heart "burst smilingly", and Pericles, who felt "the great sea of joys" might "drown him." Cymbeline exclaims, "the gods do mean to strike me/To death with mortal joy" (5.5.234–5). In these instances Shakespeare senses a limit to the extremities of hope-despair that an exhausted father can endure. And what does this father see when Imogen/Fidele revives? A daughter in son's clothing, *a twin both female and male, uplifted from the dead*. The image allows Shakespeare to picture Hamnet alive without Judith dead, and so to avoid the sense of guilt that might go with replacing his living twin with his dead one. Imogen/Fidele confirms this miracle of rebirth, saying, "I was dead," not "I was as one who had died" (5.5.259). And there is nothing in the *Folio* text to indicate that Imogen changes from her male costume by the end of the play, so we are left with the image of the divine boy that we have had for nearly half the play, just as we were left with Cesario rather than Viola at the end of *Twelfth Night.*

But despite the plentiful imagery of apparent death and rebirth, Shakespeare seems to need more, as if it creates an emotional high he cannot relinquish. The next matter to be unveiled in this very complicated ending—the killing of the villainous Cloten, which Guiderius freely confesses—leads to yet another image of a son's death, this time killed by his unaware father. Cymbeline responds to Guiderius' confession, not knowing it's his elder son speaking, "By thine own tongue thou art condemn'd, and must/Endure our law. Thou'rt dead" (5.5.298–9). Again, the wording is revealing: not "Thou must die," or "Thou wilt die," but the continuous present tense, "*Thou'rt* dead." When Cymbeline's younger son Arviragus pleads on his brother's behalf, he too is subject to a death sentence—"And thou shalt die for't," (5.6.311).[20] To avoid this, Belarius at last confesses his identity, and reveals how and why he stole Cymbeline's sons 20 years before. And through this confession, at long long last, "the more delay'd," Cymbeline has his delight, for his sons as well as his daughter are now reborn to him.

Even though we are in the pre-Christian world, the pervasive imagery of rebirth, as in other late plays, has obvious Christian overtones, reminding us that Jupiter behaved like the Christian God, *crossing* those He loved. Indeed, the choice of Cymbeline's reign for the restoration of son to father may not be accidental. Shakespeare would have read in one of his sources, Holinshed's *Chronicles*, that Jesus' birth took place "about the 23rd year of the reign of this Cymbeline."[21] Is it merely a coincidence that the miraculously reborn son and heir Guiderius, aged three when he was stolen by Belarius 20 years ago, is now 23?

Following Belarius' confession, Cymbeline realizes that his kingdom will no longer pass to a daughter when he dies, which would no doubt be pleasing to King James and the court as they watched. Indeed, Cymbeline quickly forgets Imogen in celebrating the recovery of his sons, recalling also the emphasis on male inheritance in Shakespeare's will. This focus on the father's joy, however, leads to a further problem: for most of the play Cymbeline has been in the background, so suddenly to have our attention focused on him and away from characters we have found more interesting, is unsatisfactory for many playgoers. It is another example of the incomplete fit between dramatic situation and authorial need.

Shakespeare probably wrote this play in 1610 or early 1611. As we have seen, his own Hamnet, had he lived, would have been 23 in 1608. Again, it would be a mistake to look for mathematical exactitude; but it is suggestive that Cymbeline's magically restored heir is of a similar age to Shakespeare's own "low-laid son." The restoration of the family group, however, is not for most playgoers as persuasive as in *The Winter's Tale*. There it is partial, while here Shakespeare seems to give way to unrestricted fantasy, perhaps reflecting his desire to be accepted back into his own living family, a desire to be joined again with his son, and the hope of an afterlife to make up for the sufferings of this one. Not only are Guiderius, Arviragus, and Imogen reunited with each other and with their father, but Cymbeline calls Belarius brother (despite the fact that Belarius stole his sons), and Imogen adopts him as her second father as well. Then Posthumus is also included, so the family now has a son who has a posthumous life, as Hamnet has in Shakespeare's imagination.

Stanley Wells' comment about the introspection of these last plays again comes to mind: Shakespeare is willing to risk the theatrical effectiveness of the ending to express that within which yearns for expression.

Notes

Full publication details of every source are included in the bibliography.

1. I am grateful to the editor of the forthcoming Arden edition, Valerie Wayne, for an e-mail about the likely date and political references of the play.

2. Nosworthy, *Cymbeline*, p. xi.

3. Warren, *Cymbeline*, p. 42. My italics.

4. I agree with commentators like Gary Taylor and Stanley Wells who believe the name Imogen probably results from a misreading of Shakespeare's

handwriting and should be Innogen: Innogen appears in Shakespeare's source material and also as a nonspeaking character quickly discarded in the draft version of *Much Ado About Nothing* preserved in the *Quarto* text; but as this book is aimed at the general reader as well as the specialist, I have kept to the established name of Imogen.

Imogen's name when disguised as a male is also interesting. Fidele suggests faithfulness, and there is a Fidelia in *The Rare Triumphs of Love and Fortune*; (one of several similarities Bullough establishes in *Narrative and Dramatic Sources of Shakespeare*, Volume 8, pp. 21–3, 26, 27, 34, 37). But as René Weis has noted, Fidele is almost an anagram of (Richard) Field, who was born three years before Shakespeare in Stratford and like him made a success in London, in his case as a printer, producing the first texts of Shakespeare's two early narrative poems. When Imogen/Fidele, lying next to the headless corpse of Cloten (which Imogen/Fidele thinks is Posthumus), is asked the corpse's name, the reply is Richard du Champ, Richard Field translated into French (*Shakespeare Unbound*, p. 118 and *Shakespeare Revealed*, p. 116). There is clearly a private joke here in Shakespeare identifying a Stratford and London contemporary with a headless corpse, but what exactly it portends is unclear. It is one of many examples of how Shakespeare, to whom puns were second nature, could work on several different levels simultaneously.

5. Wright, *Sudden Death*, p. 60.

6. The story of King David and Absalom is in the *Second Book of Samuel*, chapter 18.

7. It is interesting that the plays which deal most strongly with the pain of loss, especially the loss of Hamnet, all have settings in societies which preceded Christian civilization: *Hamlet* in the world of the Scandanavian revenge sagas, *King Lear* and now *Cymbeline* in pre-Christian Britain, *The Winter's Tale* in the pagan world of the oracle at Delphi. It is as if these precivilized settings act as a release for Shakespeare, allowing him to dig deeper into buried emotions. In this case the setting makes possible the creation of his own memorial to a lost boy.

8. What constitutes the ninth hour varies from culture to culture: in the New Testament the day begins with sunrise, taken to be 6 a.m., and so the ninth hour is 3 p.m.; in *Cymbeline* it means the ninth hour of the morning, that is 9 a.m. But what I think is significant is the biblical connotation of the phrase, not what the ninth hour translates into in different cultures.

9. Edward Capell is the eighteenth-century editor who substituted "as dead."

10. Warren, *Cymbeline*, p. 45.

11. When summer began and ended, like many other things, was not fixed for Shakespeare's contemporaries. "Autumn" was still a relatively new term, replacing the traditional "harvest" for the months at the end of summer (and has never caught on in the United States). Shakespeare only uses it or its cognates nine times, while winter and its cognates occur 89 times, summer and cognates

over one hundred times, and spring (as in the season) and its cognates 36 times, so autumn does not seem to have been a strong element in Shakespeare's sense of the yearly cycle: often, as in the quotation from *The Winter's Tale*, he suggests summer goes straight into winter. He does, however, seem to associate the start of summer with late April/early May, as in "A day in April never came so sweet,/To show how costly summer was at hand" (*The Merchant of Venice*, 2.9.93–4), and the link between summer and the presence of swallows and martlets in *Timon of Athens* and *Macbeth*, respectively, birds which usually arrive in April. If in Shakespeare's mind summer starts in late April/early May and usually goes straight into winter, this would make late summer August and early September.

There is evidence that mourners traditionally carried sprigs of rosemary, but there is no evidence of floral tributes being commonly placed on graves in Shakespeare's period, or of them being regularly renewed, as Arviragus and Marina suggest they will do theirs. I am again grateful to Julian Litten for an e-mail containing this information. (At least this is true for this country: Goody and Poppi, "Flowers and Bones: Approaches to the Dead in Anglo-American and Italian cemeteries," draw attention to the tradition of flowers on Italian graves from before Shakespeare's time). Perhaps Shakespeare's inability to perform the affectionate act of placing flowers regularly on the graves of his loved ones because of social pressure and, perhaps more definitely, because of his absence from Stratford, made it more important to him that some of his created characters did this.

12. And if the James Shakespeare was not his uncle's child, but Shakespeare heard about it, he is still likely to have been interested in a child who bore his own surname and was born in the same year as his own son and who died so young.

13. Cullingford, *British Chimney Sweeps*, p. 73.

14. Warren, *Cymbeline*, p. 208.

15. There is no direct narrative or dramatic source for this episode of (prehistoric) mourning. Valerie Wayne kindly sent me an unpublished paper, "Civil Rites: The Obsequies for Innogen in *Cymbeline*," in which she argues persuasively that Shakespeare may have been influenced by works such as the enlarged 1590 text of Thomas Heriot's *A brief and true report of the new found land of Virginia*, which included a chapter on, and pictures of, burial rituals amongst the Algonquin Indians. Wayne argues that the main purpose of the scene is to show the courtly and civilized response of Guiderius and Arviragus to the death of one they instinctively recognize as their sibling, which confirms for the audience that they are of noble birth, even though they have been brought up away from the court in a Welsh cave. This was a common theme in plays of the period. I certainly agree that this is one function of this scene but would argue that in the burial service for Fidele the social/political and the personal are brought together in typically Shakespearean fashion.

16. If *Cymbeline* were written after *The Winter's Tale*, or the two overlapped, "furious winter's rages" (259) and "the tyrant's stroke" (265) might be in part memories of Leontes' behavior, creating winter out of summer.

17. In *The Rare Triumphs of Love and Fortune* Hermione says, "A joy deferr'd is sweeter to the mind" (*The Rare Triumphs* online, image 23, right hand column). Of course this is a common sentiment but, given the other links Bullough notes between *The Rare Triumphs* and *Cymbeline* (see note 4 above), it's possible the phrase influenced the wording of Jupiter's speech.

18. Merrington, *Suffering Love*, p. 39.

19. Merrington, p. 59.

20. The action onstage is so complicated by this point that it is impossible to be certain whom Cymbeline is threatening. Arviragus has spoken last, and I agree with Nosworthy's suggestion that it might be aimed at him rather than at Guiderius or Belarius (*Cymbeline*, p. 187).

21. Bullough, *Narrative and Dramatic Sources of Shakespeare*, Volume 8, p. 43.

14

Grief, Art, and Letting Go; Deeper Than Did Ever Plummet Sound

In his previous two plays Shakespeare had at some level enacted the paradox that it is unbearable to think about a dead child, but that the child has to be thought about, mourned, and laid to rest, at least in fictional form. After his next play, *The Tempest*, Shakespeare collaborated three times with John Fletcher to write plays for The King's Men; but *The Tempest* is his last sole-authored play and, among many other matters, performs a leave-taking of many of the things that have dominated his life. As in *King Lear* and *Cymbeline* paternal emotions are split between two fathers, and this time their names point in opposite directions, Prospero and Alonso. Indeed, it appears that at first Shakespeare considered having a further father-son relationship, for Prince Ferdinand mentions, among those he thinks drowned, "the Duke of Milan/And his brave son being twain," but no such son appears or is mentioned again (1.2.440–41). Perhaps Shakespeare decided that a third father-child relationship would only lead to repetition and an overcomplicated structure of the kind that handicaps *Cymbeline*. Certainly he seems determined to produce a much shorter, more tightly structured and disciplined play: *The Tempest* is his second shortest play, two-thirds of the length of *The Winter's Tale*, and less than two-thirds of *Cymbeline*. But the detail about the Duke of Milan's son does con-firm how much father-child relationships are in Shakespeare's mind as he conceives this play. Further, Shakespeare has now reached a stage in his journey where he can acknowledge the link between the power of his art and the loss of his child. This has been implied before, but in this play it is made clearer. *The Tempest* was acted before King James on 1 November 1611, which may have been a first performance. It draws on accounts of a group of ships caught in a violent storm near the Bermudas in 1609. All was thought lost, but the flagship arrived in Virginia in May 1610, and accounts of the almost miraculous event became available in England from September 1610 onward. Interestingly, Simon Forman does not mention seeing the play in spring or summer 1611 as he does *The Winter's Tale* and *Cymbeline*; of course it could have been performed when he wasn't present, but it seems more likely that it was not yet in production. Although Shakespeare draws on pamphlet accounts of the shipwreck, he, unusually, devises his own plot, and sets it on a strange and magical island controlled by Prospero, who had been Duke of Milan until 12 years before when his brother Antonio, with the help of King Alonso of Naples and his brother, seized his dukedom and set Prospero and his daughter Miranda adrift in an open boat, hoping they would starve to death, as Leontes had hoped his (he thought, bastard) daughter would do. But a sympathetic courtier of Alonso's, Gonzalo, took pity on them and smuggled some provisions and books onboard, and they survived. These books are the source of Prospero's magical power to create the shipwreck that begins the play and brings these four men from Prospero's past onto his island. Tellingly, Prospero behaves like a playwright, allotting the other characters their exits and their entrances, and controlling whether they live or die.

Shakespeare again seems in retrospective mood. We've seen that Ben Jonson wrote a masque called *Oberon* in 1610, which must have reminded Shakespeare, perhaps deliberately, of his own presentation of Oberon in *A Midsummer Night's Dream*. Prospero had been a character in the first version of Jonson's *Every Man in His Humor* (as had Stephano, also used in *The Tempest*), and Shakespeare seems to be continuing the dialogue with Jonson via a name that Jonson would certainly remember. (Further possible influences on the choice of name are discussed later). Indeed, also in 1610 Jonson had produced *The Alchemist*, about a charlatan magician, so Shakespeare's creation of a genuine magician may be another contribution to dialogue. Perhaps the disciplined structure of *The Tempest*, which, unusually for Shakespeare, keeps to the classical unities of time, place, and action, was similarly a riposte to the critical Jonson that he could organize his material on classical lines when he wanted to. In creating Prospero it is also likely that he thought back to Marlowe's Dr. Faustus, who indulges in black/evil magic; Shakespeare takes pains to emphasize that Prospero, like Paulina, is a practitioner of the art of white/good magic. Katherine Duncan-Jones points out that Faustus comes from the Latin for lucky or auspicious, a pun that might have seemed appropriate to Shakespeare for his prospering protagonist. She also notes that *Dr. Faustus* had been reissued in 1609, which might have drawn it again to Shakespeare's attention. We saw in Chapter 5 how Shakespeare was still thinking of Marlowe six years after his death, and this continuation of the dialogue now, following the one with Greene in *The Winter's Tale*, reinforces the image of Shakespeare as a man who turned things around in his mind over a long period of time. Marlowe was the most adventurous playwright during Shakespeare's early years in London; and Jonson, having produced in *Volpone* and the recent *The Alchemist* exuberant and powerful satires the equal of any by previous dramatists, Aristophanes included, the nearest to a living rival as London's greatest dramatist. Shakespeare seems to be considering his own art in relation to theirs, particularly in terms of the kind of values that lie behind the magic each writer creates in the theater.

He also seems to have been influenced again by the anonymous *The Rare Triumphs of Love and Fortune*, but more so than in *Cymbeline*, in my judgment. No single feature *The Rare Triumphs* and *The Tempest* share is uncommon, but the accumulation of features shared, albeit transformed, suggests that this is the strongest catalyst yet discovered for some features of Shakespeare's invented plot. *The Rare Triumphs* is a mediocre work, but then so are most of the sources that inspired Shakespeare's previous plays; Shakespeare is generally a writer of transformations, metamorphoses, and elements that may appear on a low level in his source material are transmuted into moments and characters that reach our deepest emotions and stay with us long after we have left the theater. In *The Rare Triumphs* Bomelio has been falsely accused of treachery and thrown out of court, and has survived as a hermit who has used books to become a practitioner of magic. The supernatural forces he calls upon have black magic associations, but he is, in the main, well-intentioned in doing so. There are comic servants Lentulo and Penulo, like Trinculo, Stephano, and Caliban (although Caliban is much, much more than this); and Lentulo fears punishment from Bomelio but is forgiven curtly at the end, as Caliban does and is. At the end thoughts of revenge are replaced by pleas for forgiveness. Most interestingly, Hermione, Bomelio's son, burns his father's magic books, as Caliban tells Trinculo and Stephano they must do to gain power over Prospero. When Bomelio discovers the loss he runs mad, "the day begins to be dark, it rains, it begins with *tempests*, thunder and lightning, fire and brimstone, and all my books are gone, and I cannot help my self, nor my friends."[1] He is charmed asleep by the *mischievous and invisible* Mercury, who uses music to "recure his woe," as Prospero, through his attendant spirit Ariel, uses it to restore Alonso, Sebastian, and Antonio's senses.[2] Of course, Shakespeare uses music as a healer in other plays, but if *The Rare Triumphs* was one of the plays he encountered in his early days in London in written form or in performance it might have been another feature that drew him to the play.

Overall, then, the links are substantial, and Shakespeare may have been reconsidering what still seemed invigorating from the discarded experiences of his early days in London.[3] In deciding on a title for his play, Shakespeare may also have been looking back: as well as the reference in *The Rare Triumphs*, in *Twelfth Night* when Viola hears the name of her apparently dead brother and begins to let herself hope that he may be alive, she says, "O, if it prove,/Tempests are kind, and salt waves fresh in love" (3.4.383–4).

No source, however, has been found for the grieving Alonso. As a name Alonso derives from Alphonso or Alfonso, meaning noble and ready for struggle: Alonso has a life-and-death struggle and, through his suffering, becomes transformed from a man of sin to a penitent (albeit Prospero cuts the expression of his penitence short). Possibly the choice of name, and others in the play, were affected by the third chapter of the 1601 English translation of an Italian political discourse, *Civil Considerations upon Many and Sundry Histories*, which contains dealings between Alfonso, King of Naples, his son Ferdinand, and two nobles, Prospero and Frabritio; and/or by William Thomas' *History of Italy*, which includes the story of a Prospero who was deposed and sent into exile, and an Alfonso, King of Naples, who married the daughter of the Duke of Milan and later abdicated in favor of his son Ferdinand.[4]

But it is the shortened form Alonso, not Alphonso/Alfonso, that Shakespeare chooses, and for a writer excited by puns Alonso must have had associations with alone—a word which occurs over 200 times in his plays—for Alonso is indeed alone in his grief for his son Ferdinand's apparent death.[5] Actually Alonso would be a fitting name for many of Shakespeare's isolated fathers, for instance Lear, Gloucester, Pericles and Leontes. Alonso's simple denial of Francisco's suggestion that Ferdinand might have survived the shipwreck—"No, no, he's gone"—encapsulates his grief, although even here a euphemism is preferred to the stark truth of "dead" (2.1.123). But Alonso still needs to search the island for his son, enacting the typical behavior of a bereaved person noted in Chapter 3.

After the fruitless search, he again tries hard to let go of his son, "He is drown'd/Whom thus we stray to find, and the sea mocks/Our frustrate search on land. Well, let him go" (3.3.8–10). But he cannot let him go: in the last act he has to admit, "Irreparable is the loss, and patience/Says, it is past her cure" (5.1.140–1). Of course, he is another character to whom Shakespeare grants an apparent resurrection of a lost one, but before that occurs, this simple and direct acceptance that a father's grief will never end is a further step forward toward a new relationship with his son for Alonso's creator.

Like Leontes, Alonso feels terrible guilt. He had decided to marry his daughter to the King of Tunis, and the shipwreck has occurred on the voyage back to Naples. He sees this decision, which valued material considerations above any potential risk, as the cause of Ferdinand's death. His sense of guilt increases when Ariel reminds him of his sin 12 years before when he helped Antonio to seize Prospero's dukedom, and asserts that supernatural forces are now punishing him by taking his son: "Thee of thy son, Alonso,/They have bereft." His punishment is "Ling'ring perdition," an unending purgatory of loss (3.3.75–7). "Ling'ring perdition" is what we have seen Gloucester, Pericles, and Leontes suffer and links with the acknowledgment above, "Irreparable is the loss." As we saw in Chapter 3 Alonso then acknowledges his "trespass" and feels the only way he can atone and find release from his pain is by joining his drowned son in the ooze at the bottom of the Mediterranean Sea, and without Gonzalo's vigilance he would probably succeed in doing so. As we have seen, such a wish is a common experience for bereaved parents, "particularly among parents who have lost an older child."[6] Evelyn Gillis, for instance, says of her desire to commit suicide after her daughter's death, "At first it was just a strong urge to follow her," but then a counselor "helped me understand I really did not want to die. I just wanted the pain to stop, and suicide seemed the way to become free from this pain."[7] Such anguished admissions are frequent: "I just wanted to die ... Just to be with my son;" or "I would lie in the bath and wonder whether I had the nerve to drown myself and end it all."[8]

Just as Alonso thinks his son is drowned for most of the play, so Ferdinand thinks his father is; but in contrast with the father, the son barely suffers for it. Magical music allays his grief and turns into Ariel's reassuring song:

Full fadom five thy father lies,
Of his bones are coral made:

Those are pearls that were his eyes:
Nothing of him that doth fade,
But doth suffer a sea-change
Into something rich and strange (1.2.397–402).

And when Ferdinand sees Miranda and falls in love, his father is all but forgotten. Both father and son think the other drowned, then, but what a difference in the experience. "Full fadom five" is a measurable, containable depth—about 30 feet or nine meters. "Deeper than e'er plummet sounded," where Alonso imagines his son, is immeasurable, unnameable, a perfect representation for the unimaginable depth of a father's grief. Further, for Ferdinand Alonso under water is transformed "Into something rich and strange," his eyes beautiful pearls. The image suggests his father is weeping, but the son is shielded from the agony this realization of his father's weeping might produce by the beautiful metamorphosis. A common parental comfort enacted here and already acknowledged in the dirge in *Cymbeline* is that the (supposedly) dead child is protected from the horrors the living mourner has to endure.

So through Alonso Shakespeare goes further than ever before in acknowledging *directly* a father's suicidal, oceanic grief; but through his other, successful father he provides hope that this will not be the end of his experience. Like Pericles, Leontes, and Shakespeare himself, Prospero gains a substitute son through his daughter's marriage. Here, the hope that there will be *male* grandchildren is more explicit than before. When Gonzalo hears that Alonso's son and Prospero's daughter are to marry, he draws the strands of the play together in a striking image. He remembers how Prospero was thrown out of the dukedom of Milan, but now, when Prospero and Alonso die, their children will rule over an enlarged kingdom comprising both Milan and Naples. Gonzalo asks, was Prospero "thrust from Milan, that his issue/Should become *kings* of Naples?" (5.1.208–9; my italics). Kings, not queens (as Miranda would be), not monarchs, not kings and queens, and plural, not singular: male grandchildren and greatgrandchildren are what is required. This clearly relates to the political themes of the play, and James the First would have hoped that any kingdom linked to his own through his daughter Elizabeth's marriage would be ruled by generations of males; but the emphasis in Shakespeare's will suggests that his personal hope coincided with his monarch's, and this father, who prospers even though he is sonless, as Shakespeare has, suggests that Shakespeare has reconciled himself to the fulfillment that many parents, bereaved or not, look forward to, through the generation(s) to come. We saw this perfunctorily in *Pericles* and as a secondary element in *The Winter's Tale* but, as David Bevington suggests, here the eventual letting go of the daughter and the rejoicing in her happiness is foregrounded in a way that suggests a more positive belief. Hamnet's twin Judith had yet to marry, and hopes for this may have been in the back of his mind. So social and political and personal concerns are again combined in a typically Shakespearean manner.[9]

And just as Alonso felt he could not go on if his son were dead, so Prospero tells us that 12 years before, he could not have survived when he was set adrift in an open boat if it had not been for his daughter. Again, it is a common experience for bereaved parents that their surviving child or children helps to keep them going. Prospero tells Miranda that she was a cherubin, an angel, "that did preserve me." When Prospero "groan'd" under his burden, Miranda's smile "rais'd in me/An undergoing stomach, to bear up/Against what should ensue" (1.2.152–8). Given that Miranda can dimly remember four or five women that tended her from 12 years ago, she is probably about 14, the age Susanna was in the year after Hamnet's death, and the image reinforces the sense of hope provided by Shakespeare's daughters, and Susanna in particular, notwithstanding the evidence that Shakespeare might at moments have wished Judith had died instead of Hamnet—as we have seen, the anguish of grief does not make for consistency. Typically, though, Shakespeare gives us the other side of this hope through a daughter via Prospero's unprovoked anger with Miranda in the second scene, whose reactions to the shipwreck she has seen he seems to wish to control, and also through Alonso, who berates himself for marrying his daughter to the King of Tunis not only because the shipwreck seems to have cost his son's life but also because she is now "so far from Italy removed/I ne'er again shall see her," words that recall Lear's when banishing Cordelia from his court (2.1.111–2). Susanna and her husband lived much closer to Shakespeare when he returned to Stratford, of course; nevertheless, she now had another home and another man to look up to, so Shakespeare would have been aware of her removal from the home he had returned to. Shakespeare's feelings towards daughters remain ambivalent to the very end.

In the last part of *The Tempest* the two fathers merge, as Prospero, his dukedom now restored and his daughter soon to be married, has thoughts of death and his own sins akin to those Alonso had earlier. He tells Alonso, "Every third thought shall be my grave" (5.1.312). It is time to prepare for death. In an unusually intense epilogue he acknowledges guilt feelings. Alonso "Must ask my child forgiveness" (5.1.198); Prospero's burden takes a different form, as we saw in Chapter 3: "my ending is despair/Unless I be reliev'd by prayer," which can "free *all* faults." Of course the final lines, "As you from crimes would pardon'd be,/Let your indulgence set me free" are, as noted in Chapter 3, an invitation to the audience to show its appreciation of the play, and also may be a request to King James to indulge him by letting him resign from his position as principal playwright to the King's Men; but taken together with the reference to the centrality of prayer, it suggests that the speaker's guilt is so great that only prayer may save him—whether just his own or other people's prayers for his soul as well (as the old religion emphasized) is left ambiguous (Epilogue, 15–20; my italics). In this deep sense of guilt and personal imperfection, he resembles other fathers we have met—Lear, Gloucester, Leontes, as well as Alonso—which supports the suggestion that for Shakespeare the experience of fatherhood and its powerlessness when it came to loss is inextricably bound up with feelings of guilt.

And for the first time Shakespeare is almost explicit about the connection between Hamnet's death and his own power as a playwright, for the image of a dead son is linked to the source of Prospero's magical art. When Prospero renounces his art near the end of *The Tempest*, he almost quotes Alonso. He will "drown" his magical book "deeper than did ever plummet sound;" Alonso thought Ferdinand was drowned "deeper than e'er plummet sounded" (5.1.56–7; 3.3.101). This implies that *part* of the magic of that art finds its natural resting-place where the dead son lies, in the ooze, and indeed earlier in the play Ariel, the spirit of "aery nothing" through whom Prospero is able to work his creative magic, is pictured treading "the ooze/Of the salt deep" (*A Midsummer Night's Dream*, 5.1.16; *The Tempest*, 1.2.252–3). This art has given Prospero supernatural powers: "Graves at my command/Have wak'd their sleepers, op'd, and let 'em forth/By my so potent art" (5.1.48–50).

In other words, Prospero has raised the dead. Editors have found these lines hard to explain within the dramatic context of the play. For instance, Frank Kermode notes, "There seems to be no occasion for this; all the other magic feats" he "has performed, or could have performed, save this one."[10] In the most recent Arden edition, Virginia and Alden Vaughan write, "If these lines are taken literally, Prospero must be referring to events that occurred before he came to the island."[11] But the rest of the play suggests no such events. It might be thought that the lines refer to Prospero's saving of lives in the opening tempest (which he created and controlled); but that is not exactly opening graves. True, the phrase occurs in Shakespeare's source for Prospero's speech, Ovid's *Metamorphoses*, but not as its climax, as here. It is Shakespeare, not Ovid, who makes this claim the height of his magician's powers, and it most obviously links not to the Prospero we see in the play but to a flourishing playwright who has conjured up onstage famous dead people, like Julius Caesar, and not so famous ones, such as his own son in disguise who, like Ferdinand, has received "a second life" in this play, even if only in an "insubstantial pageant" that soon fades (5.1.195; 4.1.155). Prospero then tells us, "this *rough* magic/I here *abjure*," clearly differentiating himself from Marlowe's Faustus and Jonson's charlatan alchemist Subtle (5.1.50–51; my italics).[12] "Abjure" suggests a renunciation made under oath, as in a law court, and in this renunciation Shakespeare at last reaches a kind of resolution: his plays have frequently shown an awareness of the limitations of theatrical impersonation, but now he can acknowledge more directly than before that it was only a "rough magic" that allowed him to create an onstage world in which he could bring the dead to life. Having confessed the depth of a father's grief through Alonso as never before, and emphasized, as in all his final plays, the importance of forgiveness and the need for "spiritual regeneration," he no longer needs his art to fulfill the multifarious functions—social, financial, and personal—it has fulfilled in his life.[13] He can now take his leave of the wonderful but "insubstantial pageant[s]" he has created for us and for himself, the word "pageant" taking us back to the moving pageant invented by Julia to convey, in disguised form, the depth of her pain in one of his very first comedies, *The Two Gentleman of Verona* (4.4.159ff). It has been a long and painful journey; but it is now possible to leave this need behind.[14]

Notes

Full publication details of every source are in the bibliography.

1. *The Rare Triumphs of Love and Fortune.* Online: image 24, left hand column. My italics.

2. *The Rare Triumphs*, image 26, left hand column.

3. *The Rare Triumphs* was performed at court in 1582, and the following year Elizabeth set up her own company, The Queen's Men, comprised of the main players from the existing theatrical companies of the time. Many playscripts are thus likely to have fallen into the new company's hands, and there is evidence to suggest that The Queen's Men was one of the companies Shakespeare worked for during his early years in London; for instance, in Scott McMillin and Sally-Beth MacLean's *The Queen's Men and their Plays*, p.165.

4. Slights, "A Source for *The Tempest* and the Context of the Discorsi."

5. Given Valerie Wayne's evidence that the story of *Don Quixote* was known in England well before 1610 (see note 5 to Chapter 12), it might be worth remarking that Quixote's born name is Alonso Quixano. They are very different characters, but Cervantes' protagonist is also a (comic version of a) man alone in a world of inner experience. As Wayne notes too, the idea of burning of books, in this case Don Quixote's books of chivalry, occurs as well.

6. Merrington, *Suffering Love*, p. 58.

7. Gillis, "A Single Parent Confronting the Loss of an Only Child," pp. 315–20, in Rando, *Parental Loss of a Child.* The quotation is on p. 319

8. Merrington, *Suffering Love*, p. 58.

9. Bevington, *Shakespeare's Ideas*, p. 207. Interestingly there is no wife/mother figure here or at the end of *Cymbeline*. Perhaps Shakespeare had been spending more time in Stratford already, and he and Anne had reestablished their relationship, or at least developed a working relationship by this point; or perhaps, ultimately, that relationship was less important to Shakespeare than the one with his daughters, with its hope of grandsons.

10. Kermode, *The Tempest*, p. 115.

11. Vaughan, *The Tempest*, p. 266.

12. Of course an apparently dead person coming to life occurs in plays by other dramatists. Again, though, it is a matter of degree: Shakespeare keeps returning to this idea in these last plays and treats it here as the summit of his magician's powers.

Medea's speech about her magic powers, is in Ovid's *Metamorphoses*, Book 7. Medea speaks her incantation in response to her husband Jason's desire to rejuvenate his father Aeson, who is near to death, as so many of Shakespeare's fathers are, or feel. This might have increased the attraction of the speech for Shakespeare. Perhaps also Shakespeare felt his art had saved him from the despair that envelops Lady Constance, Gloucester, and Alonso when they think they will never see their loved son again.

13. Benson, *Shakespearean Resurrection*, p. 178.

14. After this Shakespeare collaborates with John Fletcher, but never again writes a play on his own. In the first scene of one of the collaborations, *Two Noble Kinsmen*, we hear, "O grief and time,/Fearful consumers, you will all devour!" (1.1.69–70). And in scene three we learn that Emilia lost her bosom friend, almost her twin, Flavina, "when our count/Was each eleven" (1.3.53–4; *Folio* wording). Eleven is of course the age at which Judith was parted from Hamnet. Stylistic analysis has ascribed both these scenes to Shakespeare, so perhaps unconsciously, even after the leave-taking of *The Tempest*, his writing remembered his loss.

Bibliography

There are so many thought-provoking books and articles on Shakespeare and/or on grief that it is impossible to list them all. For the sake of space I have limited myself to works directly referred to in the text, and others I have found especially helpful.

For the benefit of the general reader, I have kept to a regular order regarding places of publication: where a United States and a British place of publication or publisher are listed, the one in the United States precedes the one in Britain. Journal volume and issue numbers are in the form 32:7, meaning Volume 32, issue 7, followed by the year of publication and the page numbers of the article.

Unless otherwise stated, Shakespeare quotations are from:

Evans, G. Blakemore, and J. J. M. Tobin. (Eds.). *The Riverside Shakespeare: The Complete Works.* Second edition. Boston and New York: Houghton Mifflin Company, 1997.

* * * * * *

Ackroyd, Peter. *Shakespeare: The Biography.* New York: Anchor Books, 2006. London: Chatto and Windus, 2005.

Adelman, Janet. *Suffocating Mothers: Fantasies of Maternal Origin in Shakespeare's Plays, Hamlet to The Tempest.* New York and London: Routledge, 1992.

Aristotle. *Poetics.* Trans. S. H. Butcher. Available at: http://classics.mit.edu/Aristotle/poetics.1.1.html.

Arnold, Joan and Gemma, Penelope Buschman. "The Continuing Process of Parental Grief." *Death Studies* 32:7 (2008): 658–673.

Ashton, Gail. "Pebble on My Wing." *Therapy Today* 18:5 (2007): 7–10.

Barber, C. L. " 'Thou That Beget'st Him That Did Thee Beget': Transformation in *Pericles* and *The Winter's Tale*." In *Shakespeare Survey* 22: 59–67. New York and Cambridge: Cambridge University Press, 1969.

Barber, C. L. and Richard. P. Wheeler. *The Whole Journey.* Berkeley, Los Angeles: University of California Press, 1986.

Bate, Jonathan. *The Genius of Shakespeare.* New York and Oxford: Oxford University Press, 2008.

Batson, Beatrice. (Ed.). *Reconciliation in Selected Shakespearean Dramas.* Cambridge: Cambridge Scholars Publishing, 2008.

Bearman, Robert. (Ed.). *The History of an English Borough: Stratford-upon-Avon 1196–1996.* Dover, New Hampshire, and Stroud: Sutton Publishing, 1997.

Bearman, Robert. *Shakespeare in the Stratford Records.* Dover, New Hampshire, and Stroud: Sutton Publishing, 1994.

Beauregard, David N. *Catholic Theology in Shakespeare's Plays.* Newark: University of Delaware Press, 2008.

Beauregard, David. N. "New light on Shakespeare's Catholicism: Prospero's Epilogue in *The Tempest*." *Renascence: Essays on Values in Literature* 49 (1997): 159–74.

Benson, Sean. *Shakespearean Resurrection: The Art of Almost Raising the Dead.* Pittsburgh: Duquesne University Press, 2009.

Bergman, Martin S. "The Inability to Mourn and the Inability to Love in Shakespeare's *Hamlet*." *The Psychoanalytic Quarterly* 78:2 (2009): 397–423.

Bevington, David. *Shakespeare and Biography.* New York and Oxford: Oxford University Press, 2010.

Bevington, David. *Shakespeare's Ideas: More Things in Heaven and Earth.* Malden, Oxford and Chichester: Wiley-Blackwell, 2008.

Bloom, Harold. *Shakespeare and the Invention of the Human.* New York: Riverhead, 1998.

Bosticco, Cecilia and Teresa. L. Thompson. "Narratives and Story Telling in Coping with Grief and Bereavement." *Omega* 51:1 (2005): 1–16.

Brandes, Georg. *William Shakespeare: A Critical Study.* London: Heinemann, 1898.

Brietenberg, Mark. *Anxious Masculinity in Early Modern England.* New York and Cambridge: Cambridge University Press, 1996.

Bruce, Susan. "Mamillius and Leontes: Their Final Exchange." *ANQ* 16:3 (2003): 9–12.

Bryson, Bill. *Shakespeare: The World as a Stage.* New York and London: HarperPress, 2007.

Buccola, Regina and Lisa Hopkins. (Eds.). *Marian Moments in Early Modern British Drama.* Burlington and Aldershot: Ashgate, 2007.

Bullough, Geoffrey. (Ed.). *Narrative and Dramatic Sources of Shakespeare.* 8 Volumes. London: Routledge and Kegan Paul. New York: Columbia University Press, 1957–75.

Burrow, Colin. (Ed.). *The Complete Sonnets and Poems*. New York and Oxford: Oxford University Press, 2002.

Burton, Robert. *The Anatomy of Melancholy*. New York: New York Review Books, 2001.

Chambers, E. K. *William Shakespeare: A Study of Facts and Problems*. 2 vols. Oxford: Oxford University Press, 1930.

Chedgzoy, Kate, Susanne Greenhalgh, and Robert Shaughnessy, *Shakespeare and Childhood*. New York and Cambridge: Cambridge University Press, 2007.

Clulow, Christopher and Janet Mattinson. *Marriage Inside Out: Understanding Problems of Intimacy*. New York and London: Penguin, 1995.

Cooper, Judy and Nilda Maxwell. (Eds.). *Narcissistic Wounds: Clinical Perspectives*. London: Whurr Publishers, 1995.

Coren, Victoria. "Gilded Butterflies." *King Lear*. RSC Programme, 2004.

Cox, Murray. *Structuring the Therapeutic Process*. Oxford and New York: Pergamon Press, 1978.

Cressy, David. *Birth, Marriage and Death: Ritual, Religion and the Life-Cycle in Tudor and Stuart England*. New York and Oxford: Oxford University Press, 1997.

Cullingford, Benita. *British Chimney Sweeps: Five Centuries of Chimney Sweeping*. Lanham: New Amsterdam Books, 2000.

Dubrow, Heather. *Shakespeare and Domestic Loss: Forms of Deprivation, Mourning and Recuperation*. New York and Cambridge: Cambridge University Press, 1999.

Duncan-Jones, Katherine. *Ungentle Shakespeare: Scenes from his Life*. London: The Arden Shakespeare, 2001.

Duncan-Jones, Katherine. (Ed.). *Shakespeare's Sonnets*. London: The Arden Shakespeare, 1997.

Eccles, Mark. *Shakespeare in Warwickshire*. Madison: University of Wisconsin Press, 1961.

Eliot, T. S. *Selected Prose of T.S. Eliot*. Frank Kermode. (Ed.). San Diego: Harcourt, Inc.. London: Faber and Faber, 1975.

Ellis, David. "Biographical Uncertainty and Shakespeare." *Essays in Criticism* 55:3 (2005): 193–208.

Enterline, Lynn. *The Tears of Narcissus: Melancholia and Masculinity in Early Modern Writing*. Stanford: Stanford University Press, 1995.

Foakes, R. A. (Ed.). *Henslowe's Diary*. Second edition. New York and Cambridge: Cambridge University Press, 2002.

Foakes, R. A. (Ed.). *King Lear*. London: The Arden Shakespeare, 1997.

Fripp, Edgar. I. *Shakespeare: Man and Artist*. 2 vols. Oxford: Oxford University Press, 1938.

Gibson, James M. (Ed.) *Records of Early English Drama: Kent: Diocese of Canterbury*. Toronto: University of Toronto Press, 2002.

Goodenough, Elizabeth, Mark A. Herberle and Naomi B. Sokoloff. (Eds.). *Infant Tongues: The Voice of the Child in Literature*. Detroit: Wayne State University Press, 1994.

Goody, Jack, and Cesare Poppi. "Flowers and Bones: Approaches to the Dead in Anglo-American and Italian Cemetries." *Comparative Studies in Society and History* 36:1 (1994). 146–75.

Gossett, Suzanne. (Ed.). *Pericles*. London: The Arden Shakespeare, 2004.

Greenblatt, Stephen. *Hamlet in Purgatory*. Princeton and Oxford: Princeton University Press, 2001.

Greenblatt, Stephen. "The Death of Hamnet and the Making of *Hamlet*." *The New York Review of Books* 51(16). 21 October, 2004. Available at: http://www .nybooks.com/articles/archives/2004/oct/21/the-death-of-hamnet-and-the -making-of-hamlet. Accessed 06/08/2006.

Greenblatt, Stephen. *Will in the World: How Shakespeare Became Shakespeare*. New York: W. W. Norton. London: Jonathan Cape, 2004.

Greenfield, Matthew. "The Cultural Functions of Renaissance Elegy." *English Literary Renaissance* 28:1 (1998): 75–94.

Greer, Germaine. *Shakespeare's Wife*. New York and London: Bloomsbury, 2007.

Gurr, Andrew. *The Shakespeare Company, 1594–1642*. New York and Cambridge: Cambridge University Press, 2004.

Gurr, Andrew. *Philaster, or Love Lies a-Bleeding*. London: Methuen, 1969.

Hart, Alfred. "The Growth of Shakespeare's Vocabulary." *Review of English Studies* 19:74 (1943): 128–40.

Hays, Michael L. *Shakespearean Tragedy as Chivalric Romance: Rethinking Macbeth, Hamlet, Othello and King Lear*. Cambridge: D. S. Brewer, 2005.

Hockey, Jenny, Jeanne Katz and Neil Small. (Eds.). *Grief, Mourning and Death Ritual*. Buckingham: Open University Press, 2001.

Holden, Anthony. *William Shakespeare*. London: Little Brown and Co, 1999.

Holland, Peter. (Ed.). *Shakespeare Survey 55: King Lear and its Afterlife*. New York and Cambridge: Cambridge University Press, 2002.

Honan, Park. *Shakespeare: A Life*. New York and Oxford: Oxford Paperbacks, 2000.

Honigmann, E. A. J. (Ed.). *King John*. London: Methuen, 1954.

Houlbrooke, Ralph. *Death, Religion and the Family in England, 1480–1750*. New York and Oxford: Oxford University Press, 1998.

Jackson, MacDonald. P. "Vocabulary and Chronology: The Case of Shakespeare's Sonnets." *Review of English Studies* 52:205 (2001): 59–75.

Jones, Jeanne. *Family Life in Shakespeare's England: Stratford-upon-Avon 1570–1630*. Dover, New Hampshire, and Stroud: Sutton Publishing, 1996.

Joyce, James. *Ulysses*. New York and London: Penguin, 1971.

Kahn, Coppélia. *Man's Estate: Masculine Identity in Shakespeare*. Berkeley and Los Angeles: University of California Press, 1981.

Kauffman, Jeffrey. "Dissociative Functions in the Normal Mourning Process." *Omega* 28:1. (1993): 31–8.

Kay, Dennis. *Shakespeare: His Life, Work and Era*. New York and London: Sidgwick and Jackson, 1992.

Kermode, Frank. (Ed.). *The Tempest*. London: Methuen, 1958.

Klass, Dennis. "The Deceased Child in the Psychic and Social Worlds of Bereaved Parents during the Resolution of Grief." *Death Studies* 21 (1997): 147–175.

Klass, Dennis, Phyllis R. Silverman and Steven L. Nickman. *Continuing Bonds: New Understandings of Grief*. Philadelphia and London: Taylor and Francis, 1996.

Klausner, David N. and Marsalek Karen Sawyer. (Eds.). *"Bring furth the pagants": Essays in Early English Drama Presented to Alexandra F. Johnston*. Toronto and London: University of Toronto Press, 2007.

Klein, Melanie. *Envy and Gratitude and Other Works 1946–1963*. New York: The Free Press, 2002.

Knapp, Jeffrey. *Shakespeare Only*. Chicago: University of Chicago Press, 2009.

Knight, W. Nicholas. *Autobiography in Shakespeare's Plays: Lands So By His Father Lost*. New York and Oxford: Peter Lang, 1991.

Kozuka, Takashi, and J. R. Mulryne. (Eds). *Shakespeare, Marlowe, Jonson: New Directions in Biography*. Burlington and Aldershot: Ashgate, 2006.

Krims, Marvin. *The Mind According to Shakespeare: Psychoanalysis in the Bard's Writing*. Westport: Praeger, 2006.

Lendrum, Susan and Gabrielle Syme. *Gift of Tears: A Practical Approach to Loss and Bereavement in Counseling and Psychotherapy*. New York and London: Routledge, 2004.

Levine, Laura. *Men in Women's Clothing: Anti-theatricality and Effeminization 1579–1642*. New York and Cambridge: Cambridge University Press, 1994.

Litten, Julian. *The English Way of Death: The Common Funeral since 1450*. London: Robert Hale, 2002.

MacDonald, Michael. *Mystical Bedlam: Madness, Anxiety, and Healing in Seventeenth-Century England*. New York and Cambridge: Cambridge University Press, 1981.

Maguire, Laurie. *Where There's a Will, There's a Way or, All I Really Need to Know I Learned from Shakespeare*. Boston and London: Nicholas Brealey Publishing, 2007.

Mahon, Eugene. J. "The Death of Hamnet: An Essay on Grief and Creativity." *The Psychoanalytic Quarterly* 78:2 (2009): 425–44.

Malan, David. *Individual Psychotherapy and the Science of Psychodynamics*. New York and London: Arnold, 2001.

Marlowe, Christopher. *Doctor Faustus and Other Plays: Tamberlaine, Parts I and II; Dr. Faustus, A and B-Texts; The Jew of Malta; Edward II*. David M. Bevington and Eric Rasmussen. (Eds.). New York and Oxford: Oxford University Press, 1995.

Marston, John. *Antonio's Revenge*. W. R. Gair. (Ed.). New York and Manchester: Manchester University Press, 1999.

Mazzio, Carla and Douglas Trevor. (Eds.). *Historicism, Psychoanalysis and Early Modern Culture*. New York and London: Routledge, 2000.

McLean, Ian. *The Renaissance Notion of Woman: A Study in the Fortunes of Scholasticism and Medical Science in European Intellectual Life*. New York and Cambridge: Cambridge University Press, 1980.

McMillin, Scott and Sally Beth MacLean. *The Queen's Men and Their Plays*. New York and Cambridge: Cambridge University Press, 1998.

Merrington, Bill. *Suffering Love: Coping with the Death of a Child*. Leamington Spa: Advantage, 1995.

Nashe, Thomas. *The Works of Thomas Nashe*. 5 vols. R. B. McKerrow and F. P. Wilson (Eds.). Second edition. Oxford: Basil Blackwell, 1958.

Nicholl, Charles. *The Reckoning: The Murder of Christopher Marlowe*. Chicago: University of Chicago Press. London: Jonathan Cape, 1992.

Nosworthy, James M. (Ed.). *Cymbeline*. London: Methuen, 1955.

Ovid. *Metamorphoses*. Trans. M. Innes. Harmondsworth: Penguin, 1955.

Palliser, David M. *The Age of Elizabeth*. New York and London: Longman, 1992.

Parkes, Colin Murray. *Bereavement: Studies of Grief in Adult Life*. Third edition. New York and London: Penguin, 1998.

Partee, Morriss Henry. *Childhood in Shakespeare's Plays*. New York and Oxford: Peter Lang Publishing, 2006.

Paster, Gail Kern, Katherine Rowe and Mary Floyd-Wilson. (Eds.). *Reading the Early Modern Passions: Essays in the Cultural History of Emotion*. Philadelphia: University of Pennsylvania Press, 2004.

Payne, Martin. *Narrative Therapy: An Introduction for Counselors*. Thousand Oaks and London: Sage Publications, 2006.

Pedder, J. R. "Failure to Mourn, and Melancholia." *British Journal of Psychiatry* 141 (1982): 329–337.

Penuel, Suzanne. "Missing Fathers: *Twelfth Night* and the Reformation of Mourning." *Studies in Philology* 107:1 (2010): 74–96.

Perrett, Wilfred *Palaestra XXXV: The Story of King Lear from Geoffrey of Monmouth to Shakespeare*. Berlin: Mayer and Muller, 1904.

Pitcher, John. (Ed.). *The Winter's Tale*. London: The Arden Shakespeare, 2010.

Pointon, Clare. "The New Black: Interview with Darian Leader." *Therapy* 19:2 (2008): 18–21.

Pollock, Linda A. *Forgotten Children: Parent-Child Relationships from 1500 to 1900*. New York and Cambridge: Cambridge University Press, 1983.

Quinlan, Maurice J. "Shakespeare and the Catholic Burial Services." *Shakespeare Quarterly* 5:3 (1954): 303–6.

Rando, Therese A. (Ed.). *Parental Loss of a Child*. Champaign, Illinois: Research Press Company, 1986.

The Rare Triumphs of Love and Fortune. Available at: http://eebo.chadwyck.com/search. Last accessed: 12/12/10.

Rayner, Eric, Angela Joyce, James Rose, Mary Twyman and Christopher Clulow. *Human Development: An Introduction to the Psychodynamics of Growth, Maturity and Ageing*. New York and London: Routledge, 2005.

Rhodes, A. "Hamlet and Hamnet as Interchangeable Names." *Notes and Queries* 11(4), 4 November 1911.

Riches, Gordon and Pam Dawson. *An Intimate Loneliness: Supporting Bereaved Parents and Siblings*. Philadelphia and Buckingham: Open University Press, 2000.

Rosenblatt, Paul. *Parent Grief: Narratives of Loss and Relationship*. Philadelphia: Brunner/Mazel, 2000.

Sanders, Catherine. M. "A Comparison of Adult Bereavement in the Death of a Spouse, Child and Parent." *Omega* 10:4 (1980): 303–22.

Sannazaro, Jacopo. *Arcadia*. R. Nash (Trans.). Detroit: Wayne State University Press, 1966.

Savage, Richard. (Transcriber). *The Registers of Stratford-on-Avon: Burials 1558–1622-3*. London: Parish Register Society, 1905.

Schiesari, Juliana. *The Gendering of Melancholia*. Ithaca: Cornell University Press, 1992.

Schiff, Harriet Sarnoff. *The Bereaved Parent*. New York and London: Penguin, 1979.

Schoenbaum, S. *William Shakespeare: Records and Images*. New York and Oxford: Oxford University Press, 1981.

Schoenbaum, S. *William Shakespeare: A Compact Documentary Life*. New York and Oxford: Oxford University Press, 1987.

Schoenbaum, S. *Shakespeare: A Documentary Life*. New York and Oxford: Oxford University Press, 1975.

Schwab, Reiko. "Paternal and Maternal Coping with the Death of a Child." *Death Studies* 14 (1990): 407–422.

Scully, E. Jean. "Men and Grieving." *Psychotherapy Patient* 2 (1985): 95–100.

Shakespeare, William. *Hamlet*. First Quarto. Available at: http://internet shakespeare.uvic.ca/Library/facsimile/book/BL_Q1_Ham/

Shakespeare, William. *Hamlet*. Second Quarto. Available at: http://internet shakespeare.uvic.ca/Library/facsimile/book/BL_Q2_Ham/

Shakespeare, William. *Mr. William Shakespeare's Comedies, Histories and Tragedies*. (First Folio). Available at: http://internetshakespeare.uvic.ca/Library/facsimile/book/SLNSW_F1.

Shakespeare, William. *Much Ado About Nothing*. First Quarto. Available at: http://eebo.chadwyck.com/search/.

Shakespeare, William. *Romeo and Juliet*. Second Quarto. Available at: http://internetshakespeare.uvic.ca/Library/facsimile/book/BL_Q2_Rom/.

Shapiro, James. *A Year in the Life of William Shakespeare: 1599*. New York and London: Faber, 2005.

Shapiro, Michael. *Gender in Play on the Shakespearean Stage: Boy Heroines and Female Pages*. Ann Arbor: University of Michigan Press, 1995.

Slights, William W. E. "A Source for *The Tempest* and the Context of The *Discorsi*." *Shakespeare Quarterly*. 36:1 (1985): 68–70.

Smart, Laura S. "Parental Bereavement in Anglo American History." *Omega*. 28:1. (1993): 49–61.

Smith, Keverne. "Hamlet and After: The Presence of Absence." *Journal of Theatre and Drama*. 7/8 (2001/2): 29–48.

Spaas, Lieve. (Ed.). *Paternity and Fatherhood: Myths and Realities*. New York: St. Martin's Press, 1998.

Spurgeon, Caroline. *Shakespeare's Imagery and What It Tells Us*. New York and Cambridge: Cambridge University Press, 1935.

Staudacher, Carol. *Men and Grief: A Guide for Men Surviving the Death of a Loved One*. Oakland: New Harbinger Publications, 1991.

Stone, Lawrence. *The Family, Sex and Marriage in England, 1500–1800*. New York and London: Harper Row, 1977.

Sundelson, David. *Shakespeare's Restoration of the Father*. New Bruswick: Rutgers University Press, 1983.

Thomas, David. *Shakespeare in the Public Records*. London: Her Majesty's Stationery Office, 1985.

Thompson, Ann and Neil Taylor. (Eds.). *Hamlet*. London: The Arden Shakespeare, 2006.

Vaughan, Virginia Mason, and Vaughan, Alden T. (Eds.). *The Tempest*. London: The Arden Shakespeare, 2000.

Warren, Roger. (Ed.). *Cymbeline*. New York and Oxford: Oxford University Press, 1998.

Way, Niobe. *Deep Secrets: Boys' Friendships and the Crisis of Connection*. Harvard: Harvard University Press, 2011.

Wayne, Valerie. "Civil Rites: The Obsequies for Innogen in *Cymbeline*." Unpublished Paper, Shakespeare Association of America Conference, 2003.

Wayne, Valerie. "*Don Quixote* and Shakespeare's Collaborative Turn to Romance," in *The Quest for Shakespeare's Cardenio*. David Carnegie and Gary Taylor. (Eds). New York and Oxford: Oxford University Press, forthcoming.

Weis, René. *Shakespeare Unbound: Decoding a Hidden Life*. New York: Holt Paperbacks. In Britain, *Shakespeare Revealed: A Biography*. London: John Murray Paperbacks, 2007.

Wells, Stanley. *Shakespeare and Co: Christopher Marlowe, Thomas Dekker, Ben Jonson, Thomas Middleton, John Fletcher and the Other Players in His Story*. New York and London: Penguin, 2006.

Wells, Stanley, Gary Taylor, John Jowett, and William Montgomery. *William Shakespeare: A Textual Companion*. New York and London: W. W. Norton, 1997.

Wells, Stanley, Gary Taylor, John Jowett and William Montgomery. *William Shakespeare: The Complete Works*. Second edition. New York and Oxford: Oxford University Press, 2005.

Wheeler, Richard P. "Deaths in the Family: The Loss of a Son and the Rise of Shakespearean Comedy." *Shakespeare Quarterly* 51:2 (2000): 127–53.

White, Cheryl, and David Denborough. *Introducing Narrative Therapy: A Collection of Practice-based Writings.* Adelaide: Dulwich Centre Publications, 1998.

Wilson, Ian. *Shakespeare, The Evidence: Unlocking the Mysteries of the Man and His Work.* New York: St. Martin's Griffin. London: Headline Book Publishing, 1993.

Wilson, Richard. *Will Power: Essays on Shakespearean Authority.* Detroit: Wayne State University Press. London: Harvester Wheatsheaf, 1993.

Woodgate, Roberta L. "Living in a World without Closure: Reality for Parents who have Experienced the Death of a Child." *Journal of Palliative Care* 22:2 (2006): 75–82.

Woods, Michael. *In Search of Shakespeare.* London: BBC Books. 2003.

Worden, J. William. *Grief Counseling and Grief Therapy.* New York and London: Routledge, 1991.

Wright, Bob. *Sudden Death: A Research Base for Practice.* New York and London: Churchill Livingstone, 1996.

Yachnin, Paul and Patricia Badir. *Shakespeare and the Culture of Performance.* Burlington and Aldershot: Ashgate, 2008.

Young, Bruce. *Family Life in the Age of Shakespeare.* Westport: Greenwood, 2009.

Zisook, Sidney and Richard A. de Vaul. "Grief, Unresolved Grief and Depression." *Psychosomatics* 24:3 (1983): 247–56.

Index

Only substantial references are included. Where there are several references under a particular heading, the main one (if there is one) is printed in bold.

For ease of reference, themes linked with grieving and the process of mourning are listed under Grief.

Shakespeare's plays are listed under Shakespeare. Other plays are indexed under the author's name, or under the title if the play is anonymous. Shakespeare's source materials are listed under their titles.

About the Author

KEVERNE SMITH is Course Director for B.A. Humanities at the University Centre, College of West Anglia in King's Lynn, United Kingdom. He has published and delivered conference papers on education and on the presentation of grief in Shakespeare. His most recent article, "Almost the Copy of My Child That's Dead: Shakespeare and the Loss of Hamnet," will appear in a forthcoming issue of *Omega: Journal of Death and Dying.*